STUPID
BLACK
MEN

Also by Larry Elder

Ten Things You Can't Say in America

Showdown

STUPID BLACK MEN

How to Play the Race Card—and Lose

LARRY ELDER

ST. MARTIN'S PRESS   NEW YORK

The extract on pages 156–157 is excerpted with permission from
The Atlanta Journal-Constitution, copyright © 2006. For more
information about reprints by PARS International Corp.,
visit us online at www.ajcreprints.com.

www.stmartins.com

Design by Sarah Maya Gubkin

Library of Congress Cataloging-in-Publication Data

Elder, Larry.
    Stupid Black men : how to play the race card—and lose /
Larry Elder.—1st ed.
        p.   cm.
    ISBN-13: 978-0-312-36733-6
    ISBN-10: 0-312-36733-3
    1. African Americans—Social conditions—1975–   2. African Americans—
Attitudes.   3. African American leadership.   4. African Americans—Politics
and government.   5. Responsibility—United States.   6. Political correct-
ness—United States.   7. United States—Politics and government—2001–
8. Mass media—Political aspects—United States.   9. United States—Race
relations.   10. Racism—United States.   I. Title.

E185.615.E39 2008
305.896'07309047—dc22

                                                                    2007040916

First Edition: February 2008

10   9   8   7   6   5   4   3   2   1

To Viola Elder

(July 2, 1925–June 13, 2006)

CONTENTS

ACKNOWLEDGMENTS

I would first like to acknowledge the hard work, persistence, and dedication of my personal assistant, Dana Riley. Dana's researching and editing efforts were tireless, and her suggestions were invaluable.

I also want to thank Jennifer Hardaway and Aaron Hanscom for their assistance.

I also want to thank, for the third time, my patient and understanding editor, Elizabeth Beier. Elizabeth's enthusiasm and support make her a writer's dream to work with.

PREFACE

"[T]he greatest challenge we face . . . is the oldest, and in some ways today, the newest: the problem of race,"[1] said President Clinton at his historic "race relations" speech in 1997. "Race plays a part of everything in America,"[2] says famed O. J. Simpson defense attorney Johnnie Cochran.

Nonsense.

These statements would be funny, if not so tragic. Americans want safe streets, good schools, and economic opportunity. But safe neighborhoods, especially urban ones, need community support of the police and of the criminal justice system. Good schools place high standards on students, demand homework, and expect parental involvement. Good economic opportunities require a skilled and motivated labor force, a safe location for employees, and a business-friendly environment of low taxes and limited regulation.

The civil rights movement properly demanded justice—by government. Many of today's so-called black leaders seem incapable of distinguishing between equal rights and equal results. Results stem from hard work, focus, education and training, and the assumption of the consequences of one's own actions.

Yet racism, say "black leaders" with their co-conspiring Democratic Party, remains the real roadblock—the moat, the ditch, the barrier—to self-improvement.

On today's vital issues of crime, education, and employment

opportunities, where does the "black leadership" stand? Unfortunately, they're usually AWOL, stuck in a time-warped, decades-old "fight against racism" that vacuums up time, energy, and resources.

In reality, the formula for success is simple: work hard, make sacrifices, focus on education, delay gratification, avoid bad moral mistakes, and maintain optimism.

Bad schools, crime, drugs, high taxes, the Social Security mess, the health care "crisis," unemployment, welfare state dependency, illegitimacy—and race and racism. What do these issues have in common? So-called black leaders—aided and abetted by the mainscream media, and cheered on by the Democratic Party—lie to us about them. They lie about the cause. They lie about the effect. They lie about the solutions. They make the most outrageous statements—and get away with it. Why? Many people refuse to challenge these outrageous statements for fear that *they* will be branded as racist. Others say nothing because keeping blacks angry and unduly concerned about racism advances the political agenda of the Democratic Party.

In reality, the formula for success is simple: work hard, make sacrifices, focus on education, delay gratification, avoid bad moral mistakes, and maintain optimism.

Negative outlook produces negative results. For example, when asked whether hard work offers little guarantee of success, 27 percent of whites agree. But a whopping 41 percent of blacks agree with that statement.[3]

Overcoming laziness remains one of life's hardest challenges. Good parents tear their hair out trying to motivate their children to study. But give kids an excuse—like "The Man" holds him back—and watch them use this excuse as a badge and a shield instead of accepting personal responsibility for their own actions.

But people find ease in being a "victicrat." If The Man conspires to bring you down, why try? If The Man stands ready to block my success, why study? Why work hard? After all, what's the point? Forget, for a moment, about success. What about happiness? How can someone attain happiness if he or she feels that people and forces bigger than they are stand ready to strike them down and prevent them from succeeding?

Contrary to popular belief, most blacks lead working-class or better lives, and most live outside of the inner city. But the black so-called underclass—the 25 percent of blacks defined as living below the poverty rate[4]—are not helped by the angry, pessimistic rhetoric of those who claim to operate in their best interests. Getting ahead becomes elusive when you're trained to think like a victim.

This book calls a lot of public figures' bluffs—no more tiptoeing around. *Stupid Black Men* calls out black men and women, men and women of other races, the "empathetic" liberal media, and Democratic Party sympathizers for their racism-done-me-wrong statements and policy measures that maximize victimhood and minimize personal responsibility.

The left-leaning media happily assist. The mostly well-intentioned but condescending members of the mainscream media go the extra mile to avoid having charges of "racist" directed at themselves, so they seldom challenge "black leaders" when these race-baiters confuse equal rights with equal results. Thus, lower black college enrollment becomes "underrepresention" in higher education; the fact that white net worth exceeds black net worth becomes "disproportionate"; data showing banks decline black loans more readily than loans to whites becomes "discrimination"; blah, blah, blah.

Stupid Black Men calls for an end to BMW—Bitching, Moaning, and Whining. These so-called black leaders, mainscream media conspirators, and sympathizers in the Democratic Party send a simple, harmful message: standards of hard work and accountability do not apply to blacks. This hurts the very people they supposedly support. Because of the hard work, endurance, and suffering of many people, slavery and legalized segregation no longer exist. The racist, hard hearts and minds of an overwhelming majority of Americans is a long-gone thing of the past. While all societies have to endure a few wacko racists here and there, they don't wield power and they face great forces aligned to call them out and crush them.

Stupid Black Men calls for an end to BMW— Bitching, Moaning, and Whining.

President John F. Kennedy once described happiness as the "full use of your powers along lines of excellence."[5] Can happiness coexist alongside exaggerated claims of racism, claims that turn people into victims and pawns? This kind of thinking may benefit the we're-here-to-help Democratic Party and its pursuit of the monolithic black vote, but it downplays personal initiative and responsibility and makes people believe they are powerless to control their own lives. *Stupid Black Men* says this incessant harping about the "pervasiveness" of racism is not only wrong-headed, but downright dangerous. It diminishes personal responsibility and dupes people into thinking that their salvation rests with more government spending and the expansion of government programs.

Blaming racism is not just false, it is toxic.

It keeps races wary of each other. Watch what I say. Watch for an innocent remark that might be construed as "racist," or "racially insensitive." Unfounded charges of racism cause us to emphasize differences, rather than our broad and deep similarities.

STUPID
BLACK
MEN

1.

IT'S THE MEDIA, STUPID

White racism does exist, but its social power is weak and social power arrayed against it overwhelming.[1]

—JOHN O'SULLIVAN, EDITOR, *NATIONAL REVIEW*

Media malpractice: the shameful willingness to provide a megaphone for baseless, outlandish charges of racism; the failure to highlight the tremendous progress of minorities over the past forty years; and the unwillingness to seek out minority voices to counter the histrionics of the Jesse Jacksons, the Al Sharptons, and their willing liberal conspirators in the media and the Democratic Party.

Consider the stupid, silly, or just plain ignorant statements made by angry blacks—statements that go unchallenged by the mainscream media.

"Race stories" fill our newspapers. "Hate crimes." Unjustified accusations of "police brutality." "Cultural bias" in standardized testing. "Discriminatory" college and university admissions when some groups are admitted at higher rates than others. The alleged

Hollywood "blackout" that argues show business—despite being chock-full of liberals—discriminates against minorities.

If a black person says this, he is an Uncle Tom.

America is more inclusive and just than at any point in her history. When one considers the staggering diversity and continued prosperity of the American people, racism approaches near insignificance. If a white person says that, he stands accused of blindness, if not outright bigotry. If a black person says this, he is an Uncle Tom. Yet those who consistently—and often without evidence—cry "racism," attract attention, sympathy, and votes.

Blacks overwhelmingly vote for the Democratic Party, the party that counts on receiving more than 90 percent of the black vote.[2] Democrats need and rely on the black vote the way humans need oxygen. Thus we hear absurd, hysterical statements that racism remains the principal problem facing "black America." The Democratic Party then mounts the white horse and charges into this battle against racism. And, since racism remains enemy number one against blacks, voting for Democrats becomes not only a matter of self-interest, but a moral necessity!

But where's the proof that social programs and redistribute-the-wealth schemes work? Who cares? Social programs show that Democrats "do something." Whether by offering ineffective "jobs programs," or providing welfare without work, these programs say that Democrats are clearly here to help.

Gutless Republicans—in fear of the racist label—often keep silent rather than speak out against verbal outrages. So when black New York City Councilman Charles Barron says, "I want to go up to the closest white person and say, 'You can't understand this, it's a black thing,' and then slap him, just for my mental health,"[3] many blacks applaud.

Did Barron apologize afterward? When WABC radio's Steve Malzberg asked him for clarification, Barron said, "I think everybody knew that was what we call . . . oratorial improvision [*sic*] and black hyperbole. And y'all wouldn't understand that 'cause you're uptight and you're gonna take it where it was not intended."⁴ Oh.

The actions of the race baiters go beyond irresponsible. They border on evil. And a compliant media goes willfully along. Imagine, for example, what the media coverage would be like if a white public figure said he or she wanted to slap the nearest black person. For many days, it would be front-page news, the lead story on television news, and editorials everywhere calling for the politician's resignation.

Cosby urged blacks to embrace education, speak standard English, and obey the law. How *dare* he?

Bill Cosby, the legendary actor/entertainer/philanthropist, gets it. He said, "[I]n our cities and public schools we have fifty percent drop-out. . . . No longer is a person embarrassed because they're pregnant without a husband. No longer is a boy considered an embarrassment if he tries to run away from being the father of the unmarried child."⁵ Cosby urged blacks to embrace education, speak standard English, and obey the law. How *dare* he?

But in a book called *Is Bill Cosby Right?* author Michael Eric Dyson accused Cosby of unfairly attacking blacks, blaming "the victim." This professor from the University of Pennsylvania downplays or dismisses the tragedy of babies having babies, the 50 percent inner-city dropout rate, and the disproportionately high percentage of black youth involved in crime. Obviously, the white man made them do it.

Many in the media go jelly-legged if someone like Cosby calls on blacks to take responsibility. The *Today* show invited Dyson to discuss his book and his attack on Bill Cosby. But who conducted the interview? Cohost Matt Lauer? No. Then cohost Katie Couric? No. Al Roker, the black weatherman. Nice guy, Roker, but by using him the *Today* show protected Lauer and/or Couric from injecting themselves into a race debate. The "white man done me wrong" theme remains a staple of mainscream media malpractice, and clearly the *Today* show producers felt so uncomfortable about having one of its stars involved in this the argument that they devalued this serious issue by letting the weather guy handle the task. It went like this:

"Do you think there's any validity in some of the things he said?" asked Roker.[6]

"Oh sure . . . there's validity always," said Dyson. "Tim[othy] McVeigh had a point. The state is overreaching. But the way you do it, dropping bombs and castigating of human beings, that's terrible. . . . Let's hold the larger society accountable for creating the conditions that lead to some of the downfalls of the poor people."[7]

What? Roker said nothing.

Roker then read three quotes from Cosby: "Those people are not Africans; they don't know a damn thing about Africa. With names like Shaniqua, Shaliqua and Mohammed and all of that crap, and all of them are in jail." Next, "All this child knows is 'gimme, gimme, gimme.' These people want to buy the friendship of a child . . . and the child couldn't care less. . . . These people are not parenting. They're buying things for the kid. $500 sneakers, for what? They won't . . . spend $250 on Hooked on Phonics." And finally, "You can't land a plane with 'why you ain't'. . . . You can't be a doctor with that kind of crap coming out of your mouth."[8]

Dyson responded, "Black people have always been creative in naming their children. Africans name their kids after the days of the week, after conditions of their birth. Black people in

1930s gave their kids names after consumer products, Cremola, Listerine, Hershey Bar. So black naming has always been creative. I'm not worried about Shaniqua and Taliqua, I'm worried about Clarence and Condoleezza, who can hurt us in high places of power in America."[9]

What? Roker said nothing.

Because Cosby served as a "pitchman" for Jell-O Puddin' Pops he, according to Dyson, "created artificial desire in people to spend beyond their means."[10]

What??!! Roker said nothing.

"So I'm speaking forth," Dyson continued, "on behalf of those people who are poor, because, after all, I was a teen father, lived on welfare until I was twenty-one, then went to get a Ph.D. at Princeton. Now I'm gonna have Afro-nesia [*sic*] and forget the people from which I've emerged? No, bro, I ain't the one." To which Roker "fired back" with this show stopper: "You know, you gotta come out of your shell."[11]

Would Dyson have called Couric or Lauer "bro"?

RIP (Rest In Peace) to radio host Don Imus's CBS radio show and its simulcast. The firing of the longtime host represents another example of hypocrisy, selective outrage, and our society's obsession with the "pervasiveness" of anti-black racism. The ensuing feeding frenzy over Imus's remarks occupied the mainscream media for almost two weeks, until a horrific campus shooting pushed Imus from the front pages and lead stories.

Imus, on April 4, 2007, referred to the predominately black Rutgers female basketball team as "nappy-headed hos," after Imus's morning show executive producer, Bernard McGuirk, called the women "hard-core hos." Furthermore, McGuirk described the women's NCAA championship match between Rutgers and Tennessee as the "jigaboos versus the wannabes"—a reference to Spike Lee's movie *School Daze* about the tension between dark-skinned blacks and light-skinned blacks.[12]

After first dismissing the remark as a joke, Imus apologized several times. No doubt fearing the career-ending label of "racist," Imus agreed to go on Al Sharpton's radio show for a beat-down.

SHARPTON: What is any possible reason you could feel that this kind of statement could be just forgiven and overlooked?

IMUS: I don't think it should be. . . . I think it can be forgiven, but I don't think it can be overlooked. . . . I apologized. And I didn't say what everybody says, *"If* I offended somebody, I'm sorry," 'cause I knew I offended somebody. . . .

SHARPTON: Mr. Imus, do you think it's funny to call people "nappy-headed hos"?

IMUS: No, I don't. . . .

SHARPTON: "Nappy" is racial.

IMUS: Yes, sir, I understand that.

SHARPTON: Saying "wannabees" and "jiggaboos" is racial.

IMUS: *I* did not say that. And that was said in the context—

SHARPTON: You didn't argue with it, either, and it was the same conversation—

IMUS: No, sir, but that was presented in the context of the Spike Lee film.

SHARPTON: . . . So you made all of these analogies—let me get this right. You call these people "nappy-headed hos," but you wasn't talkin' racial when you said "nappy." "Jiggaboos" and "wannabees," but you didn't understand what you was sayin'. What are you sayin', you blacked out?

IMUS: No, don't tell me—no, I didn't say I didn't understand what we were saying. I said, I wasn't *thinking* that. Now when someone says "jiggaboos" and "wannabees," then my frame of reference is the Spike Lee film.

SHARPTON: Right, which was about light-skinned, black-skinned—

IMUS: I understand that. But I'm not thinking that it is a racial insult that's being uttered at somebody at the time. . . . There's no excuse for it. I'm not pretending that there is. I wish I hadn't said it. I'm sorry I said it.

SHARPTON:... If you realize that something must be done, why would you then feel that we are out of order to ask that you step aside?

IMUS: I didn't say that.

SHARPTON: Oh, you don't think we're out of order?

IMUS: No, sir.

SHARPTON: So you come to sign your resignation then?

IMUS: No, I'm not signing anything.

SHARPTON: So what are you saying? You want to determine what ought to happen, even though you were the one that did the wrong?

IMUS: I didn't say that, either. . . . You have the right to say and do whatever you want to do.

SHARPTON: The issue is, whether . . . somebody can say something that you admittedly say yourself is wrong, and I say is racist and sexist, and it just be glossed over. . . . Because then, if you walk away from this unscathed, the next guy can say whatever he wants, and just say, "I'm sorry."

IMUS: Unscathed? Are you crazy? How am I unscathed by this? Don't you think I'm humiliated? Don't you think I'm embarrassed? Don't you think—

SHARPTON: You're not as humiliated as young black women are.

IMUS: I didn't say I was. . . . It's not a contest as to who's the most humiliated.[13]

Yet Sharpton later said, "We had never asked him to never work again."[14] But when rumors floated about a possible Imus return to the airwaves, Sharpton promised to boycott his sponsors, "This is not a one-incident offender. This person has made a career out of this. And for him to go back to the air, we will be all over him every day and into advertisers the first time he steps over the line."[15] Imus's repeated apologies are wasted on a man who makes a living from accusing others of racism.

Now follow the bouncing hypocrisy.

Sharpton has *never* apologized for falsely accusing a white former assistant district attorney in 1987 of sexually assaulting black teenager Tawana Brawley, even though he's had twenty years—and many opportunities—to apologize. Sharpton's bellicose and fraudulent accusations thrust him into the national spotlight. A New York grand jury determined the whole Tawana Brawley affair a hoax, and the assistant DA successfully sued Sharpton and two other defendants for defamation. A unanimous, multiracial jury awarded the assistant DA $65,000 from Sharpton. No apology.[16]

In 1989, after the "Central Park Jogger" was viciously attacked and left for dead, Sharpton called the Jogger a "whore,"[17] and falsely accused her boyfriend of committing the crime.[18] No apology. And few now bring this up.

Jesse Jackson also criticized Imus. But in 1984, when the *Washington Post*'s Milton Coleman reported Jesse Jackson called Jews, "Hymie," and New York, "Hymie Town," the reverend initially denied the statement. Days later, Jackson apologized for his anti-Semitic remark, thus taking longer to apologize than did Imus for his racist, sexist remark. Again, few now bring this up. Jackson's friend and confidante, the Nation of Islam's Minister Louis Farrakhan, publicly threatened black reporter Coleman on radio and warned the Jews, "If you harm this brother [Jackson], I warn you in the name of Allah this will be the last one you harm." Jackson refused to condemn Farrakhan's remarks.[19]

Jackson, then a presidential candidate, refused to condemn Farrakhan's remarks or distance himself from his relationship with the minister.[20] Moral arbiter Jackson also "mentored" then President Bill Clinton during his Monica Lewinsky troubles. Never mind that Jackson, at this time, had an affair with a staff member from his Rainbow/PUSH organization. Incredibly, Jackson, standing next to his visibly pregnant mistress, took a picture with Clinton in the Oval Office.

And "racially insensitive" whites like Imus are compelled to apologize to these reverends.

Director Spike Lee also called for Imus's head. Lee, in a 1992 interview with *Esquire*, stated that he disliked interracial couples, "I give interracial couples a look. Daggers. They get uncomfortable when they see me on the street."[21] This puts him on the same side of the line as, say, David Duke.

Republican Senator Trent Lott (R-MS) complimented Senator Strom Thurmond (R-SC) on his hundredth birthday by saying, "I want to say this about my state: When Strom Thurmond ran for president, we voted for him. We're proud of it. And if the rest of the country had followed our lead, we wouldn't have had all these problems over all these years, either."[22]

Lott apologized and explained that he intended to flatter an old man on his hundredth birthday. He appeared on BET for an hour-long beat-down. And Spike Lee, on national television, without any evidence, called Lott a "card-carrying member of the Klan."[23]

Did Lee ever apologize for his anti-interracial remark or for the false accusation against Senator Lott? Please.

The hypocrisy does not end with this trio.

Presidential contender Senator Barack Obama (D-IL), became the only candidate to publicly call for Imus's firing, "He didn't just cross the line. He fed into some of the worst stereotypes that my two young daughters are having to deal with today in America. The notions that as young African-American women—who I hope will be athletes—that that somehow makes them less beautiful or less important. It was a degrading comment. It's one that I'm not interested in supporting."[24] Apparently the senator ignored his daughters' sensibilities when he allowed record mogul David Geffen to hold a fund-raiser for him. Geffen's company produces rappers like Snoop Dogg, who liberally uses the words "bitches" and "hos" in referring to women, brags about getting high, and produced X-rated videos. And a September 15, 2006, Associated Press dispatch noted that a hip-hop group called Nappy Roots warmed up the crowd before an Obama speech in Louisville, Kentucky.[25] Another AP dispatch on November 30, 2006, wrote that Obama met with rapper Ludacris—whose lyrics often call women "hos"—where, according to the artist, "We talked about empowering the youth."[26]

Wu Tang Clan's RZA—whose lyrics contain racial, gender, and sexual epithets too vile to repeat here—attended an exclusive Hollywood presidential campaign fund-raiser. Present at the fund-raiser—candidate Hillary Rodham Clinton (D-NY).[27] In addition, Ms. Clinton held another fund-raiser hosted by rapper/producer Timbaland. In his own music, Timbaland calls women "bitches" and "hos," as do other artists he produces. Clinton denounced Imus's words as "small-minded bigotry and coarse sexism." And in a speech delivered at Rutgers, she expanded, "Will you be willing to speak up and say, 'Enough is enough,' when women or minorities or the powerless are marginalized or degraded?"[28] Ms. Clinton, once again, committed the sin of selectivity—apparently it all depends on whether the person doing the degrading contributes to her campaign.

As for CBS, the radio network that canned Imus, they, too, showed a selective outrage. One of the network's popular syndicated radio hosts—who provides men with advice on how to handle women—routinely refers to women as "skanks" and "bitches."

A poll showed reaction to Imus's firing split down black-white racial lines, with most blacks agreeing with the firing, and most whites disagreeing. Call this another example of hypersensitivity/payback on the part of blacks, for the Rutgers basketball team represents a group of accomplished women, including a high school valedictorian, a prelaw student, and a classical music prodigy. How many of them even heard of Don Imus before his offensive remarks? Do any of these ladies have hip-hop/rap music with misogynist lyrics on their iPods? Here's a suggestion—ignore the remark. Ignore Sharpton and his ilk. After all, in the great department store of life, Imus operates in the toy section.

Another "Big Bombshell" occurred in November 2006.

Michael Richards, aka Kramer of *Seinfeld*, launched into a racist tirade against two black hecklers during a stand-up comedy show in Los Angeles. Richards, apparently irritated because the targets of his rage, among a larger group of friends that arrived late, disrupted his act.[29] Richards called the two "n——gers" numerous times, and many in the audience, appalled, began leaving. Someone called Richards a "f——ing white boy" and a "cracker-ass motherf——er."[30]

How many of them even heard of Don Imus before his offensive remarks? Do any of these ladies have hip-hop/rap music with misogynist lyrics on their iPods?

The exchange, captured on video by a comedy club patron, quickly appeared on the Internet and immediately became a "National Incident." Richards promptly appeared on Letterman and apologized profusely. He then continued the beat-down by appearing on Jesse Jackson's radio show, again apologizing. For good measure, he phoned Reverend Al Sharpton and apologized yet again.

Jamie Masada, the owner of the Laugh Factory, the comedy club where the tirade took place, refunded the distraught patrons' money and banned Richards from the club until he personally apologized to the offended patrons. Masada also called on Richards to donate millions to black charities.[31]

Hold the phone. Now, did Richards direct his unwarranted attack against two blacks in particular, or against the entire black race? When someone in the audience called Richards a "cracker," did *that* person direct that attack to the entire "white race," or to Richards in particular?

While he was under fire from the likes of Reverend Jesse Jackson, Al Sharpton and other so-called black leaders to "do something," I interviewed club owner Masada. Why, I asked him, do so many people transform an outburst from a has-been comic into the moral equivalent of let's-put-blacks-at-the-back-of-the-bus?

ELDER: I wonder why this has become this big, huge incident. I got a lot of letters from people who had seen Michael Richards perform, and several said that he teed off on a lot of people, got mad . . . he went off on Bush, went off on the troops, went off on Catholics, went off on Christians. . . . He appears to be somebody who's got a really short fuse. And I agree with you, he was just trying to hurt these two people. That's why I don't get it when he goes on Jesse Jackson's radio show and Jackson just beats him up and then starts talking about Hurricane Katrina and why there aren't more blacks on television, and why Congressman Harold Ford had a negative campaign ad that Jesse Jackson didn't like. For crying out loud! It was a guy who exploded, lost his temper, said some racist things, has apologized all over the place. You refunded everybody's money. It seems to me that should be the end of it, Jamie!
MASADA: I think you got a good point, but unfortunately, Larry, no matter what you do, there are some opportunists, there are some groups that are out there . . . they keep saying they are gonna riot, they are gonna burn up the club and they all keep calling and saying stuff. And it's unfortunate, because of some opportunists, they want to get something out of that incident and they're making it bigger than what it is."[32]

While fear of being tarnished with the same "racist" label probably kept Masada from calling the opportunists' bluff, at least he admitted that, yes, some people take advantage and exaggerate a "racial" situation for their own gain. For many nonblacks *wanted* to believe that the Richards incident produced positive proof of the remaining virulence of racism in America—as opposed to a dried-up comedian and an apparently unfunny standup who lost his temper and expressed it in a vulgar way. One of the hecklers accused him of failing at everything post-*Seinfeld*, a dispiriting—even if accurate—hurtful shot that contributed to Richards's outburst.

However, when a black guy uses the "n-word" against another black guy—even in anger—different rules apply. In January 2005, black NBA Portland Trail Blazers player Darius Miles defiantly shouted at his black coach, Maurice Cheeks, reportedly calling him "n——ger" during a team film session. Miles's punishment? A two-day suspension.[33]

Miles later released a statement: "Things were said in frustration and I am sorry for that. It is very important to me that our fans understand that I am committed to winning and that the losses we have had this season have been difficult for all of us. My entire focus when I return to the team will be on winning and helping us make a run for the playoffs."[34] Notice anything missing? An apology to the "victim," his coach, Maurice Cheeks.

However, when a black guy uses the "n-word" against another black guy—even in anger—different rules apply.

The Kramer flap continues a tradition of "beat whitey" when whites make a racially insensitive comment. For their "racially insensitive" remarks, golfer Fuzzy Zoeller, former CBS sports analyst Jimmy "the Greek" Snyder, former Los Angeles Dodger general manager Al Campanis, and former baseball pitcher John Rocker all lost sponsors or found themselves out of work—repeated apologies not accepted.

How bad did it get for Michael Richards? Richards left the country on a spiritual journey to Cambodia. He claimed the sojourn had nothing to do with his meltdown at the Laugh Factory, yet somehow his trip, undoubtedly via his press agent, made it into the *Los Angeles Times*. So now in addition to undergoing counseling and therapy to exorcise inner racist demons, you've got to do penance by leaving the country to contemplate life on mountaintop temples.

After the Michael Richards incident, Jackson, Sharpton, and others put out a covenant urging rappers, comics, and other performers to cease the use of the n-word.

I once attended a comedy club performance by Paul Mooney, a talented comedian who once wrote for the late Richard Pryor. He liberally used the n-word throughout his act. A white guy in the audience heckled him. Mooney went absolutely ballistic, launching into a racist tirade. He called the heckler "white boy," and called himself "one n——ger you can't push around." Guess who, after Richards' outburst, appeared in print and on television to say that Richards convinced *him* to stop using the n-word? Mr. Mooney.

This raises an interesting issue. If so-called black leaders and other influence-makers can simply halt the widespread use of the n-word by rappers and others, why not use this power to deal with urban crime? Or to halt the unacceptably high 50 percent inner-city high school dropout rate? Or to lower the 70 percent of today's out-of-wedlock black births?[35] Or do something about the estimated 25 to 30 percent of young black men who possess criminal records?[36]

And how about this proposal to the mainscream media: Please discontinue the use of the phrase "black leader"—a phrase used ad nauseam by the sympathetic media in reporting the reaction to Richards's outburst. The term "black leader," at some point, simply becomes a catchall statement—no credentials required. Why doesn't the media use the term "white leader"? The media's condescending, paternalistic attitude toward blacks considers them gullible or rudderless, so that, unlike other groups, blacks *need* a leader. Never mind that when asked, blacks reject the very "black leaders" that the media calls "black leaders."

The term "black leader," at some point, simply becomes a catchall statement—no credentials required.

An Associated Press–AOL Black Voices survey shows that when asked to name the "most important black leader," the highest percentage of blacks—about one-third—named . . . nobody. Jackson was named by 15 percent of respondents, 11 percent chose Secretary of State Condoleezza Rice, 8 percent named former Secretary of State Colin Powell, 6 percent chose Senator Barack Obama, 4 percent named Louis Farrakhan, 3 percent selected Oprah Winfrey, another 3 percent picked the late Dr. Martin Luther King Jr., Reverend Al Sharpton received 2 percent, and 14 percent picked someone other than the above. This means that nearly 50 percent of blacks named no one or someone other than these usual suspects.[37]

The National Association for the Advancement of Colored People (NAACP), ever eager to show its continued significance, put out a post-Kramer outburst statement, saying the incident reflects deep-seated, pervasive racist feelings in America.[38] The NAACP could have titled the memo, "Hot Damn! We're Still Relevant!"

But the evidence refutes the NAACP's assertion about America's continued racism. Black home ownership—all-time high. The employment rate for a married black man versus the employment rate for a married white man—almost identical. The black middle class continues to thrive, with blacks serving as CEOs of Time Warner, American Express, and more. Indeed, the fact that Richards rushed out and hired a publicist to do damage control shows the opposite of what the racism-is-under-every-rock crowd claims. Golfer Fuzzy Zoeller, following Tiger Woods's first Masters win, told reporters, "Tell him [Woods] not to serve fried chicken next year . . . or collard greens or whatever the hell they serve,"[39] a reference the winner's traditional selection of the clubhouse food for next year's event. Zoeller's $2 million loss in endorsements[40] after this rather innocuous "racially insensitive" comment demonstrates the truth of John O'Sullivan's statement. The social power against white racism is simply overwhelming.

When black PBS commentator Tavis Smiley hosted a Democratic presidential debate in front of a mostly black audience, C-Span host Brian Lamb asked Smiley why he failed to request and enforce a no-applause rule, as is customary. Tavis replied, "Because black people are an emotional people. *I know it would not have worked.*"[41] [Emphasis added.] Imagine if CNN's Wolf Blitzer, who also moderated a debate, failed to give the customary admonition before a predominately black audience, explaining that black audiences can't control themselves, or be expected to follow rules. How dare Lamb expect blacks to follow the same rules as everybody else. Doesn't Smiley owe blacks an apology?

And so, in the spirit of apologies, how about some other long-overdue gestures of contrition:

> *Dear Anti-Defamation League,*
> *Once again, please accept my apology for calling Jews*
> *"Hymies" and referring to New York City as "Hymie Town." As I*
> *said at the time, "Charge it to my head . . . not to my heart."*[42]
> *Sincerely,*
> *Reverend Jesse Jackson*
>
> *Dear NAACP, Urban League, and Congress of Racial Equality,*
> *Please accept my apology for—during concerts in which I*

sang my song, "Gold Digger"—giving whites permission to sing along and use the "n-word." Obviously, Michael Richards misused the license that I temporarily granted whites. Please accept my apology.

Kanye West, hip-hop/rapper

Dear Jewish Defense League, Korean-American Grocer Association, and Council on American-Islamic Relations,

Please accept my apology for, while serving as a spokesperson for Wal-Mart, condemning Jewish, Korean, and Arab inner-city merchants for "overcharging" blacks. I also inexcusably said that these merchants sell "stale bread and bad meat and wilted vegetables."[43] Charge that to my head, not my heart.

Sincerely yours,

Andrew Young, former U.N. ambassador for the United States, former mayor of Atlanta, and former colleague of Martin Luther King Jr.

Dear Republican National Committee,

I note that in last year's election cycle, the Republican Party ran a number of blacks—among them Maryland Lieutenant Governor Michael Steele for Senate, Ohio Secretary of State Ken Blackwell for governor, and Lynn Swann for governor in Pennsylvania. So please accept my apology for saying Republicans have a "white-boy attitude," which means, "I must exclude, denigrate, and leave behind."[44]

Sincerely yours,

Donna Brazile, former Al Gore 2000 campaign manager

Dear White Community,

Please accept my apology for my statement during the 2002 Millions for Reparations rally, in which I said, "I want to go up to the closest white person and say, 'You can't understand this, it's

a black thing,' and then slap him, just for my mental health."[45]
There goes my head!

Sincerely,

Charles Barron, New York City councilman

Dear Anti-Defamation League,

Please accept my apology. I lost my temper during my
husband's unsuccessful 1974 campaign for Congress. Bill's
campaign advisor, Paul Fray, and his wife publicly claim that I
referred to Fray as a "f——ing Jew bastard."[46]

I don't recall this, but assuming I did, what was I thinking? It
wasn't my heart.

Sincerely yours,

Senator Hillary Rodham Clinton

Dear Jesse Jackson and local Little Rock, Arkansas, black activist Robert "Say" McIntosh,

Former Arkansas state trooper Larry Patterson publicly
claims I referred to the two of you as "n-words."[47]

Ditto what Hillary just said.

Former president of the United States Bill Clinton

Dear NAACP, Congress of Racial Equality, Urban League,
and Reverends Jackson and Sharpton,

Please accept my apology for the allegations made by Jay
Homnick in an American Spectator article dated January 12,
2006. Homnick says that when I ran for State Assembly in 1974,
residents in the Flatbush area of Brooklyn held a meeting. The
mostly Italian, Jewish, and Slavic immigrant white residents
wanted to get rid of the apartment buildings on Avenue K
populated almost completely by blacks. According to Homnick,
who, as a teenager, attended the meeting, I promised, if elected,
to proclaim those building "dilapidated," move the blacks out, and
then—nudge, nudge, wink, wink—expensively refurbish their

apartment buildings and price the blacks out of the buildings. After renovations the blacks, whom we would have "temporarily" relocated, would have been unable to afford to move back into the more expensive and valuable apartments.[48] Voilà, no more blacks! I don't recall engaging in such a racist scheme, but if I did, it was a mistake of the mind, not of the heart.

Sincerely yours,

Senator Chuck Schumer (D-NY)

Dear Ward Connerly and anyone engaged in an interracial relationship,

When you led the successful campaign in California to get rid of race-based preferences, I criticized you, a black man, saying, "He's married a white woman. He wants to be white. He wants a color-less society. He has no ethnic pride. He doesn't want to be black."[49] Furthermore, please accept my apology, for, when offered an opportunity to explain or apologize, I said, "That's right. I said it."

Sincerely,

Congresswoman Diane Watson (D-CA)

Dear Colin Powell, Condoleezza Rice, and other minority members of the Bush administration,

Please accept my apology for, while cohosting the Allred & Taylor radio show in 2001, calling Bush's minority appointees, "Uncle Tom types."[50] Since I represent the two young men whom Michael Richards called n-words, I know my having called some blacks "Uncle Tom types" might seem hypocritical. But I made a mistake of the head, not of the heart.

Sincerely yours,

Gloria Allred, attorney-at-law

Dear Republican National Committee,

Please accept my apology for saying, after the Republicans

took over Congress in 1994, "It's not 'spic' or 'nigger' anymore. They say 'let's cut taxes.' "[51] Also, please accept my apology for, following Katrina, publicly saying, "George Bush is our Bull Connor"[52]—referring to the former Birmingham, Alabama, police commissioner, who turned water hoses and dogs on civil rights workers.

Sincerely,

Representative Charlie Rangel (D-NY), chairman of the House Ways and Means Committee

Dear Colin Powell, Condoleezza Rice, and any other blacks who served in the Bush administration,

Please accept my apology for calling you a house "slave" serving the "master."[53]

Sincerely,

Harry Belafonte, singer/activist

Dear Anti-Defamation League and white community,

Please accept my apologies for calling whites "interlopers," and referring to Jews as "diamond merchants,"[54] and, during a conflict between Jews and blacks, saying, "If the Jews want to get it on, tell them to pin their yarmulkes back and come over to my house."[55]

Reverend Al Sharpton, civil rights activist and former host of Saturday Night Live

Dear Anti-Defamation League and Jewish Community,

Please accept my apology for the title of my new book, Palestine: Peace Not Apartheid. On reflection, likening the condition in the Palestinian territories to South Africa's apartheid was a bit much. In 1947, the U.N. divided the area be-tween a Palestinian state and a Jewish state, after which several Arab countries attacked the new state of Israel. Furthermore, as

Alan Dershowitz recently pointed out, following the U.N. mandate, Arabs met in Khartoum and agreed "no peace, no recognition, no negotiation."[56] I made mistakes of the head, not the heart.

    Sincerely yours,
    Former President Jimmy Carter

What about *those* apologies?

Why tell your viewers about an increasing problem with gang violence, when you've got two and a half minutes of grainy video taken on a cell phone, showing Richards during his meltdown?

Don't hold your breath, for debacles like the Kramer matter trigger wall-to-wall, headline, stop-the-presses coverage that seems to last for weeks, including never-ending apologies. Real news of the day got shoved aside for the "racist Kramer" coverage. Why tell your viewers about an increasing problem with gang violence when you've got two and a half minutes of grainy video taken on a cell phone, showing Richards during his meltdown?

Media make this sort of decision every day. With only so many minutes of airtime, or so many column inches of print available, the decision of what to report and what to ignore exposes media's perception of race and racism. Decision after decision show that many in the liberal media—despite evidence to the contrary—believe racism against blacks remains a big deal in today's America.

If the media *truly* care, they ought to reconsider the damage done by perpetuating the I-am-a-victim attitude. According to a long-term study recently published in the *Journal of Epidemiology and Community*, a victicrat mentality can give you a heart attack. People who reported high levels of unfair treatment in their lives were 55 percent more likely to suffer a coronary event than the ones who did not complain of unfairness. Even people who reported low levels of unfair treatment experienced a 28 percent greater rate of cardiac problems than the ones who reported no unfairness.[57]

The study was based on the participants'—all British civil servants—perceived and self-reported *feelings* of being unfairly treated. Yet, in reporting the study findings, the *Los Angeles Times* swiftly made it an issue of racism. "Nancy Krieger," reported the *Times*, "a professor at the Harvard School of Public Health, said the study added to a growing field of research linking poor cardiovascular and mental health to racial and gender discrimination—two significant sources of unfair treatment. People who think they are victims of discrimination often respond by drinking, smoking, or overeating. 'They do things that take the edge off,' Krieger said. 'If you do those things, those will have health consequences.' "[58]

Angry black economist and frequent television pundit Julianne Malveaux often writes for *USA Today* and other prestigious magazines and newspapers. She deserves a special place in the Victicrat Hall of Fame for her book, *Sex, Lies and Stereotypes: Perspectives of a Mad Economist*.

I once got into it with Malveaux on the *Charles Grodin Show* on CNBC:

JULIANNE MALVEAUX: Race is a factor and you could watch all the conservative sort-of rap that you want to put out there about unwed mothers and about prisons and you're failing to look at some of the institutional issues that are extremely important.

LARRY ELDER: Let me respond and let me make it very simple. Today in America if you have an education, if you're willing to work hard, if you have drive, if you have energy, you can make it, whether you're black, whether you're white, whether you're Asian, whether you're male, whether you're female. *The Wall Street Journal* had a poll. They asked blacks and Hispanics and Asians and whites whether they felt confident about their prospects for promotion in their corporations. Asians and blacks and Latinos were more confident about their prospects for promotion than were whites. I think you and people like you do a great deal of damage by constantly looking for the Great White Bigot instead of telling people, "Work hard!" "Get an education!" "Learn how to speak standard English!"

MALVEAUX: You don't know what I say to people. I talk about working hard and about education and there's no Great White Bigot, there's just about two hundred million Little White Bigots out there.

ELDER: Two hundred million Little White Bigots? Do you realize how appalling that statement is?"[59]

Conservative commentator Sean Hannity interviewed Malveaux a few years later. Malveaux said, "Terrorism in the United States is as old as we are. You want me to give you a litany of terrorism? You want me to start with what's happened to the Indian population? You want to go on to what happened in Tulsa, Oklahoma, in 1921? . . . We are terrorists." Hannity asked her if the United States was a "terrorist nation," and she answered, "Oh, absolutely . . . the chickens have come back to roost," obviously referring to 9/11. Hannity then asked if America was "a good country." Her response? "We're a country." And when asked why she omitted the word "good," she said, "I can't answer that. I think we have some good and I think we have some evil."[60]

Finally, toward the end of the interview, the ever angry Malveaux, referring to "the weapons of mass distraction," said, "You know they weren't there. I know they weren't there. George Bush is evil. He is a terrorist. He is evil. He is arrogant. And he is out of control."[61] Oh.

"Two-hundred-million-little-white-bigots" Malveaux isn't

alone in using her media spotlight to find racism everywhere. Media malpractice helps blacks to think like victims, even when the victims fail to grasp their own victimization.

Take the case of the infamous Harold Ford "call me" political attack ads. In 2006, black Representative Harold Ford (D-TN) ran for Senate. His opponent ran an ad that purported to unmask Ford—running as a kind of Democratic centrist—as your basic Democratic lefty. The ad showed a bunch of Tennesseans criticizing Ford for his stances on everything from taxes to North Korea. In the beginning of the ad, a ditsy blonde said she met Harold Ford at a "Playboy party." At the end of the ad, the same woman appears and whispers, "Harold, call me."

Without skipping a beat, critics cried racism!

MSNBC's Chris Matthews said, "Well, that was a racist ad, and it ripped the scab off the old racial animosities in this country and fears. You see a very attractive—sexy, if you will—white woman, a blonde, a floozy, saying that you don't have to come for me, I'm coming for you. And after the commercial, she pops back in after the Republicans have said we agree with the content of this ad, she pops around the corner and says, 'I'll call you later, Howard.' In other words, she's throwing herself at a black guy. You're talking about opening up all the old fears and angers. That was the most racist ad I think I've ever seen. And anybody that doesn't see it is either not born in America or refuses to accept the reality."[62]

Washington Post writer E. J. Dionne Jr. also pronounced the ad racist. "And there is what will, sadly, become the most famous advertisement of this election cycle, the 'Harold, call me,' ad run by the Republican National Committee against Representative Harold Ford Jr., the Democratic candidate for Senate from Tennessee. To claim that an ad depicting a pretty blonde woman coming on to an African-American politician does not play on the fears of miscegenation on the part of some whites is to ignore history."[63]

A *New York Times* editorial, too, read, "The sleazy way in

which U.S. political parties use loopholes in the campaign fi-
nance laws to evade responsibility for their attack ads is on full
display in the Tennessee Senate race. Slick as a leer, pernicious
as a virus, a campaign commercial transparently honed as a racist
appeal to Tennessee voters has remained on the air, despite as-
surance from Republican sponsors that it was pulled down."[64]

Never mind that Ford added to the "controversy" by first
denying ever attending a party at the Playboy Mansion. He later,
however, admitted attending a "Playboy-sponsored Super Bowl
party," an admission that, if made right away, might have headed
off the entire "controversy."

But guess who failed to call the "Harold, call me" ad racist?
Harold Ford. He said, "I don't think race had anything to do
with that ad."[65]

In "racist America," interracial relationships supposedly
drive the sheet-and-hood crowd absolutely crazy.

Tiger Woods, arguably the most recognizable athlete in the
world, dominates the sport of golf, a pastime that, unlike other
sports, likely appeals to a disproportionately conservative,
upper-income crowd. Tiger, a multiethnic man who calls himself "Cablinasian"[66]—Caucasian, black, American Indian, and
Asian—married a white woman. He lost no endorsements; his
TV ratings remained through the roof.

After winning the January 1, 2007, Fiesta Bowl, black Boise
State running back Ian Johnson dropped to one knee and proposed to his white cheerleader girlfriend on national television.
Giddy fans and viewers cheered wildly as print and television
media soaked up the feel-good story. But what about the black
groom/white fiancée angle? Nobody seemed to care.

The black population in Idaho checks in at a mere 0.6 percent.[67] And former L.A.P.D. "racist cop" Mark Fuhrman moved to
that state after the O. J. Simpson trial. Undoubtedly, Boise State
University's fan base is probably pretty "lily-white." But the Fiesta
Bowl proposal played out—as it should—like a fairy-tale love story,
and none of the fans grabbed their sheets and hoods. Although

one wonders how black Congresswoman Diane "he's-married-to-a-white-woman, he-wants-to-be-white"[68] Watson, and black director Spike "I-give-interracial-couples-a-look, daggers"[69] Lee reacted to the proposal.

But the hunt for racism as a debilitating factor continues. Black *USA Today* columnist DeWayne Wickham wrote about the reaction to Mexican postage stamps that show a cartoonish, monkeylike black character with oversized lips. Black advocacy groups and "leaders" like the NAACP, the Urban League, Al Sharpton, Jesse Jackson, and others denounced the Mexican government's "racism." Wickham shared their outrage.

But, in a twist, Wickham also took these groups and leaders to task for turning a blind eye when blacks distort their *own* images. "I am dumbfounded," wrote Wickham, "by their failure to just as loudly challenge some more prominent warped images of blacks that have surfaced recently in this country." Wickham, for example, pointed to the July 2005 "Jail Issue" of *XXL* magazine, which "contained interviews with some of what it calls hip-hop music's 'incarcerated soldiers.' " Incarcerated soldiers? The interviewed "soldiers" included black rap artists Corey "C-Murder" Miller (convicted of second degree murder), Michael "Mystikal" Tyler (pled guilty to sexual battery), and Antron "Big Lurch" Singleton (guilty of murdering a woman and then eating part of her lung). Charming guys. But hey, according to *XXL*, "the startling number of imprisoned rappers is ultimately a product of a nation that funnels a third of its black males ages 20–29 through jail, the penitentiary, parole or probation."[70]

"Making these thugs the focus of sympathetic coverage," writes Wickham, "ought to enrage civil rights leaders more than an offensive Mexican stamp. But they've yet to call a press conference to blast the damage these warped images can do to the psyche of young blacks in this country."

Racism provides a convenient way of avoiding serious examination of issues. Crying racism takes less effort than, for example, examining the data that show why black loan applications get turned down at a greater rate. Crying racism takes less effort than exploring why black children underperform compared to their white and Asian counterparts. Crying racism avoids the awful, horrible truth that maybe, just maybe, the "victim's" action or inaction accounts for disparate outcomes.

Racism provides a convenient way of avoiding serious examination of issues. Crying racism takes less effort than, for example, examining the data that show why black loan applications get turned down at a greater rate. Crying racism takes less effort than exploring why black children underperform compared to their white and Asian counterparts. Crying racism avoids the awful, horrible truth that maybe, just maybe, the "victim's" action or inaction accounts for disparate outcomes.

Although they pronounced Republicans "racist" for the "Call me" Harold Ford ads, there's no word yet from Chris Matthews or E. J. Dionne on the black-on-black celebration of the thug culture.

Where were Matthews and Dionne when Chrysler began running television ads pairing Lee Iacocca with dope-toking rapper Snoop Dogg? The commercial shows the twosome riding in a golf cart at a country club, while Snoop praises Chrysler cars. Iacocca said later he didn't know anything about Snoop Dogg. "He's just a good kid," said Iacocca. "I didn't understand half the things he was telling me, but it was fun."[71]

Well, Lee Iacocca, at eighty years old, probably knows little about rap music artists. So for the record, Snoop Dogg openly raps about drug use, filmed an X-rated video, and has a rap sheet that includes multiple felony arrests and convictions. He records "songs" filled with vulgar words like "f——ed up," "bitch," "ho," and "nigga," glorifying violence toward women. Apparently, "racist" corporate America found this pretty inoffensive.

But there might be some racism—against *whites*—when it comes to using pitchmen with similarly thuggish backgrounds. Automaker Ford, for example, pulled the plug on a deal to loan white rapper Eminem a Ford vehicle for his new video, after hearing Eminem's new song was about, among other things, urination. It's hard out there for a thuggish white rapper who wants to endorse mainstream products in America.

"Obstacles" faced by today's blacks shrivel in comparison to those faced by millions of black men and women of yesterday, who still managed to overcome and thrive. Think of the struggles endured by people like black baseball Hall of Famers Henry Aaron and Frank Robinson. They worked their way up through segregated minor leagues before breaking into the major leagues. Robinson became Major League Baseball's first black manager.

Black Hall of Fame first baseman Eddie Murray had an older brother named Charles, who played in the minor leagues in the '60s. Charles quit baseball and never made it to the major leagues, emotionally crushed by the segregation he endured in fighting his way up.

A reporter asked Frank Robinson about Charles Murray. Robinson responded with the kind of grit and attitude that made him great: "He wasn't strong," Robinson said. "He went home. He didn't pursue what he wanted to do in life. He let a barrier prevent him from doing that. If that was the case, then there would have been no blacks in baseball, because the barrier was there."[72]

Robinson's response surprised the reporter, who apparently empathized with Charles Murray's decision to quit. According to *The New York Times*, "The reporter seemed taken aback; he apparently saw quitting in this case as a sign of quiet dignity. In Robinson's world, successful struggle is built upon resistance and tenacity of purpose."[73]

People like Aaron and Robinson realized that, even then, they had opportunities. Today's generation must now make use of the opportunities denied to those who came before. How insulting and dismissive of the deep, hardcore racist abuse dealt with by the Aarons and the Robinsons—when the mainscream media writes article after article expressing sympathy for the alleged racist "plight" of blacks in contemporary America.

2.

DEMOCRATS, STUPID BLACKS, AND REPUBLICANS

Politically, black America is almost socialistic. There's a feeling that the government is the vehicle that's going to lift us to equality, and without the government, we'll never make it. Black America has suffered from this delusion since the 1960s. It's gotten to the point where we've now made affiliation with the Democratic Party an aspect of the black American identity. No matter who the Democratic nominee is, they get 90 percent of the black vote in every single election. If you are black and not a Democrat, it's said that you're not authentically black—the civil rights leadership vigorously enforces that. So you have this disjuncture in black life: we're culturally conservative, but politically, we are far, far left.[1]

—SHELBY STEELE, SOCIOLOGIST

When you look at the way the House of Representatives has been run, it has been run like a plantation, and you know what I'm talking about. It has been run in a way so that nobody with a contrary view has had a chance to present legislation, to make an argument, to be heard.[2]

—SENATOR HILLARY CLINTON,
TO A MOSTLY BLACK HARLEM CHURCH AUDIENCE

Democrats need blacks. It is not the other way around. Democrats need blacks to continue to believe that racism remains America's number-one problem.

When someone—especially a black person—says otherwise, he or she must be demeaned in the most profane of ways. Janeane Garofalo, for example, broadcasting her Air America show from the Democratic National Convention, called me a "fascist," a "racist," and a "douche bag." After a caller informed me of her attack, I invited her on my show, and she agreed to come on. She, in turn, invited me on her show, and I agreed. When, for example, I informed her that, as a percentage of the party, more Republicans voted for the passage of the Civil Rights Act than did Democrats, she simply asserted that was untrue. Why let the facts get in the way of an attack on the Republican Party, or, for that matter, on anyone who dares to question the smug liberal orthodoxy?

Like a magician using misdirection, Democrats avert blacks' attention from other relevant issues. Blacks, for example, stand to benefit disproportionately more from the privatization of Social Security, a Republican idea. Black men receive the lowest rate of return, and pay more into Social Security than they receive. Why? They die at a younger age than black females or whites. "African-Americans understand this," writes the Cato Institute, "and are increasingly coming to embrace Social Security privatization. According to a Zogby International poll conducted for the Cato Institute, African-Americans support privatization by a margin of 58 to 30 percent. Other polls show similar results."[3]

Republicans are more "prolife" than Democrats. So are blacks. A 2004 Zogby poll found 56 percent of all Americans believe abortion should never be legal, or legal only if the mother's life is in danger, or legal in cases of rape or incest, compared to 62 percent of blacks.[4]

Republicans support education vouchers to empower parents to choose school for their children, rather than for government to make that decision. Urban blacks overwhelmingly support education vouchers, so they can have some choice in how and where their child is educated.[5] A 1999 National Opinion Poll found 87 percent of black parents, ages twenty-six to thirty-five—those most likely to have school-age children—want vouchers.[6]

While polls show Americans are frustrated with the government's failure to control our borders, Republicans—more so than Democrats—seem determined to do something about it. Illegal workers compete against legal workers in America, especially "unskilled" legal workers. Labor attorney and U.S. Commission on Civil Rights member Peter Kirsanow writes, "It's no secret that black workers are more heavily concentrated in unskilled occupations—the very occupations in which the greatest amount of displacement by illegal immigrants has taken place. It's not unreasonable, then, to infer that workforce displacement caused by illegal immigration has a far more pronounced effect on blacks than whites."[7]

During Labor Day, 2006, the government cracked down on the Georgia-based Crider corporation, a chicken processing company, for hiring illegal aliens. Their mostly Hispanic workforce of nine hundred promptly declined some 75 percent. "Until the late 1990s," says *The Wall Street Journal*, "the plant employed a majority black production line, with whites and some blacks as supervisors, according to current and former employees. By 2000, Latino migrant workers who had long come and gone with the cotton and onion seasons were putting down roots, part of a national trend. . . . The presence of so many illegal workers became routine at Crider."[8]

When the Republican-led House of Representatives, in 2006, passed a tough anti-illegal alien bill, protestors took to the streets and staged rallies in several cities. Democratic Los Angeles Mayor Antonio Villaraigosa appeared at one protest, thundering, "There are no illegal people here today!"[9] *What?*

Democrats know that if blacks ever stop believing that racism holds them down, stop thinking like victicrats, stop looking at the world through race-tinted glasses and start looking at the things issue by issue, then the Democratic Party—especially at the national level—is doomed. Democrats, for their very preservation, need to cry "racism" in order to keep blacks angry and keep their minds closed and eyes shut towards Republican policies.

One Sunday morning, as I drove to my local tennis court to play a match, I heard a black radio commentator give this assessment of the now late, great fortieth president: "Ronald Reagan tortured blacks." Imagine my conflict. Here I am heading to the tennis court, wanting to work on my backhand, with Reagan, all the while, "torturing" members of my race.

For many blacks who hate Republicans, this dislike of Republican icon Ronald Reagan is rabid. But this raises a question. How *did* blacks fare under President Reagan?

During the Reagan years, federal spending for social programs increased from $344.3 billion in 1981 to $412 billion in 1989, a 19.7 percent increase using 1982 dollars. Yet Reagan's critics explain away the rise as driven simply by increased spending on the elderly—primarily Social Security and Medicare. This, according to the Reagan-haters, was "offset" by the reduction in spending on the poor. Not true. Spending on programs to provide income support, food, housing, health care, education, training, and social services to poor families rose from $104 billion in 1981 (using 1989 dollars) to $123 billion in 1989—an 18 percent increase. As a percentage of Gross National Product (GNP), such means-tested social spending during Reagan's two terms averaged 1.73 percent. By contrast, during the Carter years, social spending, as a percentage of GNP, averaged 1.65 percent.[10]

From the end of 1982 to 1989, black unemployment dropped 9 percentage points (from 20.4 percent to 11.4 percent), while white unemployment dropped by only 4 percentage points.[11] Black household income went up 84 percent from 1980 to 1990, versus a white household income increase of 68 percent.[12] The number of black-owned businesses increased from 308,000 in 1982 to 424,000 in 1987, a 38 percent rise versus a 14 percent increase in the total number of firms in the United States.[13] Receipts by black-owned firms more than doubled, from $9.6 billion to $19.8 billion.[14]

If this is "torture," more, please—and a side of fries.

But actor Danny Glover, like many blacks, when hearing of the death of Ronald Reagan, seemed gleeful: "We all know Reagan's legacy, from the Iran-Contra affair to the funding of the Nicaraguan military in which over two hundred thousand people died. The groundwork for the move steadily to the right happened with the Reagan administration. People want to elevate him to some mythic level; they have their own reason for doing that."[15] Of course, no one *ever* elevated JFK or Bill Clinton—our first "black" president—to some mythic level. Oh, well, while he didn't attempt to hide his disgust, at least Glover didn't use the occasion of the president's death to claim Reagan was a hood-wearing Klansman.

The "torture" theme continues for George W. Bush.

Coretta Scott King, the wife of civil rights icon Martin Luther King Jr., died January 30, 2006. Former Presidents Jimmy Carter, George H. W. Bush, and Bill Clinton, along with their wives, attended her funeral. President George W. Bush and the First Lady also came to the funeral. In blatant disrespect to President George W. Bush—who sat right behind them—speaker after speaker condemned the president in the harshest of terms.

Never mind that this president appointed more blacks to positions of true responsibility than any other president in history. Or that he supported and signed the extension of the Voting Rights Act, despite its obsolescence and violation of Republican principals of states' rights. Or that much of his spending contradicted core Republican values. Bush authorized $15 billion to combat HIV/AIDS in Africa, more money than allocated by any president in history. He increased social spending, a disproportionately high percentage of which goes to blacks. Bush also publicly supports an increase in the minimum wage, something Reagan successfully thwarted during his entire eight-year tenure.

Yet, at the Coretta King funeral, the church crackled with Bush and Republican Party–bashing.

Coretta's daughter, Reverend Bernice King, delivered the eulogy, comparing her mother's ovarian cancer to the "materialism . . . greed, elitism, arrogance, militarism, poverty," and racism that are allegedly overtaking the country.[16]

Former President Jimmy Carter drew cheers when he alluded to President Bush's surveillance of terrorists by comparing it to when the government spied on Martin Luther King Jr.: "It was difficult for them personally," said Carter, "with the civil liberties of both husband and wife violated as they became the target of secret government wiretapping, other surveillance, and as you know, harassment from the FBI."[17]

Reverend Joseph Lowery continued the pounding. Lowery, cofounder—along with Martin Luther King Jr.—of the Southern Christian Leadership Conference, castigated Bush for insufficient disaster relief, failing to provide health care, and failing to cure poverty. He said, "We know now there were no weapons of mass destruction over there. But Coretta knew there were weapons of misdirection right here. Millions without health insurance, poverty abounds. For war, billions more. For poor, no more."[18] Yet President Bush, remaining on stage during these attacks, kept his grace and cool, even giving Lowery a standing ovation and a bear hug at the conclusion of the reverend's remarks.[19]

But it got worse.

Entertainer/activist Harry Belafonte accused Bush of preventing him from speaking at the funeral. When Coretta Scott King died, Belafonte cancelled a speech scheduled at Cleveland's Case Western University, saying, "Due to a recent tragic unfolding, the death of Mrs. Martin Luther King Jr., I have been requested by the family and my fellow leaders from the civil rights movement to deliver a part of the eulogy on the occasion of her burial on Tuesday, February 7, 2006, in Atlanta, Georgia. The loss of Mrs. King is profound. My relationship to Dr. King and Mrs. King and with their children since the time of their birth has always been evident. I could not imagine being required to speak in the church at her service and not be in attendance."[20]

But Belafonte did not speak at the funeral. When President George W. Bush decided to attend the funeral, Belafonte accused the White House of interfering, pressuring the King family into disinviting him from Mrs. King's funeral because of Belafonte's well-known hostility toward the Bush administration. "I called Belafonte to find out for myself," said Reverend C. T. Vivian a few days after the funeral. "I asked, were you disinvited, and he said, yes. The reason is that the president was not coming if Belafonte was going to be there."[21] Or perhaps even the King family considered it disrespectful to include Belafonte.

Why? Belafonte, only weeks earlier, while visiting Venezuela and President Hugo Chavez, called Bush "the greatest terrorist in the world."[22]

Few would blame Bush for not wanting to hang around Belafonte, given this singer's odious comments and Bush's probable fear that Belafonte might pull a repeat performance at the funeral. But what about the facts? Did Bush stop Belafonte from speaking?

The publicist who assisted the King family in putting on the funeral said no: "The rumor Harry Belafonte was disinvited to the King funeral is one hundred percent inaccurate. The only individuals with the authority to take such action were the King family. The White House did not have the authority, nor did anyone else—again, only the family. It is ridiculous and insulting to suggest that they would treat someone so close to them and their mother in such a manner. It is up to Mr. Belafonte to answer the question of why he was not in attendance. The King children would have welcomed his presence. In fact, he was listed in the program as an honorary pallbearer. Additionally, the rumor is very suspect because no one, including Mr. Belafonte, can explain exactly who it was that supposedly disinvited him. The reason for this is, of course, the fact that he was always welcome."[23]

The controversy continued, and so almost *two months* after the funeral, the King family issued a statement blaming an unnamed aide for "uninviting" Belafonte without their knowledge.[24] Sounds like a conspiracy on the part of the racist, dastardly George W. Bush.

If blacks dislike white Republicans, consider their attitude toward *black* Republicans. In 2001, 9,101 blacks held elected office.[25] Of that number, care to guess how many were Republican? Approximately fifty.[26] Consider what a black Republican politician faces.

Michael Steele grew up in a poor area of Washington, D.C. His dad drove a limo. Mom did laundry. Both were Democrats. But he became a Republican. Why? In his neighborhood, says Steele, "everyone—cousins, friends and neighbors—was always asking [my mother] why she didn't take public assistance. 'Why don't you stand in line and get a check?'" His mom, says Steele, would always give the same answer: "Because I don't want the government raising my kids." Later, when he first heard Ronald Reagan, Steele realized that Reagan's message of self-reliance was just like his mother's. A personalized, autographed photograph of The Gip, says Steele, "is one of my proudest possessions."[27]

In his neighborhood, says Steele, "everyone— cousins, friends and neighbors—was always asking [my mother] why she didn't take public assistance. 'Why don't you stand in line and get a check?'" His mom, says Steele, would always give the same answer: "Because I don't want the government raising my kids."

Lieutenant Governor Mike Steele became the first black person elected to a statewide office in Maryland. In 2005, Steele announced his candidacy for the U.S. Senate. Almost immediately, a doctored photo showed up on a popular liberal news blog, showing Steele as a minstrel and using racial slurs to describe him. The blog's headline: "Simple Sambo Wants to Move to the Big House."[28] But, by then, Steele was probably used to it. A few years earlier, in 2001, the president of the Maryland State Senate called Steele "an Uncle Tom." During the gubernatorial campaign in 2002, the *Baltimore Sun* wrote that Mr. Steele "brings little to the team but the color of his skin." During a campaign debate, detractors threw Oreo cookies at the candidate for lieutenant governor.[29]

"Delegate Salima Siler Marriott, a black Baltimore Democrat," wrote the *Washington Times*, "said Mr. Steele invites comparisons to a slave who loves his cruel master or a cookie that is black on the outside and white inside because his conservative political philosophy is, in her view, anti-black."[30]

When asked about the fairness of these attacks on Steele, the black Democratic state senator from Baltimore, Lisa A. Gladden, said, "Party trumps race, especially on the national level. It's democracy, perhaps at its worst, but it is democracy."[31]

Senator Barack Obama traveled to Maryland and spoke at Bowie State University to rally support for the white Democratic senatorial candidate, Ben Cardin, Steele's opponent. "The nation's best-known black elected official, Illinois Sen. Barack Obama," wrote the Associated Press, "on Friday urged hundreds of blacks not to vote along racial lines next week in Maryland's Senate race. . . . 'Listen, I think it's great that the Republican Party has discovered black people,' Obama said to laughter from students at the predominantly black school. 'But here's the thing . . . you don't vote for somebody because of what they look like. You vote for somebody because of what they stand for.' "[32] And what they—Republicans—stand for is, by definition, hurtful and antithetical to the interests and needs of blacks.

But two days later, Obama journeyed to Tennessee and asked voters at two black churches and a Nashville rally to elect

Harold Ford, a black Democrat running for the Senate. But here, instead of encouraging blacks to vote their interests and *not* down racial lines, he gave the opposite message. "I know that all of you are going to work the next couple of days to make sure it happens, because I'm feeling lonely in Washington," Obama said at the Mount Zion Baptist Church.[33] If Obama means his "loneliness" would be cured by the election of another black to the Senate, why not support Steele?

Steele, despite receiving support from many black religious, business, and political leaders, lost his race. Given the "R" next to his name, Steele failed to muster the black vote, especially in the heavily black Prince George's County, Steele's home for twenty years. Despite targeting Prince George's growing middle and upper classes, he took only 26 percent of the vote there, with his white Democrat opponent getting 76 percent.[34] Black voters, irrespective of class and income, simply do not trust Republicans—black or white.

Maryland Bishop Harry Jackson, one of Steele's supporters, said, "In the post-civil rights era, there has been a feeling by blacks that the Republican Party was anti-the little guy and pro-state's rights." State's rights, he explained, "is for many blacks still a code word for segregation."[35]

Of black conservatives, *St. Petersburg Times* black columnist Bill Maxwell said: "Take the wildebeest, the warthog, the hyena, the brown pelican, the Shar-Pei. These animals, seemingly wrought by committee, make us laugh or shake our heads. Another such creature, of the human kind—and perhaps the strangest of all—is the black Republican. . . . Black Republicans fail to understand that white Republicans will never accept them as equals. Although they will not acknowledge the truth, white Republicans, like most other whites, view black Republicans as strange creatures. . . .

"Some blacks, like General Powell, become Republicans because they see clear political advantage or because they work for Republicans. Most others, however, are mean-spirited self-loathers who rarely find anything positive to say about fellow blacks. They out-nasty the worst white racist, calling the likes of

Jesse Jackson, the NAACP's Kweisi Mfume and the Urban League's Hugh Price evil men hell-bent on destroying America. White Republicans love this kind of stuff. They wink and nod each time black Republicans claim that racism is a thing of the past, that whites and blacks are free to compete equally. Black Republicans have fooled themselves into believing that white Republicans are their brethren. And, of course, black Republicans delude themselves into believing that they alone are responsible for their success."[36]

These same liberal black Democrats found no quarrel with white cartoonist/writer Ted Rall when he called Condoleezza Rice a "house nigga,"[37] but the most heinous condemnation of black conservatives or black Republicans usually comes from other blacks.

More viciousness? Consider black writer Erin Aubry Kaplan's article about George Bush's former domestic policy advisor Claude Allen, who is black. Few even heard of Claude Allen—at least, not until March 9, 2006. On that day, police arrested the adviser for allegedly stealing $5,000 in store refunds.[38]

According to the police, Allen's modus operandi went like this. He purchased items, brought them out to his car, and then returned to the store with the receipt. He then chose a similar item from inside the store, and took the item and receipt in hand for a "refund." Authorities said over a period of several months, Allen scammed and cheated stores like Target out of $5,000.[39]

President Bush said upon learning of the arrest, "If the allegations are true, Claude Allen did not tell my chief of staff and legal counsel the truth, and that's deeply disappointing."[40] Allen, for what it's worth, had resigned from his position some three weeks earlier.

Writer Kaplan nearly snapped an Achilles tendon as she jumped with glee and pronounced Allen "sick." Ideologically sick, that is, for only an internally tortured black would join the Bush administration. Thus Allen's thievery simply showed the sheer incompatibility of being both black and conservative. In an article subtitled: "Did the Pressures of Being a Black Conservative Take a Toll on the Former Bush Aide?" Kaplan wrote, "I don't support conservatism in its current iteration, and I support black conservatives even less, but we cannot ignore the racial implications of this latest Republican fall from grace." Later she offers a diagnosis of Claude Allen: "Was he fatally overconfident—fatal indeed for a black man—that his position shielded him from the consequences of crime, or at least the consequences of petty theft?"[41] Always a mistake for a black man to be *that* confident—at least a Republican black man.

Incredible.

Let's try to unravel this. Apparently black conservatives, not so very deep down inside, consider their artificially adopted ideology as evil, as an attack on "my own people." So their inner turmoil, goes Kaplan's psychological analysis, will inevitably result in an explosion or a meltdown of sorts. Thus, Kaplan writes of Claude Allen, "After a career of always conducting himself appropriately, as his mentor Clarence Thomas reportedly advised, did he finally crack under the pressure? . . . It's hard to imagine that such compromises and cognitive dissonance don't exact a psychological toll at some point, and Allen's alleged dabbling in crime might have been that point for him."[42]

This does not, of course, explain the travails of black *liberal* politicians.

Let's examine a few of those in the Clinton administration. At the time of his death, Commerce Secretary Ron Brown was under investigation for corruption by the Office of the Independent Counsel. Agricultural Secretary Mike Espy resigned from his position because of an independent counsel's investigation of allegations that he improperly accepted gifts from businesses and lobbyists. (Espy was indicted, but a jury acquitted him.)

Independent counsel Ralph Lancaster investigated Labor Secretary Alexis Herman for allegedly soliciting illegal campaign contributions while working as a White House aide. (Lancaster eventually announced he would not seek an indictment of Herman.)

How does Kaplan's psychotic black conservative syndrome square with, say, black Representative William Jefferson (D-LA)? The feds reportedly videotaped Jefferson accepting $100,000 in bribes.[43] This led to a search of Jefferson's home. During the FBI search, Jefferson asked to take a look at the subpoena that authorized the search. An agent handed him a copy of the subpoena. As Jefferson reviewed it, he took other documents from a table, inserted them among the subpoena pages and placed them in the blue bag, which had already been searched.[44] An agent caught him, potentially setting up the congressman for an obstruction of justice charge. In any case, the FBI agents found $90,000 in cash—in his freezer, wrapped in aluminum foil and stuffed in frozen food boxes.[45]

Did Jefferson's *liberalism* push him to allegedly steal and attempt to hide evidence?

Or perhaps Kaplan might help us explore the apparent "neurosis" of black long-time Congressman John Conyers (D-MI). Former staffers charged that Conyers used them for personal errands, forced them to baby-sit, chauffer, and tutor his children, and demanded his staff to work in election campaigns for his family and friends. Deanna Maher, one of the aides, wrote to the House Ethics Committee, "I could not tolerate any longer being involved with continual unethical, if not criminal, practices which were accepted as 'business as usual.' "[46]

And if you think Kaplan hates Claude Allen, the writer absolutely, positively loathes Secretary of State Condoleezza Rice. Surely Kaplan expects, at some point, for Rice to psychologically "melt down" and engage in a drive-by shooting. Any day now, expect Colin Powell to climb a water tower with an AK-47 to start mowing down innocent citizens.

Writing for the leftwing alternative newspaper *L.A. Weekly*, Kaplan wrote: "Alas, Rice *is* the bullshit we all need to be guarding against now, along with a string of other so-called history-making Negroes."[47] Kaplan even attacked Rice's physical appearance: "With her tight smirk, serpentine gaze and hopelessly immutable hairdo, she's been Bush's black doppelgänger to a tee, albeit better-spoken."[48] She also attacked Rice's predecessor, Colin Powell, as a "sell-out."[49]

Rice gets no credit for defending the University of Michigan when it was challenged by the government for its use of race-based preferences. Rice said, "I believe that while race-neutral means are preferable, it is appropriate to use race as one factor among others in achieving a diverse student body."[50] And during the 2000 Republican Convention, the future Secretary of State Colin Powell said, "[S]ome in our party miss no opportunity to roundly and loudly condemn affirmative action that helped a few thousand black kids get an education."[51] But Kaplan gives no credit to Rice or Powell for taking stands supporting race-based preferences, in defiance of their party.

So exactly what is Kaplan complaining about? Apparently, one can't be black and Republican even with moderate social views. Powell, for example, criticized Newt Gingrich's Republican Contract With America, saying, "Some parts I find a little too hard, a little too harsh, a little too unkind. We do not yet have a level playing field in our society."[52] On the issue of abortion, Condoleezza Rice calls herself "libertarian on this issue, and meaning by that, that I have been concerned about a government role in this issue. I'm a strong proponent of parental choice, of parental notification. I'm a strong proponent of a ban on late-term abortion. These are all things that I think unite people and I think that that's where we should be. I've called myself at times mildly pro-choice."[53]

White liberals, on the other hand, apparently suffer no internal conflicts.

The Whitewater investigation resulted in fourteen convictions, including Democratic governor of Arkansas, Jim Guy Tucker.[54]

Webster Hubbell held the number-three job in Clinton's Justice Department when the Whitewater probe began. Hubbell, a Clinton friend from Arkansas and Mrs. Clinton's former law partner, received a plea-bargained twenty-one-month prison sentence for fraud and tax evasion. Surely the crimes of these

Democrats, like those of black Republicans, stem from their inner turmoil over their true conservative instincts—instincts they cast aside for money and power.

Give me a break.

Kaplan's attack against Bush policy advisor Allen, if made by a white writer, would be called racist. Kaplan's race doesn't change things. It is still racist. Kaplan apparently believes blacks are capable of individual thought, provided the individual thought leads them to the Democratic Party. If you oppose race-based preferences—as most Republicans do—you cannot be black and sane. If you agree with lower taxes and less business regulation, you cannot be black and sane. If you believe in a strong national security and support the War on Terror—including the war in Iraq—you cannot be both black and sane.

If you oppose race-based preferences—as most Republicans do—you cannot be black and sane. If you agree with lower taxes and less business regulation, you cannot be black and sane. If you believe in a strong national security and support the War on Terror—including the war in Iraq—you cannot be both black and sane.

Former Democratic presidential candidate Jesse Jackson, like Kaplan, sees no redeeming qualities in the Republican Party. Oh, sure, Colin Powell, a black man, served as secretary of State. And yes, Condoleezza Rice, a black woman, also serves in that position. Then there's Alphonso Jackson, the black secretary of HUD, or Elaine Chao, the Asian-American who serves as secretary of

Labor. The Bush Republican administration named Alberto Gonzales as White House counsel, and later made him the first
Latino attorney general. And President George W. Bush, unlike
his predecessor,[55] called the slaughter in the Darfur region of Sudan "a genocide."[56]

Nevertheless, Reverend Jackson accuses Republicans of
pushing a Confederate ideology. "The ideological right in control of our nation knows what it wants," says Jackson. "The right
wing fights for a series of constitutional amendments. They intend to have their ideology protected by law. They intend to
push the ideology of the Confederacy and continue to challenge
the vision of the Union."[57]

Insulting—indeed, racist—language leveled by Democrats
against blacks gets a pass. But when Republicans show "racial insensitivity" it becomes front-page news. During Senator George
Allen's (R-VA) 2006 reelection campaign, he caught fire when
he used the term "macaca."

Shekar Ramanuja Sidarth, who worked for Allen's opponent,
followed and filmed Allen during the senator's campaign stops.
Sidarth's parents came from India, but he was born in Fairfax
County, Virginia. At a campaign rally, Allen pointed to the man
and said, "Let's give a welcome to Macaca here. Welcome to
America and the real world of Virginia."[58] Apparently, the term
can mean "monkey." Allen publicly and privately apologized,
personally calling the young man to express his regrets. Asked
the meaning of macaca, Allen said, "I don't know what it means."
He thinks he meant to say "mohawk," because Sidarth's haircut
inspired Allen's staff to bestow that nickname on the young man.
As for welcoming him to America, Allen meant "just to the real
world. Get outside the Beltway and get to the real world."[59]

Newspapers also reported that, as a college student in the
early 1970s, he used the "n-word,"[60] and, during the campaign,
Allen learned that one of his grandparents is Jewish. The
"n-word" plus "macaca" plus Allen's less-than-artful response to
the revelation of his grandparent's heritage caused Allen's campaign to reel.

But what about the allegations that Allen's Democratic opponent, Jim Webb—who subsequently defeated Allen—also used the "n-word"? According to a former acquaintance, Dan Cragg, Webb says in his freshman college year, he used to drive through Watts, a predominately black area of Los Angeles, pointing rifles and shouting the "n-word" at blacks.[61]

Today, few mention that the so-called "conscience of the Senate," Senator Robert Byrd (D-WV), once belonged to the Klan. Not merely a rank-and-file member, Byrd served as a Kleagle, a Klan recruiter. Back then, Byrd called American blacks "race mongrels, a throwback to the blackest specimen from the wilds."[62]

Arkansas State Trooper Larry Patterson, who guarded then governor Bill Clinton, claims Clinton frequently used the "n-word," using it to describe Reverend Jesse Jackson as well as a local black civil rights leader. Said Patterson, "When [Bill Clinton] had black political leaders in the state and he disagreed with them, he would frequently use the 'N' word."[63]

Clinton's wife allegedly called Clinton's congressional campaign advisor, who failed to secure her husband's election to Congress, an "f——ing Jew bastard."[64] Not only did Paul Fray—the target—go public, so did his wife, as well as campaign aide and businessman Neil McDonald.[65]

What about more recent examples of "racial insensitivity"? As first lady, Hillary Rodham Clinton gave a speech on behalf of an organization called EMILY's List. EMILY stands for Early Money Is Like Yeast. In her speech, Hillary mocked black then mayor Willie Brown, who, according to Ms. Clinton, did not know this "person" called "Emily," and asked to be introduced to her. First Lady Clinton, according to the *Los Angeles Times*, used a "mock African-American accent," to imitate Brown saying, "She's supportin' all these people. She's supportin' Senator Dianne Feinstein. She's supported Senator Barbara Boxer. . . . She supported everybody. Why won't she support me?"[66]

Even more recently, during a large fund-raiser for her 2008 presidential campaign, Senator Clinton compared her fight to win the White House to the struggle and bravery of Harriet Tubman. "Harriet Tubman," said the unabashed senator, "made it to freedom after having been a slave and she got to New York and she could have been so happy . . . but she kept going back down South to bring other freed slaves to freedom. And she used to say, 'No matter what happens, keep going.' So we're going to keep going until we take back the White House!"[67]

A little perspective, please. Harriet Tubman—arguably one of our most heroic Americans—worked tirelessly in her efforts to free slaves, making nineteen dangerous trips on the Underground Railroad over a ten-year period, leading more than three hundred slaves to freedom. John Brown consulted with "General Tubman" about his planned raid on Harpers Ferry, and said Harriet Tubman was "one of the bravest persons on this continent." Frederick Douglass said of her, "Excepting John Brown—of sacred memory—I know of no one who has willingly encountered more perils and hardships to serve our enslaved people."[68] Isn't it just a bit condescending to compare Ms. Tubman's efforts to the presidential bid of a privileged former first lady in 2008?

Then there's the successful congressional candidacy of Keith Ellison, a black man who ran in Minnesota's Fifth District. In 1990, Ellison, then a member of the Nation of Islam (NOI) and a law student at the University of Minnesota, wrote an article for the school's newspaper, defending NOI's Minister Louis Farrakhan against charges of racism.[69] (Farrakhan called Judaism a "gutter religion,"[70] pronounced Adolf Hitler "wickedly great,"[71] claimed that whites are the devil, condemned gays, and, on their Web site, his organization still calls for a separate region in America so that blacks may relocate and live there.) Ellison now denounces Farrakhan's views, claiming that he, at the time, did not know enough about them.[72]

Moral to the story? Anti-Semitism and anti-black rhetoric count against you—but not so much if you're a Democrat.

Voting for a Republican can kill you—at least in Atlanta, Georgia. During the 2006 elections, a radio advertisement recorded by three prominent local "black leaders" warned voters not to cast their ballots for a Republican candidate for the Fulton County Commission, because, Representative John Lewis (D-GA) concluded in the advertisement, "Your very life may depend on it."[73] Your *life?*

Lewis, along with Atlanta Mayor Shirley Franklin and former ambassador, mayor, and Martin Luther King Jr. colleague Andrew Young, held nothing back. Lewis said, "On November 7 we face the most dangerous situation we ever have. If you think fighting off dogs and water hoses in the '60s was bad, imagine if we sit idly by and let the right-wing Republicans take control of the Fulton County Commission." Mayor Franklin explained, "The efforts of Martin and Coretta King, Hosea Williams, Maynard Jackson, and many others will be lost." Then Andrew Young gravely warned that votes must be cast for the Democratic candidate, "unless you want them to turn back the clock on equal rights and human rights and economic opportunity for all of us."[74] Wow. For the record, the Republican candidate—who lost the election—describes himself as a moderate, pro-choice environmentalist who supports gay rights. Not that it matters.

The offensive ad fanned racial tensions in the county, and it is blamed for spurring a movement to break large Fulton County into two separate counties. Residents of the more affluent northern suburbs say they want a more responsive, localized government. But because of the northern suburbs' affluence and predominately white makeup, the movement to break up the county must, of course, be about race. The offensive ad prompted a white lawyer from Buckhead (one of the communities that would secede to the new county) to say, "When the day comes that the city of Buckhead opens its doors, I will gladly tell Franklin, Lewis, and Young, and all others who've used race to obtain and keep political power for thirty years—in the words of the Reverend Martin Luther King—'Free at last, free at last, thank God almighty, I'm free at last.' "[75]

NAACP Chairman Julian Bond, at a gathering before September 11, 2001, compared the Republican Party to the totalitarian Taliban regime in Afghanistan: "[Bush] has selected nominees from the Taliban wing of American politics, appeased the wretched appetites of the extreme right wing, and chosen Cabinet officials whose devotion to the Confederacy is nearly canine in its uncritical affection."[76] Worse, in December 2001, almost three months after the terrorist attacks on our soil that killed more than three thousand, Bond repeated the charge, again comparing the Republican Party to the Taliban. Speaking about then Attorney General John Ashcroft, Bond said, "He knows something about the Taliban, coming from as he does from that wing of American politics."[77]

The NAACP chairman, while speaking at historically black Fayetteville State University in North Carolina, said, "The Republican Party would have the American flag and the swastika flying side by side."

Bond, almost three years after 9/11, on June 2, 2004, did it again. At a Take Back America conference, Bond said, "[Republicans] draw their most rabid supporters from the Taliban-wing of American politics."[78]

The NAACP chairman, while speaking at historically black Fayetteville State University in North Carolina, said, "The Republican Party would have the American flag and the swastika flying side by side." He referred to former Attorney General John Ashcroft as J. Edgar Ashcroft, compared Bush's judicial nominees to the Taliban. He also called President Bush a liar, and said that this White House's lies are more serious than the lies of his predecessor, because Clinton's lies didn't kill people. When later accused of comparing the Republican Party to Nazis, Bond denied making these remarks. The university, however, taped his speech. Though the school said that Bond did not equate the Republican Party with the Nazi Party, the tapes confirmed the accuracy of the American flag and swastika quote.[79]

For votes, Democrats exploit and fan blacks' rabid contempt for Republicans. Senator Joseph Biden (D-DE) quite inadvertently exposed this game. In an interview with a reporter from the *New York Observer*, Biden, commenting about black presidential aspirant Senator Barack Obama, said, "I mean, you got the first mainstream African-American who is articulate and bright and clean and a nice-looking guy. I mean, that's a storybook, man."[80]

Let's analyze this.

Obama follows a list of former black presidential aspirants that includes Representative Shirley Chisholm (D-NY) (1972), Republican former Ambassador Alan Keyes (1996, 2000), former Senator Carol Moseley Braun (D-IL) (2004), and Reverends Jesse Jackson (D) (1984, 1988) and Al Sharpton (D) (2004). Yet the liberal, condescending Biden seemed utterly amazed at the notion of a black person being both "clean" and "articulate."

During the 1984 convention, presidential candidate Walter Mondale's nice-looking and well-educated children spoke. No pundit, at least while I watched, described them as "articulate." But then Jesse Jackson's children spoke. Also nice looking and well educated. The mainscream liberal anchors and analysts fell all over themselves describing Jackson's kids' articulateness. During Supreme Court Justice Clarence Thomas's 1991 nomination hearings, black speaker after black speaker appeared, and, again, observers seemed astonished at their "articulateness." How condescending to laud a black person simply because he or she speaks proper English. You wouldn't hear a pundit declare, "Them kids sho' 'nuff is actin' white!" yet that's the implication of their praise.

Biden's comment ripped the lid off another one of his party's dirty little secrets—their not-so-very-deep-down disrespect for the antics and extremism of co-party race-baiters like Al Sharpton and Jesse Jackson, both of whom ran for president. When Biden called Obama "mainstream," the Delaware Senator not only took a slap at the bombast of the likes of the Sharptons and Jackson, but also at black flame-throwers like Representative Charlie Rangel, Representative Maxine Waters (D-CA), and most of the other members of the Congressional Black Caucus.

But does Biden ever publicly describe the Sharptons and the Jacksons as nonmainstream? Of course not. The Democratic Party uses them, indeed, *needs* them. The flame-throwing, racism-under-every-rock crowd keeps a black voter focused laserlike on race and racism. Again, this diverts attention from other issues, such as improving schools through vouchers and increasing net worth through privatization of Social Security—issues that threaten to peel away support from the Democratic Party.

Democrats portray themselves as caring about the "little guy," especially minorities. Why, then, the Democrats' crusade against Wal-Mart? Wal-Mart wanted to build a store in Inglewood, California, a city adjacent to Los Angeles, where unemployment stood at 8.1 percent in 2004,[81] with over 22 percent of residents living below the poverty line.[82] Its population is just about evenly divided between blacks and Hispanics.[83]

Building the shopping center on an empty, undeveloped lot, Wal-Mart expected to bring an estimated 2,500 temporary construction jobs, 1,500 permanent new jobs, and anticipated employing 600 or more full- and part-time workers at an average pay of $9.88 an hour.[84] But because Wal-Mart remains non-unionized, reasoned logic and convenience for those in the community don't matter.

"Community leaders" attack Wal-Mart for failing to offer "sufficient" health-care benefits. Wal-Mart, for its part, says that about half of its employees subscribe to their health-care benefits package, consistent with the average for the retail industry. And, true, Wal-Mart does have relatively high deductibles, but once an employee reaches $1,750 a year in out-of-pocket expenses, the company steps in and picks up 100 percent of medical charges.[85]

Despite the promised economic benefits, a union and "community leader"–led campaign denounced the proposed Inglewood Wal-Mart as "ugly," "devastating," creating "poverty-wage jobs," and "one of the real ugly chapters of American capitalism," which would spark a "race to the bottom."[86] Reverend Jesse Jackson thundered, "It [Wal-Mart] is a confederate economic Trojan horse."[87] Confederate? True, Wal-Mart *is* headquartered in Arkansas. But then, isn't Bill Clinton from there as well? Oh, never mind.

Democrats in the California State Assembly also targeted Wal-Mart and other "big-box" stores. One bill mandated that "large grocery stores" (more than seventy-five thousand square feet) would have to pay the state for any health care provided to their workers by state and local government agencies. So, if an employee decided not to subscribe to the company health-care plan, then sought medical treatment at a county hospital, Wal-Mart gets stuck with the hefty medical bill. Another Democrat's bill requires that a big-box store, before it could receive approval to build, must pay for a study of their store's economic and other impacts, including the share of retail sales it captures, its effect on local wages and benefits, the costs of public services, and so on. The bills sought to pile cost upon cost for Wal-Mart, in hopes to force the company to look elsewhere.[88]

One Los Angeles City councilman, black former L.A.P.D. Chief Bernard Parks, expressed some sanity. Parks's district already built a new Wal-Mart, and he considered the proposed store construction in nearby Inglewood a no-brainer. "For years the complaint has been that many small mom-and-pop stores often provide poor quality at high prices and in many instances with service that is not acceptable," said Parks. "But you go into Wal-Mart and you find the prices are good, the service is great, and the store is spotlessly clean."[89] Parks said the Wal-Mart in his own district paid to upgrade the shopping center where it was located, and in only the first month it was open, it brought as many as a million people into the area, boosting other local businesses.[90]

During the battle, Wal-Mart purchased sixty acres of land in Inglewood. But the City Council countered by passing an ordinance requiring "superstores" of more than a hundred thousand square feet to get a conditional use permit, forcing them to go before the planning commission, hold open forums with the public, and submit to a review process with an outside consultant who has the responsibility to determine the positive and negative impact of the superstore.[91]

During open hearings, a longtime resident tried to explain Wal-Mart's benefits to the City Council, including providing employment opportunities for black and Hispanic kids. But the City Council sided with the likes of Sylvia Hopper, a resident and local grocery store clerk, who said, "If they sell groceries it would undercut the market share. There are not enough grocery stores in our city. If quality grocery stores started closing down, then other grocery stores would close down."[92] Wait a minute. There are not enough grocery stores? So keeping Wal-Mart out solves the shortage?

In the end, who lost out? The mostly black and brown consumers and potential workers living in an area with a higher-than-average unemployment rate.

The same thing happened to Wal-Mart in New York City, when it tried to open its first Big Apple store in Rego Park, Queens. Incredibly, while Wal-Mart operates 3,800[93] stores nationwide, New York City, so far, shuts out the chain.

The company argued that Wal-Mart+jobs+increased tax base+lower prices+convenience=a win, win, win, win. But no dice. Why? Nonunion workers.

Again, "black leaders" and Democrats used Wal-Mart as an example of the continued victimization of blacks. But today, how bad is it?

In 1967, Dr. Martin Luther King Jr. made his fifth appearance on *Meet the Press*. He was asked if the American racial problem could be solved. His response—less than a year before his assassination—was optimistic and uplifting: "Yes, I do. I refuse to give up. I refuse to despair it in this moment. I refuse to allow myself to fall into the dark chambers of pessimism, because I think in any social revolution, the one thing that keeps it going is hope. And when hope dies, somehow the revolution degenerates into a kind of nihilistic philosophy, which says you must engage in disruption for disruption's sake. I refuse to believe that. However difficult it is, I believe that the forces of good will, white and black, in this country, can work together to bring about a resolution of this problem. We have the resources to do it. At present, we don't have the will, but certainly the Negroes and the decent, committed whites—maybe they're in a minority now, but they're there—must work together to so arouse the conscience of this nation."[94]

Today, are "decent, committed whites" still in the minority? Of course not. A recent *Los Angeles Times*/Bloomberg poll asked that assuming a presidential candidate agrees with you on most issues, which of the following types of candidate could you *not* vote for? Respondents were given several choices: "Woman," "African-American," "Mormon," "seventy two years old," "could not vote for any of them," and "could vote for all of them."[95]

The result? Only 4 percent of registered voters ruled out voting for a woman. Only 3 percent of voters said they would not vote for an African-American candidate. Interestingly, more Democrats (at 4 percent) than Republicans (at 3 percent) ruled out voting for a black candidate. Almost five times as many registered voters—14 percent—said they could not vote for a Mormon or a seventy-two-year-old. Interestingly, though, more Democrats (17 percent) than Republicans (13 percent) wouldn't vote for a Mormon. Likewise for seventy-two-year-olds—again, more Democrats (19 percent) than Republicans (12 percent) refused to vote for someone that age. Asked about voting for a Mormon, a seventy-two-year-old, a black, or a woman, 63 percent of Democrats said they would "vote for all of them." But when Republicans were asked the same question, 71 percent said they would "vote for all of them."[96] So, which party appears more tolerant and open-minded?

In the 2006 off-year election, Democrats repeatedly accused the Republican Party of a "culture of corruption." When a young Ted Kennedy (D-MA) was running for Senate in 1962, he made his first appearance on *Meet the Press*. There had been a lot of corruption in Massachusetts, and Kennedy was asked, "Will the Democratic

Party be harmed this year by these scandals?" Kennedy replied, "Well, I think the question of whether individuals who have come up, who've been indicted, have been Democrats, I think are irrelevant, really, any more than you can say that because certain of these people belong to a certain racial group, a religious group . . . or from a certain city and town are necessarily all evil."[97]

See, for Democrats, Kennedy is saying, "Judge us on the content of our character." You have to look at Democrats as individuals. But as for Republicans, "Judge them on the content of their 'racist' ideology." So if you have an "R" after your name, you need to be judged collectively, because you're all evil.

But historically, to catch up with Democrats, Republicans need to get busy. The House Committee on Standards of Official Conduct, popularly known as the House Ethics Committee, publishes a "Historical Summary of Conduct Cases in the House of Representatives," available on their Web site. Last updated in 2004, it lists every ethics case in the House since 1798. As far as investigations go, Democrats leave Republicans in the dust. Okay, Democrats have been around longer. So take a look at the past thirty years. Of the seventy members investigated for serious offenses—some involving criminal charges and jail time—only fifteen have been Republicans. The remaining fifty-five were Democrats.[98]

This brings us to the sordid history of the Democratic Party concerning race. Once, a prominent black businessman told me he found voting Republican "no different than voting for the Klan." Well, at one time, a voter who cast his ballot for the Democratic Party effectively *did* vote for the Klan. Democrats founded the Klan, not just to stop blacks and Jews, but to halt the spread of Republicanism. Abraham Lincoln became the first Republican to win the presidency, and he ran on a platform of halting the spread of slavery. The Republican Party originally counted many blacks within its ranks.

"Black History Month" has been observed for thirty years, yet many blacks know little to nothing about the parties' respective roles in advancing or hindering the civil rights of blacks. How many blacks know that following the Civil War, twenty-two blacks—thirteen of them ex-slaves—were elected to Congress, all as Republicans?[99] The first black Democrat was not elected to Congress until 1934, from the state of Illinois.[100] The first black congressional Democrat from a Southern state was not elected until 1973.[101]

See, for Democrats, Kennedy is saying, "Judge us on the content of our character." You have to look at Democrats as individuals. But as for Republicans, "Judge them on the content of their 'racist' ideology." So if you have an "R" after your name, you need to be judged collectively, because you're all evil.

Democrats, in 1854, passed the Kansas-Nebraska Act.[102] This overturned the Missouri Compromise and allowed for the importation of slaves into the territories. Disgusted with the passage of this Act, free-soilers and antislavery members of the Whig and Democratic parties founded the Republican Party—not just to stop the spread of slavery, but to eventually abolish it.

How many blacks know that blacks founded the Texas Republican Party? On July 4, 1867, in Houston, Texas, 150 blacks and 20 whites formed the party.[103] No, not the *Black* Texas Republican Party, they founded the Texas Republican Party.

Fugitive slave laws? Democrats passed the Fugitive Slave Act of 1850. If merely *accused* of being a slave, even if the person enjoyed freedom all of his or her life (as approximately 10 percent of blacks did just before the Civil War),[104] the person lost the right to representation by an attorney, the right to trial by jury, and the right to habeas corpus.

Emancipation? Republican President Abraham Lincoln issued the Emancipation Proclamation during the Civil War. In 1865, the Thirteenth Amendment emancipating the slaves was passed with 100 percent of Republicans (88 of 88 in the House, 30 of 30 in the Senate) voting for it.[105] Only 23 percent of Democrats (16 of 66 in the House, 3 of 8 in the Senate) voted for it.[106]

Civil rights laws? In 1868, the states ratified the Fourteenth Amendment, to give newly emancipated blacks full civil rights and federal guarantee of those rights, superseding any state laws. Every single voting Republican (128 of 134—with 6 not voting—in the House, and 30 of 32—with 2 not voting—in the Senate) voted for the Fourteenth Amendment. Not a single Democrat (zero of 36 in the House, zero of 6 in the Senate) voted for it.[107]

Right to vote? When Southern states balked at implementing the Fourteenth Amendment, Congress came back and passed the Fifteenth Amendment in 1870, guaranteeing blacks the right to vote. Every single Republican voted for it, with every Democrat voting against it.[108]

Ku Klux Klan? In 1872 congressional investigations, Democrats admitted beginning the Klan as an effort to stop the spread of the Republican Party, and to reestablish Democratic control in Southern states. As PBS's *American Experience* notes, "In outright defiance of the Republican-led federal government, Southern Democrats formed organizations that violently intimidated blacks and Republicans who tried to win political power. The most prominent of these, the Ku Klux Klan, was formed in Pulaski, Tennessee, in 1865."[109] Blacks, who were all Republican at that time, became the primary targets of violence.

Jim Crow laws? Between 1870 and 1875, the Republican Congress passed many pro-black civil rights laws. But in 1876, Democrats took control of the House, and no further race-based civil rights laws passed until 1957.[110] In 1892, Democrats gained control of the House, the Senate, and the White House, and repealed all the Republican-passed civil rights laws. That enabled the Southern Democrats to pass the Jim Crow laws, poll taxes, literacy tests, and so on, in their individual states.

How many blacks know that only 64 percent of Democrats in Congress voted for the 1964 Civil Rights Act (153 for, 91 against in the House; and 46 for, 21 against in the Senate)? And that 80 percent of Republicans (136 for, 35 against in the House; and 27 for, 6 against in the Senate) voted *for* the 1964 Act?

The black shift toward the Democratic Party began in the 1930s, during President Franklin Roosevelt's New Deal. The black Republican exodus continued throughout the twentieth century. Still, Eisenhower managed to win nearly 40 percent of the black vote in 1956. Four years later, in 1960, Nixon got 33 percent of the black vote against Democrat John F. Kennedy. Another four years passed, and Lyndon B. Johnson—after signing the 1964 Civil Rights Act—scored a whopping 94 percent of the black vote.[111]

How many blacks know that only 64 percent of Democrats in Congress voted for the 1964 Civil Rights Act (153 for, 91 against in the House; and 46 for, 21 against in the Senate)?[112] And that 80 percent of Republicans (136 for, 35 against in the House; and 27 for, 6 against in the Senate) voted *for* the 1964 Act?[113]

Many blacks refuse to vote for the Republican Party because of the reviled, allegedly anti-black, Republican "Southern strategy." The narrative goes like this: Southern whites, contemptuous of the Democratic Party's embrace of the civil rights movement—bolted the party and became Republicans.

But it's not that simple. Indeed, many racist Southern whites opposed, on racial grounds, the Civil Rights Act of 1964, the Voting Rights Act of 1965, the Open Housing Act of 1968, and race-based preferences. But the Southern defection from the Democratic Party to the Republican Party took place for *many* reasons. Unlike many people in the Democratic Party, most Southerners attend church on a regular basis, and many vehemently oppose abortion and the *Roe v. Wade* decision. Southerners are more pro-military, with a disproportionately higher percentage of Southerners serving in our all-volunteer military than those from Northern or Western states. While Southern states comprise approximately 38 percent of the U.S. population, they provide about 44 percent of military recruits.[114]

But what about this "Southern strategy"? Pundit Pat Buchanan, then serving as a speechwriter for Richard Nixon, codeveloped Nixon's "Southern strategy" in 1966—two years before Nixon's presidential run. They expected the "strategy" to ultimately result in the complete marginalization of racist Southern Democrats. "We would build our Republican Party on a foundation of states' rights, human rights, small government, and a strong national defense," said Buchanan, "and leave it to the 'party of [Democratic Georgia Governor Lester] Maddox, [1966 Democratic challenger against Spiro Agnew for Maryland governor George] Mahoney, and [Democratic Alabama Governor George] Wallace to squeeze the last ounces of political juice out of the rotting fruit of racial injustice.'"[115] And Republican President Richard Nixon implemented the first federal affirmative action (race-based preference) laws with goals and timetables.

Staunchly pro-choice, the Democratic Party supports a woman's right to choose. How many blacks know, however, that the founder of the American Birth Control League (which became Planned Parenthood), Margaret Sanger, avidly supported eugenics? She considered some races and individuals genetically superior to others, and eugenics enthusiasts supported abortion to decrease the number of poor, inferior minorities. Sanger bluntly stated, "Our failure to segregate morons who are increasing and

multiplying . . . demonstrates our foolhardy and extravagant sen-
timentalism. . . . Philanthropy . . . encourages the healthier and
more normal sections of the world to shoulder the burden of un-
thinking and indiscriminate fecundity of others; which brings
with it, as I think the reader must agree, a dead weight of human
waste. Instead of decreasing and aiming to eliminate the stocks
that are most detrimental to the future of the race and the world,
it tends to render them to a menacing degree dominant. . . . [W]e
are paying for, and even submitting to, the dictates of an ever-
increasing, unceasingly spawning class of human beings who
never should have been born at all."[116] Blacks, at this time, were
considered by many to be disproportionately "dead weight."

Many blacks also know nothing of the racist history of gun
control.

Remember the Supreme Court Dred Scott case, which decreed that blacks must be returned to slave owners since they
were not considered persons, but property? Then Chief Justice
Roger Taney wrote that if blacks were "entitled to the privileges
and immunities of citizens, . . . [i]t would give persons of the
negro race, who were recognized as citizens in any one state of
the union, the right . . . to keep and carry arms wherever they
went. And all of this would be done in the face of the subject
race of the same color, both free and slaves, and inevitably producing discontent and insubordination among them, and endan-
gering the peace and safety of the state."[117]

After the Civil War, gun control regulation began as a means
to prevent black ex-slaves from getting their hands on guns and
exacting revenge on their white oppressors. But since the Fourteenth and Fifteenth Amendments stopped racists from writing
gun control laws aimed only at blacks, they had to restrict gun
access to everyone.[118]

Until then, the Second Amendment's right to "keep and bear
arms" had been unchallenged for about a century. Today, we
have more than twenty thousand gun control laws on the
books.[119] Yet today's Democrats and "black leaders" applaud gun
control, blithely ignorant of the racist history of that movement.

Director Spike Lee went to the Cannes Film festival in 1999 to promote his movie, *Summer of Sam*, a partly fictionalized picture about New York City during 1977, when the "Son of Sam" killed several New Yorkers. When someone asked Lee his opinion of gun-advocate/actor Charlton Heston, Lee replied, "Shoot him—with a .44-caliber Bulldog."[120]

Does Lee know that racist whites pushed gun control to keep guns out of the hands of blacks, making them more vulnerable to attacks by racist groups like the Ku Klux Klan?

At 1:45 AM on Sunday morning, July 17, 2005, Meleia Willis-Starbuck, a popular young black woman and an Ivy League scholarship recipient, was shot to death while standing outside her Berkeley, California, apartment with five female friends. The shooter, Christopher Hollis, and the driver of the car Hollis rode in, Christopher Wilson, knew the victim from high school. The community grieved, and blamed the gun. "I know all of them," said Arnold Perkins, Alameda County Health Care Services director, also a Berkeley resident and a black man. "They are all good kids. Chris Wilson was like another son to me. This is a community tragedy, one of those terrible situations where friends end up hurting friends. No one blames anyone in this. We are all caught up in this matrix created by too many handguns."[121]

The NAACP and much of the "black leadership" routinely call for more gun control legislation while attacking the Republican Party for its resistance. In a 2003 presidential debate, Reverend Sharpton said, "I think that we must do whatever we can to regulate how guns are used."[122] Never mind that blacks living in the inner city suffer disproportionately from crime. Many live in cities with restrictive gun laws, followed by the law-abiding but ignored by the criminals. Residents of Washington, D.C., a city that's 60 percent black, live under some of the nation's most restrictive anti-gun laws. Any civilian D.C. resident who owns a handgun—unless registered before 1976—commits a crime. The laws require that owners keep their guns unloaded and disassembled or trigger-locked in the home. Yet Washington, D.C., per capita, suffers from an extremely high murder rate. As former D.C. mayor

Marion Barry once incredibly put it, "Outside of the killings, Washington has one of the lowest [crime] rates in the country."[123]

Powerful evidence indicates that restrictive gun laws do nothing to deter bad guys, while making it more and more difficult for good people to defend themselves. Criminals don't walk into gun stores, politely fill out registration forms, and then use those very same guns in crime. But so-called black leaders shower wrath on Republicans who resist further gun control laws.

Democrats and "black leaders" ignore studies showing that violent crime rates have fallen faster and further, for the most part, in the thirty-four "shall issue" states that allow citizens to carry concealed weapons. Japan and England now see crime rates increasing, despite bans on private ownership of guns.

Powerful evidence indicates that restrictive gun laws do nothing to deter bad guys, while making it more and more difficult for good people to defend themselves. Criminals don't walk into gun stores, politely fill out registration forms, and then use those very same guns in crime.

Crime in America remains disproportionately an urban affair. Therefore, the ones who most need protection from bad guys remain most vulnerable to crime, due in large measure to liberal government gun control policies. Maybe someone should tell the "black leadership" and the Democrats.

Today, the Democratic Party desperately, intensely needs the black vote for its very survival. President Lyndon B. Johnson became the last Democrat to carry the white vote, back in 1964. JFK's Democratic Party is not the Democratic Party of today. The majority of whites now vote Republican.[124] "[I]f Republicans can get just a fourth or a fifth of the black vote nationwide," writes economist Thomas Sowell, "that can shift the balance of power decisively in their favor."[125] In Midwestern states like Michigan and Ohio, even a small shift among black voters could have enormous consequences. According to Republican strategists, if their candidates could pick up as little as 2 to 4 percent of the black vote, the Republicans would win those states.[126]

But blacks' near-monolithic allegiance to the Democratic Party seems almost inconsistent with other complaints. Many black Democrats favor reparations, affirmative action, or some other redress as a means to undo years of repression and discrimination against blacks. But if blacks knew of the true history of the Democratic Party, they would also know the Democratic Party helped lead the way for the repression and discrimination.

So, next "Black History Month," pass some of this stuff along.

3.

STUPID BLACK LEADERS

For me this is a time . . . when we have to turn the mirror around, because for me it is almost analgesic to talk about what the white man is doing against us. And it keeps a person frozen in their seat, it keeps you frozen in your hole you're sitting in.[1]

—BILL COSBY

Julian Bond, after he became head of the NAACP in 1999, announced his agenda—going after "the new racists." These "new racists," explained Bond, attributed the problems in the black community to "family breakdown," the "lack of middle-class values," the "lack of education and skills," and the "absence of role models." Nonsense, said Bond. The real cause of the problem was "epidemic racism."[2]

Bond apparently believes that the "segregation now, segregation tomorrow, segregation forever" generation is not dying off, but handing down their racism to a newer, younger generation.

He hired Bruce Gordon, a former Verizon executive, to serve as president of the NAACP. They clashed. After just nineteen months, Gordon was out.

Gordon objected to the organization's emphasis on racism,

clearly considering it a fading issue, and that values, behavior, and culture constitute a far greater threat to the continued success of blacks: "[It is not enough for the NAACP] simply to push the government . . . to institute policies that matter. I think it's also important for us to step out into our communities and . . . deliver services. To be totally reliant on what the government does for us, instead of also doing for ourselves what we have the capacity to do for ourselves, is, to me, too narrow a focus."[3]

Bond was more blunt: "We want [the NAACP] to be a social justice organization; he wanted it to be more of a social service organization. Our mission is to fight racial discrimination and provide social justice. Social service organizations deal with the effects of racial discrimination. We deal with the beast itself. There are many organizations that provide social services. We say, 'Good for them.' But we are one of the very few that provide social justice. It is popular to say that we are in a post–civil rights period, but we don't believe that." Social justice?

In 2005, the NAACP decided to target large, private business. The civil rights organization wanted reparations from companies with historical ties to slavery, and threatened boycotts for companies that wouldn't participate in the NAACP's annual business diversity report card.

"Absolutely, we will be pursuing reparations from companies that have historical ties to slavery," announced interim NAACP president and CEO Dennis C. Hayes. "Many of the problems we have now including poverty, disparities in health care and incarcerations can be directly tied to slavery."[4]

The NAACP planned to lobby for laws requiring businesses to complete extensive slavery studies or find themselves excluded from government contracts. Even before the NAACP announced its new efforts, JPMorgan Chase completed a self-examination of its own history. The banking giant found that two companies it had absorbed long ago, Citizens Bank and Canal Bank of Louisiana, had, prior to the Civil War, procured more than 1,250 blacks as collateral on defaulted loans.

JPMorgan Chase apologized for its "ties to slavery" and set up a $5 million scholarship program for black Louisiana students.[5]

"Black leaders" applauded the JPMorgan Chase apology and scholarship program, as if they somehow caught the company buying fresh slaves off the boat. "It's definitely a reparations success, and we anticipate many more after this," said Ms. Deadria Farmer-Paellmann, executive director of New York nonprofit Restitution Study Group, an organization dedicated to securing reparations for slavery for blacks that has also targeted companies like Aetna, Lloyd's of London, New York Life Insurance Company, FleetBoston Financial Corporation (Bank of America), Lehman Brothers, RJ Reynolds Tobacco Company, and many more. She said JPMorgan Chase's action "confirms that the corporations can be held accountable for their roles in slavery. They've been brought to realize that they owe something."[6] Ms. Farmer-Paellmann and other "black leaders" never seem to realize that the cost of scholarships or other reparations will be borne by black customers and black shareholders, too.

To call JPMorgan Chase's slavery tie "tenuous" would be a gross overstatement. Two pre–Civil War slave-owning banks, Citizens Bank and Canal Bank, merged in 1924 to form Canal Commercial Trust & Savings, a business later liquidated during the Great Depression. In 1933 the National Bank of Commerce in New Orleans assumed some of the failed bank's assets. The National Bank of Commerce preceded Bank One Corporation, later purchased by JPMorgan Chase in 2004.[7] Follow that?

After the fall of "overt" racism practiced during slavery and Jim Crow, "black leaders" began calling racism "covert." Nelson B. Rivers III, the chief operations officer of the NAACP, characterizes it as "stealth racism"[8]—presumably more subtle and difficult to detect than old-fashioned overt racism, but just as prevalent.

Rivers says that white Americans have "an absolute blind spot" when it comes to identifying racism. For proof, he points to a CNN poll showing 49 percent of blacks say racism is a "very serious" problem, while only 18 percent of whites agreed. The poll shows that white people, says Rivers, operate from "the prism of the powerful." In other words, just because whites refuse to acknowledge racism, it still exists. "Racism requires accountability," Rivers said. "No one wants to acknowledge they are racist or have benefited from a racist system."[9] It can't be that on the issue of race, America moved, and continues to move, from its racist past? That times have changed? That societal forces no longer tolerate racism?

As far back as 1911, Booker T. Washington recognized that some people had an incentive to exacerbate racism: "There is [a] class of colored people who make a business of keeping the troubles, the wrongs, and the hardships of the Negro race before the public. Having learned that they are able to make a living out of their troubles, they have grown into the settled habit of advertising their wrongs—partly because they want sympathy and partly because it pays. Some of these people do not want the Negro to lose his grievances, because they do not want to lose their jobs. . . . There is a certain class of race-problem solvers who don't want the patient to get well, because as long as the disease holds out they have not only an easy means of making a living, but also an easy medium through which to make themselves prominent before the public."[10]

It can't be that on the issue of race, America moved, and continues to move, from its racist past? That times have changed? That societal forces no longer tolerate racism?

Project 21, a black conservative group promoting entrepreneurism, commitment to family, and individual responsibility, considers the howlings of the NAACP counterproductive in today's world. Project 21 chairman Mychal Massie interpreted the CNN survey far differently. Massie says that many blacks unfairly blame whites for the problems in their lives and in their communities, an ingrained conditioning that starts when they are very young. Massie also calls upon blacks to admit their *own* racism toward whites. "Many black people have a raw, visceral contempt for whites, and they are much more vocal than what I hear or experience from whites," Massie said. "To suggest only whites are racist is just wrong."[11] Indeed, blacks are often more racist than whites, and far less likely to be held accountable for racist remarks.

Further, Massie questions CNN's motive in organizing and releasing the survey. "I think all of this had a pre-determined outcome, needing only anecdotal comments to lend a veneer of credibility," Massie said in a press release. "The CNN report serves only one purpose, and that is to convince the public at large—specifically, white people—that they are evil racists. It is a vulgar exercise to try to find racism in the fiber of every white."[12]

The NAACP, says Massie, uses terms like "stealth racism" to justify their own existence. "The NAACP sees racism behind every tree and every bush."[13] And no racism, no job for Rivers.

Motivational speaker Tony Robbins spoke before a capacity crowd during a eulogy at the 1,500-seat black Bethel AME Church in South Los Angeles, and posed the question, "What's a white boy doing here who's supposed to be a motivational speaker?" The "white boy" went on to explain that he was there because of the deceased: "That man was love."[14] The "love" man, by the way, was Stanley Tookie Williams, cofounder of the nefarious Crips gang. Williams had just been executed for committing four murders.

If you are white, and want to endear yourself with some blacks, call yourself a "white boy." The term "boy" heralds back to the dark and ugly days of the Jim Crow South, when a black man—regardless of his age, education, or status—was derisively called a black "boy," not a man. The term is as derogatory as the word "n——gger."

But the rules are somewhat confusing.

Famed Michael Jackson defense attorney Tom Mesereau was recently lauded by Brian Dunn, a black attorney at the late defense attorney Johnnie Cochran's law firm, because Mesereau *doesn't* try to act black. Dunn observed Mesereau's easy manner at a dinner party of six, where Mesereau was the only white person. "He was being himself," said Dunn. "He wasn't trying to sound like a black man. He sounded like a white man."[15]

But for someone like President Bush, a dastardly Republican who wants to turn back the clock on civil rights, nothing would work. He could call himself "boy" or "sound like a white man"—for him, nothing would work.

President Bush, in 2006, addressed the National Association for the Advancement of Colored People, after five years of invitations. He pandered, he condescended, he told the room that he felt their pain—still, no love.

"I consider it a tragedy," said President Bush, "that the party of Abraham Lincoln let go of its historic ties with the African-American community. For too long my party wrote off the African-American vote, and many African-Americans wrote off the Republican Party."[16]

At last, cried the mainscream media, Bush addressed the NAACP! As one news anchor put it, the president's speech was an attempt to show blacks that he "cares" about them. A breathless Associated Press headline read, "Bush Acknowledges Racism Still Exists."[17]

Well, call off the hunger strike. Shut down the Internet. Break up the New York Yankees. President Bush "acknowledges" racism still exists. Excuse me, please, but when did Bush state, suggest, or imply that racism *didn't* exist? It's not number one on his agenda because it's not the number-one problem facing this country, whether you are black or white or Hispanic or Asian. But of course it exists.

"Civil rights leader" Reverend Al Sharpton weighed in on Bush's speech on the *The O'Reilly Factor*. Did anything about the president's speech impress him? "I think," Sharpton said, "the fact that he said what many people will not say around the right, and even on this station, that there's still racism in America. It's going to make it hard for a lot of people that said that's in the past. Even George Bush admits that."[18]

Excuse me, please, but when did Bush state, suggest, or imply that racism *didn't* exist? It's not number one on his agenda because it's not the number-one problem facing this country, whether you are black or white or Hispanic or Asian.

Even George Bush . . . ? Again, when did . . . oh, never mind.

The *Los Angeles Times* took the cake. In a lengthy article about the speech, the *Times* reporter wrote that the reason Bush took so long before addressing the NAACP was "the result, in part, of bad blood between the President and Julian Bond, the longtime chairman of the [NAACP]."[19] Bad blood?

The paper failed to explain exactly why "bad blood" exists. On at least three occasions—two of them *after* September 11, 2001—Chairman Bond said that Bush nominees and Republican supporters were from the "Taliban wing" of politics.[20, 21, 22]

Now get this. In an editorial about the president's NAACP address, the *Los Angeles Times* wrote, "[F]ormer NAACP Chairman Julian Bond memorably referred to the 'the Taliban wing' of the GOP in 2001 (he spoke before 9/11)."[23] Jeez. The venerable paper needs to do some homework. As we know, Bond said this before *and* after 9/11. And the description of Bond as "former" chairman—that must be news to current chairman Bond.

On the other side of the country, the *New York Times* told its readers that Bush irritated some people in the audience. "Bush repeatedly referred to the group as the N-A-A-C-P, attracting some notice from those who use the more traditional pronunciation of N-double-A-C-P."[24] Good grief, why the President practically uttered the "n-word"! Someone call Jesse!

With nothing to lose, why not turn this into a truly memorable and important speech? Instead, President Bush ran off a litany of federal programs designed to "help" blacks—No Child Left Behind Act, Pell grants, loans for black businesses, and so on.

Why not grab the NAACP—and indeed, "black America"—by its lapels and say:

"Ladies and gentlemen, good news. While racism can never be purged from the hearts of all people, it no longer represents a force potent enough to hold back anyone in America who works hard, invests in education, and avoids making poor moral choices. Because of the decades of hard work by your organization and countless men and women of all races, America has come a long way. Despite America's flaws, we can now say that we have the fairest, most free, more upwardly mobile and more open society in all of human history. We have black CEOs of *Fortune* 500 companies. Black people occupy positions in government at the very highest levels. The black middle class grows and thrives. It is an insult to hard-working black men and women by suggesting that, but for race-based preferences, they never would have made it.

"The real problem facing this country is a growing sense of entitlement—of you owe me, blaming slights of the past on those living in the present. Well, all a state can be, is just in its *own* time. As Bill Cosby once said, America has done its part. Now we must do our part."

Now *that* would show how much Bush "cares."

Instead, the attitude engendered by the NAACP makes blacks thin-skinned, causing them to apply a microscope to everyday incidents in search of a racial explanation. I received the following letter from a woman who calls herself and her sales associate Hispanic-Americans:

I work for a very well-known retail store and yesterday I had a black mother come in with her two teenage daughters, who were shopping earlier in the day (without their mom).

The teenagers had each made a separate purchase and the associate who rung them up put their one item (each purchased one item) in a brown bag that we use for small items.

Later that day their mom came in wanting to speak to the manager/supervisor and the associate who rang up her daughters, to complain on how biased the sales associate was because she put her daughters' purchases in a paper bag while other customers' (meaning white) items were put in a plastic bag!

She accused the associate of being biased because all the other customers received plastic bags . . . uh, probably because they had more than one item!

Her complaint was that everyone should be given the same type of bag and not be biased based on someone's skin color. . . .

The mom wanted an apology from the sales associate who refused to apologize for something so ridiculous.

I tried explaining to her that the paper bags are used for small items and not because of her daughters' skin color. The mother insisted that we place each of her daughters' one item into a plastic bag.

As I was placing the items in a plastic bag the mom was scolding her daughters on how they shouldn't be taken advantage of, and next time they should speak up.

The sad thing was seeing the embarrassment and shame on the daughters' faces.

I thought you would like to know about this one . . .
Thanks,
Anonymous (due to not getting in trouble from management)

Years ago, when promoting my first book, *The Ten Things You Can't Say in America*, I appeared on television with Lena Williams, a *New York Times* reporter, author of a book called *It's the Little Things: Everyday Interactions That Anger, Annoy, and Divide the Races*. One of the "problems" Williams complained about included the fact that white women routinely tossed or curled their hair as they speak—apparently a rude affront to black women whose natural black hair doesn't "flip." *What?* I couldn't take it, so I turned to her and said, "Is that it?"

Think of the true "inconveniences" endured by people like my ninety-one-year-old dad who grew up in Athens, Georgia, and those of my mom who grew up in a small town outside of Huntsville, Alabama, called Toney.

Jim Crow–era blacks, like my parents, routinely experienced blatant insults, indignities, and outright acts of white treachery that today's so-called oppressed never have—nor ever will— experience. Separate drinking fountains, separate hotels, sepa- rate restrooms, NO BLACKS ALLOWED signs posted in stores, seats for blacks only at the back of the bus, separate public parks and separate drinking facilities, separate schools and universities, separate houses of worship, separate sporting teams.

When my grandfather took my mom and her sister to shop, they entered through the back entrance of the department store. Should a garment touch my aunt's or mom's clothing, the store owner forced my grandfather to pay for the dress. Whether it fit or not, despite its cost, once that garment touched my mother or my aunt's black skin, she owned it.

My mom told the story to me at the dinner table. I turned to my dad and said, "Were you treated this way too?" My dad took his index finger, pointed to his head, and simply said, "Hats, too."

My father wanted a "jitney" business as a freelance taxi driver. He bought a beat-up car, but he needed to go to the local judge and get a court-granted taxi license to drive the cab. Un- beknownst to my dad, the judge before whom he had to appear already hired blacks for his own jitney company, servicing the black side of town. It also provided the judge a nice side income. So, in open court, the judge rejected my father's application, saying, "There are too many niggers right now who claim they want to work but don't. Permission denied."

My mother flew on a commercial flight in 1951, carrying my older brother, then two years old. Given that, at the time, few blacks traveled by airplane, the airport officials hadn't gotten around to cordoning off a separate area for blacks. So when my mother arrived at the airport, an airport worker suggested she stand "over there"—pointing to an area in the corner. They provided no chair for mother or toddler, but at least she now could stand "over there."

My dad said, as a child and during his teen years, if he walked down the street and saw one white person about his own age approaching him, he expected no trouble. If, however, two whites approached him, there would be a fight. If two blacks and two whites approached each other, no problem. If two blacks were approached by three whites, however, big problem.

My uncle Thurman, my mother's youngest brother, walked nearly five miles each day to school. Buses, however, took the local white kids to their school *three* miles away. If a black walked too close to the bus as it drove by, expect taunts of "nigger" and a pelting with rotten eggs and tomatoes.

I told my uncle about the times people—in almost every case, someone sitting safely in a moving vehicle—called me "nigger" or made other racist comments. Once, dressed casually in a T-shirt and a pair of jeans, I walked into a Mercedes dealership. The salespeople, apparently sizing me up as a nonbuyer, paid little attention to me. One finally—almost reluctantly—approached me. He found out I meant business when I whipped out my checkbook. Those kinds of things.

But much more serious indignities and abuses failed to break the spirit of America's blacks. My parents were no exception. In 1951, long before the Civil Rights Act of 1964, the Voting Rights Act of 1965, or the Open Housing Act of 1968, my dad wrote a letter to my older brother, then a two-year-old. Dad feared that if something happened to him, my brother would lack guidance and wisdom.

May 4, 1951
Kirk, my Son, you are now starting out in life—a life that
Mother and I cannot live for you.

So as you journey through life, remember it's yours, so make it a good one. Always try to cheer up the other fellow.

Learn to think straight, analyze things, be sure you have all the facts before concluding, and always spend less than you earn.

Make friends, work hard, and play hard. Most important of all remember this—the best of friends wear out if you use them.

This may sound silly, Son, but no matter where you are on the 29th of September, see that Mother gets a little gift, if possible, along with a big kiss and a broad smile.

When you are out on your own, listen and take advice but do your own thinking, and concluding, set up a reasonable goal, then be determined to reach it. You can and will, it's up to you, Son.

Your Father,

Randolph Elder

The first black female judge in the United States, Jane Bolin, recently passed away at the age of ninety-eight. Because of Bolin's gender and race, her college advisor attempted to dissuade her from pursuing a law degree. But Bolin graduated from Yale Law School in 1931, the first black woman to do so. Then in 1939, New York City Mayor Fiorello H. La Guardia appointed her as judge. How did she feel about being the first black female judge in America? "Everyone else makes a fuss about it, but I didn't think about it, and I still don't," she said in a 1993 interview. "I wasn't concerned about first, second or last. My work was my primary concern."[25]

Ms. Bolin's attitude shows how and why so many blacks endured and ultimately prospered. Black folks of my parents' generation persevered. They never gave up. They stayed focused. They retained pride in who and what they are.

NAACP member Prentice McKinney fought for civil rights in marches and rallies, speaking out against racism and segregation in Milwaukee during the late 1960s. "Back then, the enemy was clear, it was white racists, and racist police officers," said

McKinney. "It was a legalized system of segregation. And so, the challenge was between the white establishment and the African-American population."[26]

But four decades later, McKinney reexamined things. "Today, the African-American population is being destroyed by its own youth . . . an enemy from within. You have a population of older African-Americans . . . who are now afraid of the children in their neighborhoods."

Ten months after Hurricane Katrina, crime continued to rise in New Orleans. Many residents, quoted in a *Los Angeles Times* article, talked about young residents' poor attitude and irresponsibility. The *Times* wrote:

> *Businessman Sharif Nadir, 59, who was raised in the C.J. Pete housing projects, lamented the get-rich-quick, "don't want to work for nothing" attitude of many of the neighborhood's youngsters, which he attributed largely to poor upbringing.*
>
> *"I don't think it's a lack of opportunity," said Nadir, whose day care center on Oretha C. Haley Boulevard has been burglarized three times in recent years. "The old had the will, but no way. This generation has the way, but not will.*
>
> *"This generation has misplaced priorities."*
>
> *And they lack respect for their elders, said community organizer and youth worker Bertrand Butler.*
>
> *"Back then, neighbors had your mother's permission to spank your behind," said Butler. "And a person a certain age could discipline you. Even the drug dealers had discipline. They wouldn't sell in front of you.*
>
> *"Now, they call the kids to them."*
>
> *During the day, the blast of boom-box music permeates the air on certain neighborhood side streets. At night, it is the sound of gunfire that often dominates, residents said.*
>
> *"They even shoot at the cops," Jeffery Vannor, 17, said of the neighborhood gangsters. There's no respect."[27]*

Older blacks consider respect something one earned. They endured verbal and physical abuse virtually incomparable to any indignity suffered by today's generation of blacks. When I talk to older black men and women, many feel saddened by the wide-open opportunities that today's youth often fail to seize.

Years ago I met an elderly black man, an aeronautical engineer, in Dayton, Ohio. He worked for years at Wright-Patterson Air Force Base, in addition to teaching at a local university. "You must have been one of just a handful of black aeronautical engineers in the entire country," I said. "I would be surprised if there were more than fifty," he replied. After he graduated from school, corporations refused to even accept his resume. Finally, he heard that contractors in Mexico hired blacks, and he prepared to hobo-hop a freight and travel to Mexico. But the U.S. government called and offered him a position that he kept until retirement.

As he and I stood on the sidewalk in front of his house, discussing his career, a black teenager with a blasting boom box the size of Delaware walked toward us with a scowl. His demeanor told us, "Stand apart, so I can walk through." He clearly did not intend to go around us. We complied, and let the angry young man walk through. Mr. Stevens, the engineer, turned to me and said, "Larry, I don't get it. What's the problem? The sky's wide open."

That conversation took place nearly twenty years ago. But today, the anger in many still rages. So-called black leaders continue their chant: No justice, no peace. The "battle against racism" takes precedence over personal responsibility, hard work, pursuing an education, and breeding children only when capable of assuming this responsibility. Anger can become the enemy of success and of productivity. Those who fan this anger create an emotional and psychological trap of weights and barriers.

The 1992 Los Angeles riots broke out after the officers' acquittals in the first Rodney King beating trial. The riots left fifty-four people dead, more than three thousand stores looted or burned and an estimated billion dollars in damage. During the tenth anniversary of the '92 riots, Cecil "Chip" Murray, a prominent black Los Angeles clergyman, provided excuses for the rioting thugs. "How ridiculous it was to set those fires," Murray said. "How understandable, but how ridiculous."[28] Understandable? How about "just plain wrong"?

So-called black leaders continue their chant: No justice, no peace. The "battle against racism" takes precedence over personal responsibility, hard work, pursuing an education, and breeding children only when capable of assuming this responsibility.

Blaming something or someone else gets he-feels-our-pain votes for black politicians, and a quote from one of the "community activists" may find itself in the morning newspapers. But how does this help, or bring about change in a culture that does not emphasize education and where too many people refuse to take responsibility for the children they bring into the world?

The 1965 Watts riots in Los Angeles resulted in thirty-four people dead, more than one thousand injured, and $40 million in property damage.[29] Sociologists call it one of the worst "race riots" ever.

At the time the Watts population was 90 percent black, 8 percent Hispanic, and 2 percent "others." Now, due to middle-class "black flight" to the suburbs and immigration—much of it illegal—the racial composition of Watts has changed dramatically. Today Watts is 38 percent black, 61 percent Hispanic, and 2 percent other. Unemployment has increased from 14 percent to 21 percent for men, and from 14 percent to 25 percent for women.[30]

How did the riots affect the economics of that community? Economic historian and professor Robert A. Margo, with his colleague William J. Collins, studied the economic effect of the late '60s riots and their impact on income, employment, and property values. They found that the riots' destruction depressed incomes and property values in the inner city for decades. Median black family income in cities that rioted dropped by 9 percent from 1960 to 1970, compared to that of black families in similar cities with no riots. Comparing cities with riots to similar cities without riots, the median value of black homes in cities with severe riots dropped 14 to 20 percent during the '60s. And the median value of all central-city homes—regardless of the race of the owner—dropped 6 to 20 percent in cities that saw rioting.[31]

The researchers found that the property-value declines continued over the long term. "This effect," they write, "could work through any number of the channels that feed into the net benefit stream: personal and property risk might seem higher; insurance premiums might rise; taxes for redistribution or more police and fire protection might increase, and municipal bonds may be more difficult to place; retail outlets might close; businesses and employment opportunities might relocate; friends and family might move away; burned-out buildings might be an eyesore; and so on."[32]

Local Los Angeles television channel KTLA aired a piece on the Watts riots in which a roundtable of a dozen "community leaders" gathered to discuss Watts forty years after the riots.

One "leader" said, "We been struggling for over two hundred years in this country for our freedom, and we will continue to struggle." Another said, "Have we gone forward with the march of time, or have we gone backwards? In some ways, we've done both." One "community leader" said, "Racism's as alive and well today as it was forty years ago. The emphasis now is over [sic] profits over people, and the Christianization of racism through the conservative right."[33]

Christianization of racism? Does the Watts resident know that people of faith, including so-called Christian conservatives, per capita, give more of their money and volunteer more of their time than do non-religious Americans? And the giving goes beyond simply donations to their church. Religious people also donate more of their money and volunteer more hours to non-religious causes than do secularist people.[34] So those being accused of placing "profit over people" believe strongly in philanthropy, frequently directed toward minorities and the underprivileged. Most "Christian conservatives" both talk the talk and walk the walk.

The KTLA reporter concluded, "From 1965, until 2005, for those who survived, the stigma of racial and social unrest in Watts is hard to erase. Forty years later, it remains a symbol of tough life in urban America."[35]

Really?

According to the U.S. Census Bureau, the number of black-owned businesses increased 45 percent from 1997[36] to 2002,[37] a growth rate far higher than for any other race or ethnicity, including whites. The revenues of the black businesses also grew faster, increasing by 30 percent compared to a 5 percent increase for whites.[38] While many problems remain with the so-called underclass, the black earned income in America continues to rise, standing at $656 billion in 2003.[39] Put another way, this "black GDP"—if blacks represented their own country—places them within the top sixteen countries in the world. While only 12 percent of America's population, U.S. blacks would displace all of Australia from the number sixteen slot.[40]

Look around. A black man, Kofi Annan, just ended his term as the United Nations secretary general, a black woman serves as secretary of State, a black man sits as one of nine justices on the United States Supreme Court, and the state of Illinois elected a black man to the United States Senate. Blacks comprise roughly 10 percent of the U.S. House of Representatives, and blacks are CEOs of major companies like American Express and Time Warner.

If racists hold blacks back, they're doing a bad job.

But as for the so-called underclass—the 20 percent of blacks living below poverty level—welfare dependency, poor school standards, gang membership and violence, teen pregnancy, and drug use prevent them from joining the middle class.

As economist Walter Williams notes, if by tomorrow the hearts of whites became as pure as that of Mother Teresa, these problems would go nowhere.

The mainstream media's constant paternalism and condescension toward blacks never ceases. First, "leaders" like Jesse Jackson complain that lending institutions fail to provide blacks "access to capital." Never mind that, a few years ago, Freddie Mac released a report showing almost twice as many blacks have bad credit histories than whites, 48 to 27 percent, respectively.[41] At the same time, the *Washington Post* reported that whites making $25,000 per year or less had better credit histories than blacks earning $65,000 to $75,000 a year.[42] Asian applicants have their loans granted at a higher rate than whites or blacks. Why? Asians, especially those of Japanese, Korean, and Chinese ancestry, live further below their means than do other groups. Therefore, an Asian applicant is, more likely, a "creditworthy" borrower. Blacks, on the other hand—again, speaking broadly—have poorer credit histories.

The spending habits of some blacks hurt creditworthiness. *USA Today* columnist Yolanda Young wrote, "According to Target Market, a company that tracks black consumer spending, blacks spend a significant amount of their income on depreciable products. In 2002, the year the economy nose-dived, we spent $22.9 billion on clothes, $3.2 billion on electronics, and $11.6 billion on furniture to put into homes that, in many cases, were rented.

"Among our favorite purchases are cars and liquor. Blacks make up only 12 percent of the U.S. population, yet account for 30 percent of the country's Scotch consumption. Detroit, which is 80 percent black, is the world's No. 1 market for Cognac. So impressed was Lincoln with the $46.7 billion that blacks spent on cars that the automaker commissioned Sean 'P. Diddy' Combs, the entertainment and fashion mogul, to design a limited-edition Navigator replete with six plasma screens, three DVD players and a Sony PlayStation 2.

"The only area where blacks seem to be cutting back on spending is books; total purchases have gone from a high of $356 million in 2000 to $303 million in 2002. . . .

"According to published reports, the Ariel Mutual Funds/ Charles Schwab 2003 Black Investor Survey found that when comparing households where blacks and whites had roughly the same household incomes, whites saved nearly 20 percent more each month for retirement, and 30 percent of African-Americans earning $100,000 a year had less than $5,000 in retirement savings."[43]

The former head of the National Urban League, Hugh Price, rejected the they-won't-lend-us-money-because-we-are-black theory. He said, "If people have bad credit, they'll be denied loans, end of story."[44] Price understands that banks and mortgage companies—just like any other business—need to make a profit to stay in business. They make profit by charging interest. If interest is too low, no profit. If the loan is not repaid, no profit—plus a substantial loss. This is not rocket science.

Yet people like Jesse Jackson accuse lenders of racism because of blacks' higher loan rejection rates. The ever-sympathetic *Los Angeles Times* makes another charge—that lenders exploit black and minority borrowers by charging higher rates of interest. The *Times* ran an article in September 2005, with the following headline: "Racial Gap in Loans Is High in State." "The study by the Association of Community Organizations for Reform Now (ACORN)," said the writer, Jonathan Peterson, "looked at the percentage of higher-cost loans issued in minority communities compared with nonminority neighborhoods in the same metropolitan area. Residents of predominantly minority districts in the Los Angeles metro area were more than nine times more likely to get high-cost loans to refinance their homes than residents of predominately white communities.[45]

The article referred to a Federal Reserve study, showing that across the country blacks and Hispanics were more likely to receive so called subprime loans—that charge a higher rate of interest—compared to whites. This difference, according to the *Times*, could not be explained by differences in income. This, of course, reeks of . . . racism! No mention that better loan rates go to less-risky, creditworthy borrowers with better credit histories. "ACORN," wrote Peterson, "said its study raised concerns that minority group members might be paying unfairly high interest rates and thousands of dollars in extra upfront costs by being pushed into refinancing their homes in the sub-prime market." The article quoted one ACORN official as saying, "Increases in home ownership can help stabilize families and communities, but not if home equity is drained away by unfair loans."[46]

"Drained away"? What about the responsibility of the borrower? Do banks lure dummies in by putting a fishhook through their noses and forcing them to sign for pricey loans?

But wait. One month later, the *LA Times* broadened its concern. In a front-page article called, "More Homeowners with Good Credit Getting Stuck with Higher-Rate Loans," the *Times* alerted us to yet another scandal. "Increasingly," we learn, "Americans with good credit are being saddled with loans designed for high-risk borrowers." The *Times* notes, "Companies and independent brokers generally are not legally required to tell customers that they might get a better deal elsewhere, and regulations have not kept pace with the booming mortgage refinancing market and skyrocketing home prices."[47]

So now lenders get blamed because apparently some borrowers refuse to engage in comparative shopping. When borrowers fail to go online to shop for competitive rates, blame the lenders. Kathleen Keest, senior policy counsel at the Center for Responsible Lending, said, "The reality is, if you happen to walk into the wrong door, you can be trapped."

So, in just one month, the *LA Times* went from protecting minority borrowers from exploitation, to protecting nonminority borrowers with good credit from exploitation. Now, everyone is a victim—not just blacks and Latinos. Maybe this is good news.

But the blacks-are-children-who-cannot-help-themselves theme continues. "Payday Loans Blamed for Trapping Poor in 'Quicksand,'" read the *CyberNews* headline of December 1, 2006. "Thirty-nine states still allow payday lending in some fashion, prompting liberal, consumer and civil rights groups Thursday to urge a national crackdown on the practice."[48]

Guess which "black leader" profited by serving as a spokesperson for a "predatory lender" who exploited the poor and minorities by forcing subprime loans down the throats of unsuspecting borrowers?

Answer: Reverend Al Sharpton.

LoanMax, which specializes in high-interest auto title loans, hired Sharpton to pitch their products on television. "When I'm out fighting for the little guy and I need quick cash, I find comfort in knowing that LoanMax is here for me,"[49] said Sharpton in one ad. "Finally, there's someone in Virginia who will loan money to people the big guys won't loan to," said Sharpton, in another.[50] But Sharpton's home state of New York refuses to allow LoanMax to operate in that state. Why? New York sets an interest rate cap at 16 percent, but LoanMax's rates exceed that.[51] "LoanMax interest rates would make even Tony Soprano green with envy," wrote the *Chicago Sun-Times*.[52] So, Sharpton pitched a product to three other states that is illegal in his own state.[53]

According to the *Sun-Times*, "LoanMax makes 500,000 title loans a year through 200 stores in 21 states. Its average car title loan is $400, and at a 30 percent monthly interest rate, it makes $120 on a $400 loan for 30 days. Since LoanMax claims that most borrowers repay their loan in two to three months, in only 90 days the average customer pays $360 in interest on a $400 loan. If customers take a year to pay off the debt, they'll spend a whopping $1,440 in interest on a $400 loan. Borrowers also pay title recording fees, plus some lenders add a $50 annual membership fee."[54]

A *New York Post* editorial entitled "Loan-Shark Sharpton" slammed Sharpton for his practice of simultaneously criticizing those who purportedly prey on minorities and benefiting from those very same people. "Al Sharpton is the type of guy who might prompt many New Yorkers to ask: 'Would you buy a used car from this man?' But never in their wildest dreams would they imagine that the Reverend would become an actual shill for a real-life car financing company. Yet that's just what he's done. And the move surely bespeaks the preacher's rank hypocrisy. . . . [55]

"Actually, there's nothing illegal about what LoanMax does,

as far as anyone knows. And, it's not terribly surprising that Sharpton, on one day, would bash such companies for exploiting the poor and then, on another, take their money and push their services on the very people he claims to champion. After all, Sharpton is not generally known for his principles. Except for one: Al Sharpton will do what is best for . . . Al Sharpton. And nothing else matters."[56]

And, it's not terribly surprising that Sharpton, on one day, would bash such companies for exploiting the poor and then, on another, take their money and push their services on the very people he claims to champion. After all, Sharpton is not generally known for his principles.

Congresswoman Stephanie Tubbs-Jones (D-OH) carried the theme still further. She called predatory lending "the civil rights issue for this century."[57] Guess Sharpton didn't get the memo.

Confused? Let's recap: Lending institutions exploit. They lend money at exorbitant rates of interest. In particular, they exploit blacks and Hispanics while doing so. But they'll exploit nonblacks, too, even when they have good credit histories, if the loan-seekers don't bother to comparison shop and make informed decisions or to seek expert advice. Even though banks engage in this dastardly exploitative practice, Reverend Sharpton, civil rights leader—protector of all things black—serves as a pitchman for LoanMax, a company accused of exploiting the very same people Reverend Al claims to protect. Got it?

How does one explain the ink former presidential candidate Reverend Al Sharpton gets? He's a shallow, unreasonable, race-card-playing victicrat—a caricature, a clown, an embarrassment.

When the Teflon Reverend Al Sharpton ran for president in 2004, virtually no one in the mainscream media raised the issue of his false accusation of Tawana Brawley. Recall that in 1987, Tawana Brawley, a fifteen-year-old black girl, claimed that white men abducted her, scrawled racist slogans on her body, covered her in feces, and sexually assaulted her. A grand jury later called the entire incident a complete hoax, made up by a young teen afraid of punishment for staying out too long. But not before Sharpton leaped into the fray and actually named an individual—former assistant district attorney Steven Pagones—as one of the culprits! When he denied it, Sharpton literally begged Pagones to sue him for defamation, "We stated openly that Steven Pagones did it. If we're lying, sue us, so we can go into court with you and prove you did it. Sue us—sue us right now."[58]

Pagones obliged. Despite receiving death threats, and threats against his child, Pagones sued Sharpton and two others for defamation. A multiethnic jury unanimously convicted Sharpton and two codefendants of defaming Steve Pagones, and ordered Sharpton to pay the plaintiff $65,000.

The reverend promptly announced his intention not to pay. After nearly two years of nonpayment, Pagones finally received Sharpton's portion, but only because Sharpton's rich friends—right before his run for president—passed the hat and kicked in the money, which now totaled $87,000 with interest and penalties, to clean up the reverend's resume.

To this day, Sharpton refuses to apologize, "I did what I believed. . . . They are asking me to grovel. They want black children to say they forced a black man coming out of the hard-core ghetto to his knees. . . . Once you begin bending, it's 'did you bend today?' or 'I missed the apology, say it again.' Once you start compromising, you lose respect for yourself."[59]

Beyond the Pagones allegation, any number of the following offenses, run-ins, and clownishness would have and should have killed anybody else's legitimacy, let alone candidacy for president of the United States:

Convicted for tax evasion: In a 1988 interview, Sharpton said he saw no reason why blacks should pay taxes. "If we do not have a justice system that protects us, what are we paying for?"[60] Sharpton has faced multiple charges—and one conviction—of tax evasion.[61]

Organized *protests hostile to rape victim*: In 1989 the "Central Park Jogger," a young white woman, was monstrously raped and nearly beaten to death in Central Park. Sharpton organized protests outside the courthouse, where his supporters chanted, "The boyfriend did it!" and denounced the victim as a "Whore!" He brought Tawana Brawley to the trial, to show her "white justice" and arranged for her to meet the attackers. Sharpton appealed for a psychiatrist to examine the victim, generously saying, "It doesn't even have to be a black psychiatrist. . . . We're not endorsing the damage to the girl—if there *was* this damage."[62] (While it doesn't excuse anyone from calling the victim a whore and denigrating any damage to her, nor does it excuse any accusations against the boyfriend, Sharpton may have been right about one thing: the innocence of the accused. In 2002, another man—a convicted rapist and murderer whose DNA matched—confessed to the rape, and the original convictions were vacated.)

Called Jews "diamond merchants" and instigated the Crown Heights riots: In 1991, Gavin Cato, a seven-year-old black child was killed in a traffic accident in Crown Heights (in Brooklyn), when a car driven by a Hasidic Jew went out of control.[63] Sharpton turned it into a racial incident. Sharpton led four hundred protesters through the Jewish section of Crown Heights, with one protester holding a sign that read, THE WHITE MAN IS THE DEVIL. There were four nights of rock- and bottle-throwing, and a young Talmudic scholar was surrounded by a mob shouting, "Kill the Jew" and stabbed to death.[64] A hundred others were injured. Sharpton said, "The world will tell us that [Gavin Cato] was killed by accident. . . . What type of city do we have that would allow politics to rise above the blood of innocent babies? . . . Talk about how

Oppenheimer in South Africa sends diamonds straight to Tel Aviv and deals with the *diamond merchants* right here in Crown Heights. . . . All we want to say is what Jesus said: If you offend one of these little ones, you got to pay for it. No compromise. Pay for your deeds."[65] Later Sharpton said, "If the Jews want to get it on, tell them to pin their yarmulkes back and come over to my house."[66]

Consorted with Arafat: When Sharpton announced a 2001 trip to the Middle East, Rabbi Shmuley Boteach helped plan his itinerary. Sharpton, according to the rabbi, promised not to meet with Yassir Arafat, yet only days later, Jewish New Yorkers opened the morning paper to see a smiling Arafat and Sharpton, meeting and shaking hands in Israel. Furious, Rabbi Boteach said, "Prior to our recent trip to Israel, U.S. black leader Reverend Al Sharpton and I discussed several times that there were to be no meetings with Arab or Palestinian leaders, not because I wished to set preconditions for our travel, but because the express objective of our mission was to show solidarity with Israeli victims of terror. The idea was to provide a magnanimous gesture of friendship and solidarity with the Jewish nation that would hopefully have strong reverberations for the relationship of the Jewish and black communities back home."[67]

Called a Jewish storeowner a "white interloper": In 1995 a Jewish store owner in Harlem was accused of driving a black record store owner out of business, when the United House of Prayer, one of the largest black landlords on 125th Street, raised the rent on the Fashion Mart owned by a Jew, Freddy Harari, who then raised the rent on his subtenant, Sikhulu Shange, who ran a record store.[68] At one of many rallies meant to scare the Jewish owner away, Sharpton said, "There is a systematic and methodical strategy to eliminate our people from doing business off 125th Street. I want to make it clear . . . that we will not stand by and allow them to move this brother so that some *white interloper* can expand his business." Following a demonstration three months later, one of the protestors, a black man with a pistol, stormed Freddy's Fashion Mart, screaming, "It's on now! All blacks out!" In addition to shooting several people, he set fire to the building, eventually killing himself and seven others. Initially, Sharpton denied having spoken at any rallies. When tapes surfaced, he said, "What's wrong with denouncing white interlopers?" Eventually, he apologized—but only for saying "white," not "interloper."[69]

Claims criminal justice system is racist: During the Million Man March in Washington, Al Sharpton thundered, "O. J. is home, but Mumia Abu Jamal [convicted of murder, on death row for many years] ain't home. And we won't stop till all of our people that need a chance in an awkward and unbalanced criminal justice system can come home."[70]

Caught on tape discussing cocaine deal: In 2002, HBO aired a nineteen-year-old FBI video surveillance of Sharpton with self-described mobster Michael Franzese and an undercover FBI agent posing as a Latin American drug dealer. HBO's *Real Sports* got the hidden camera video, showing undercover agent Victor Quintana posing as a drug lord trying to convince Sharpton to be middleman in a large cocaine deal.[71]

Sharpton asks the undercover agent, "What kind of time limit are we dealing with?"

"Coke?" the agent asks.

"Yeah." Sharpton says.

The phony drug dealer says, "Could be about the same time we have four million coming to us."

Sharpton: "End of April?"

"End of April. Six weeks from now. Is that a good time you think?" the agent asks.

"Probably," Sharpton replies.[72]

The undercover agent offers Sharpton a commission in exchange for his help with the drug deal. The agent says to Sharpton, "I can get pure coke for about $35,000 a kilo. . . . Every kilogram we bring in, $3,500 to you. How does that sound?" Sharpton nods in response.[73]

How does Sharpton explain away the videotapes? He says he simply played along with the undercover agent because he was afraid. "And I'm in his office," Sharpton told Fox News. "I don't know whether this man is armed. I don't know what's going on. So I kind of say, 'Yeah, yeah, yeah,' to get out of there." Sharpton claimed somebody from law enforcement leaked the tape to disrupt his 2004 presidential run. He unsuccessfully sued HBO, its parent company AOL Time Warner, and several individuals who worked on the story. But the feds never brought charges against Sharpton because, allegedly, the sting was intended to get Sharpton to act as an informant for the feds into an investigation into corruption by Don King and the boxing industry. The HBO report featured former Mafia captain Michael Franzese saying that the FBI was on the right track when it targeted Sharpton in a sting back in 1983 in an effort to root out corruption in boxing.[74]

Sharpton even admitted in 1988 that he informed for the government in order "to get rid of drugs and election fraud" in black neighborhoods. He denied informing on civil rights leaders and organized crime figures.[75]

Caught on tape with "shady fund-raisers": After Sharpton's name surfaced on wiretaps in an unrelated Philadelphia City Hall corruption case, the FBI launched a probe into Sharpton's fundraising for his failed 2004 presidential run. According to the *New York Post*, the FBI secretly videotaped Sharpton on May 9, 2003, "pocketing campaign donations from two shady fund-raisers"[76] in a New York City hotel room, and then demanding $25,000 more. The two fund-raisers were La-Van Hawkins and the late Ronald White. A later wiretap recorded Hawkins telling White that they had raised more than $140,000 for Sharpton the previous quarter, but Hawkins was concerned that Sharpton had only reported about $50,000 to the Federal Elections Commission, as required by law. Sharpton said the allegations were a "politically motivated smokescreen" to hide the fact the Justice Department is out to get him. He ripped the probe and the secret videotaping, saying, "Can you imagine what would happen if it was a white presidential candidate?"[77]

Actually, Reverend, we *can* imagine what would happen to a white candidate. And it would have been ugly

Not only does the so-called black leadership fight battles won long ago, but their rhetoric, nastiness, mean-spiritedness, and anger fail to improve things. Their failure to even consider something like vouchers or private savings accounts makes things worse, and will widen the have/have not gap that they claim to care about. Whether education, health care, gun control, the war on drugs, taxes, spending, or regulations, the so-called black leadership not only takes the wrong position, but condemns as a racist or an Uncle Tom anyone who dares to suggest that Republican ideas deserve consideration.

Alphonso Jackson, Bush's secretary of the Department of Housing and Urban Development (HUD), grew up in a Jim Crow environment in segregated Dallas. His father, suffering from cancer and with almost no income, refused to take welfare or food stamps. Why? "Never take anything you didn't earn," explained Alphonso's father. "That's close to stealing."[78]

As a college freshman, the future HUD secretary stood on the Edmund Pettus Bridge during the infamous Selma-to-Montgomery March on "Bloody Sunday" in 1965, when troopers attacked the six hundred civil rights marchers with dogs and tear gas and billy clubs. But Alphonso Jackson is not bitter or angry. His father—like my own—taught him that in America skin color is not a barrier to success, and that hard work reaps rewards.[79] His father never finished high school, juggled three jobs to feed his family, and—despite struggling with his health and the yoke of Southern segregation—still instilled in his children the importance of giving back.[80]

"I never went to school with my brothers and sisters of the lighter hue until I got off to college," said Jackson. "But I'm sitting here [as Secretary of HUD]. . . . And I'm sitting here because I believe that the American system might not be the panacea, but it's the best system that I've ever been able to live in."[81]

Given his values and upbringing, Alphonso Jackson—not surprisingly—dismisses the Jesse Jacksons, the Al Sharptons, and the Julian Bonds. "They [black leaders] have created an industry," says Secretary Jackson. "If we don't become victims, they have no income. They have no podium." He denounces "leaders" who insist "it's racism that's stopping everything we're doing. They are in the business of making excuses. White folks have nothing to do with the fact that seven out of every ten black children born in this country are born out of wedlock."[82]

Secretary Jackson also attacks the victicrat mentality. "I am not going to let the black leadership—*the so-called leadership*—of this country tell me that I am a victim. I believe that if you work hard, strive to do the very best, things will work out for you. [That] doesn't mean you won't have obstacles—you will. But we can't keep living in an era that is bygone. We need to begin today to teach blacks that they can look in the mirror—and that they have the ability, once they look in that mirror, to achieve."[83] In other words, as Dionne Warwick sang, "A fool will lose tomorrow reaching back for yesterday."

Wonder why?

Surely a secretary of HUD and a presidential cabinet member is, by definition, a leader. Yet, for some reason, the mainscream media does not anoint Secretary Jackson a "black leader." Apparently, "black leadership" requires anger and a victicrat mentality. A "black leader" must engage in and encourage BMW—Bitch, Moan, and Whine.

Take, for example, "Richard" from Brooklyn, a caller to my radio program. How bad is it to be black in America? To Richard it's awful. He said he wanted to go to Africa. Not just anywhere in Africa, he wanted to go to Senegal, offering a lack of funds as the only reason he remained in America. Fine, I said.

I suggested to my listeners that we raise money to sponsor Richard's move to Africa. Even Richard's employer called and said he often complained of living in America. She said that she made him the same bargain: Go, I'll pay.

My listeners accepted the challenge to set Richard free. We accepted only pledges rather than money, for despite Richard's whining and moaning about the horrors of being a black man in racist America, I suspected that when push came to shove, he would likely back down.

So we posted Richard's request for funds on my Web site and the pledges flew in.

To avoid being the victim of a Richard rip-off, we asked him to answer questions and agree to conditions. Basic stuff, like are you current in your taxes? Are you a party to a lawsuit? Do you have any outstanding warrants or are you otherwise under the criminal justice system? Do you owe any debts? Are you current in your rent? Mortgage? Will you agree to stay for at least five years, and agree to monthly check-ins with my radio show? We waited for a response. And waited. And waited. And waited.

For what it's worth, in Senegal—Richard's African country of choice—unemployment is at 48 percent, 54 percent of the population lives below the poverty line, per capita GDP is $1,800, and the principal occupation (77 percent) of people is agriculture.[84] It should be interesting to watch a New York City boy adjust to a garden hoe.

Did Richard go? Well, let me put it this way: Next time you're in Brooklyn, ask around for Richard. I'm sure he'll still be there . . . complaining.

4.

STUPID BLACK POLITICIANS

You think the Republican National Committee could get this many people of color in a single room? . . . Only if they had the hotel staff in here.[1]

—HOWARD DEAN, DURING A MEETING WITH THE CONGRESSIONAL
BLACK CAUCUS

Representative Melvin Watt (D-NC), a Congressional Black Caucus member, serves the Charlotte/Greensboro/-Durham area, in a serpentine-shaped district that includes parts of ten counties. It is 57 percent black, 42 percent white, and has an overwhelming four-to-one Democratic registration advantage.[2] When Representative Watt appeared on C-SPAN with Brian Lamb, he offered his formula for black success:

> **LAMB:** If you had—I don't know how many—five, six black young men sitting in front of you, you're just in a room, and they say to you, Congressman, tell me what I have to do—based on your success—to do what you've done? . . . What advice would you give young men

today—or women, for that matter—how . . . in this society today, how can they become Mel Watt?

WATT: I would say, you've got to achieve to your potential. And I would say, you've got to work hard, you've got to study hard, you've got to build on every day, because tomorrow is going to be a function of what you did today and yesterday. And you've got to keep building on that. . . . But the country has to understand that if I'm giving that lecture to five black boys whose parents are not educated, who don't have adequate nutrition and background, who don't have equal opportunities in their schools and materials and technology access, and are growing up in a neighborhood at the end of school where they go in and there's no recreation activities, no after-school activities and there are gangs and violence going on around them—regardless of how hard they work, regardless of how hard they study or how much they try to stay on track—the odds are going to be stacked against them. . . . I would say with integrity to those students, you've got to work. But if you're honest with them, you've got to tell them, you've got to work five times as hard as your white counterpart. Otherwise, it ain't going to happen.

LAMB: Is that what you did?

WATT: I guarantee you, that's exactly what I did. . . . But, you know, I worked probably five times as hard in college and law school as most of my counterparts did. You're absolutely right.[3]

Watt attended University of North Carolina at Chapel Hill and Yale Law School. He clearly worked hard to achieve his lofty level of success.

But, "five times harder"? Talk about a dispiriting message! Besides, do the math. If his counterparts spent only six hours a day on classes and schoolwork, this means, as a student, Watt worked thirty hours a day. This means he got a negative six hours of sleep every day, but managed to pull through. Impressive.

Does Watt really believe this? Or does Watt represent another example of not preaching what he practices? Making it to the House ranks as a major achievement. Through hard work and a willingness to put himself out in the public fishbowl, Watt attained an impressive level of power and achievement. But now he says, in essence, I worked really, really hard to get where I am, but I cannot and do not expect the same of you.

When I grew up, my grandparents, as well as many other relatives, told me that I had to work harder that the average white kid "to get ahead." I know that meant that I had to be as good or better than anyone else.

But "five times harder"? Watt said it with a straight face. Lamb gave him a chance to say, "Well, I simply mean that you've got to work harder in order to overcome obstacles." But, no, Watt beat his chest to heroically tell us that he overcame obstacles as high as Mount Everest.

Through hard work and a willingness to put himself out in the public fishbowl, Watt attained an impressive level of power and achievement. But now he says, in essence, I worked really, really hard to get where I am, but I cannot and do not expect the same of you.

John Conyers, a black representative from Michigan, was first elected to the United States House of Representatives in 1964. His Fourteenth District in Wayne County includes Highland

Park, the poorest city in Michigan, with a poverty rate near 40 percent.[4] Poverty rating in his district stands at about 17 per-cent.[5] The Census Bureau estimates that 20 to 25 percent of adults in the Fourteenth District never finished high school.[6]

As one white e-mailer recently wrote me: "Larry, I'd be happy to pay reparations for slavery. Just tell all the ex-slaves to come over to my house and line up at the front door."

Every congressional session since 1989, Congressman Conyers goes up to the House podium and introduces a bill for . . . repara-tions: "It is a fact that slavery flourished in the United States and constituted an immoral and inhumane deprivation of African slaves' lives, liberty, and cultural heritage. As a result, millions of African-Americans today continue to suffer great injustices."[7]

Yes, reparations. When looking at the poverty in his district, Conyers fails to look at the failure of the domestic auto makers to remain competitive, a bloated local government that vastly overtaxes its citizens, the underperforming schools, lack of em-phasis on education from far too many people in his district, the phenomenon of children having children, the negative effects of the war on drugs, and the victicrat mind-set that rejects per-sonal responsibility. No, his district suffers from the lack of reparations for slavery.

Well, fine. As one white e-mailer recently wrote me: "Larry, I'd be happy to pay reparations for slavery. Just tell all the ex-slaves to come over to my house and line up at the front door."

A few years ago, white rapper Eminem made a movie called *8 Mile*, a reference to Eight Mile Road, which more or less divides the better area of Detroit from the downtrodden areas. In this area of Conyers's district, one cannot find a large retail store, and there is only one movie theater. It is filled with abandoned housing and overflows with criminals and drug addicts. Storefront after storefront stands empty or is boarded up, and graffiti-lined walls abound. Seventy percent of children here are born into single-parent households.[8]

Immediately adjacent to Eight Mile lies East Dearborn, a bustling one-hundred-thousand-member Arab community. The Arab residents hail from all over the Middle East, and built a community with thriving grocers, stores, and restaurants. Despite some anti-Arab sentiment after the terrorist attacks of September 11, 2001, in the next fourteen months twenty new businesses were opened on one three-mile stretch of road.[9] The predominately working-class Arabs who call East Dearborn home truly seize and exemplify the American Dream. Police call crime in the Arab area tame compared to that of the black area of Eight Mile.

When asked to explain why the Arab area next to Eight Mile prospers and the black one suffers, Congressman Conyers replied, "Racism."[10] This, of course, fails to explain the neighboring communities like Southfield, a prosperous suburb immediately northwest of Detroit that is 54 percent black.[11] Nor does this explain Dearborn, a community that is 30 percent Arab.[12]

For black Democratic politicians, double standards abound. They simply do not have to endure the same scrutiny as white politicians.

For example, will the last white politician with a resume like this please stand up?

Representative Maxine Waters:

- Condemned the CIA for its alleged role in the creation of urban America's drug problem: "If I never do anything else in this career as a member of Congress—I'm gonna make somebody pay for what they've done to my community."[13]

- Accused by law enforcement—on the record—of interfering with a legitimate probe by writing a letter to Attorney General Janet Reno, asking her to back off of a joint federal Justice Department/local DEA probe centered on her husband's childhood friend who was suspected of drug trafficking.[14]

- Likened former Black Panther Joanne Chesimard—who was convicted of murdering a New Jersey State Highway Patrol Officer—to Martin Luther King.[15] Sent a letter to Fidel Castro, urging him to let Chesimard stay after she escaped from prison and fled to Cuba, stating Chesimard was persecuted for her political beliefs and affiliations.[16]

- Justified the 1992 Los Angeles riots by calling them a "rebellion,"[17] while bellowing, "No justice, no peace."[18]

- Called President George Bush-41 a "racist" and refused to apologize for it.[19]

Will the last white politician with a resume like this please stand up?

Representative Alcee Hastings (D-FL):

- Charged (although acquitted in a criminal trial) with conspiring with a friend to take a $150,000 bribe and give two convicted swindlers light sentences.[20]

- Impeached, convicted, and kicked off the bench by Congress, in a move done only six times in history.[21]

- Only member of Congress ever to have been previously impeached and removed from office as a federal judge.[22]

- Following impeachment and conviction, declared himself a victim of a witch hunt, "institutional racism," and an unfair judicial system.[23]

- Played the race card to turn disgrace into triumph by running for and getting elected to the House of Representatives as a congressman in the heavily black-populated Twenty-third District[24] in Miramar, Florida, in 1992.[25]

- Now serving in the same hypocritical Congress that expelled him as a federal judge but allows him to serve today as a congressman in its self-proclaimed distinguished body. Hastings said, "I bring with me the added notoriety of being impeached and re-moved from office by the same body that I now get to serve in."[26]

Why do these people get reelected? Answer: They effectively convince their constituents that a racist criminal justice system unfairly went after them.

And let's not forget the always angry, ever-bombastic Senator Charlie Rangel. *NewsMax.com* reports that the senator received money from Castro's Cuba. Originally, Rangel listed a bird conservation group as the sponsor of his 2002 trip to Cuba. After a watchdog group raised questions, Rangel changed his disclosure form and, wrote *NewsMax*, "reimbursed the Cuban government and a New York grocery store owner $1,922 for his son's expenses after the Center for Public Integrity raised questions about the trip." The reimbursement was necessary, because House ethics rules only permit sponsors to cover the cost of one relative—and Rangel took his wife, too. But House rules also require an additional report when a foreign government pays for part of a trip. According to *NewsMax* and the Center for Public Integrity, Rangel has not filed that report. "Calls to the congressman's office," writes *NewsMax*, "were not returned."[27]

Aided by a willing media, a desperate Democratic Party, and guilty white liberals, angry, finger-waving, black Democratic politicians get a pass on the same behavior that would fry their white counterparts.

Because of the success of the "get Whitey" mentality, black Senator Barack Obama poses a serious dilemma. He shot to national prominence during the 2004 Democratic Convention, where he spoke of an undivided America. He said, "[P]eople don't expect government to solve all their problems,"[28] and he did not play the white guilt game. So how do the "old guard" activists regard him?

Reverend Al Sharpton and "activist" Harry Belafonte showed near contempt for Obama's sudden rise in popularity. The *Times of London* described the reaction to Obama as "unexpected."[29] Unexpected? No, it was entirely predictable.

For Obama represents a threat to the power, stature, and legitimacy of the Sharptons and Belafontes who huff, puff, and finger-point, standing on the twin pillars of white guilt and black anger. No doubt, in part, jealousy plays a role in the "coolness,"[30] as the *Times* described, that Sharpton and friends show toward Obama.

A black president will force at least some black victicrats to rethink the "white man continues to hold me down" theme. So why doesn't a civil rights leader like Sharpton enthusiastically embrace Barack Obama, the first black candidate with a serious shot at the presidency?

Sharpton disavows any jealousy toward Obama. "Why shouldn't the black community ask questions? Are we now being told, 'You all just shut up'?" Sharpton said in response to a published report that he was jealous of Obama's campaign—an accusation that, according to Sharpton, came from the Obama camp. "Senator Obama and I agree that the war is wrong, but then I want to know why he went to Connecticut and helped [Senator Joseph] Lieberman, the biggest supporter of the war." Sharpton called the jealousy assertion a ruse, an effort by Obama's people to get an early endorsement from Sharpton.

"I'm not going to be cajoled or intimidated by any candidate, not for my support," Sharpton said.[31]

Yet an editorial in the *New York Observer* states that "a petulant Mr. Sharpton is telling people that Mr. Obama is 'a candidate driven by white leadership.' "[32] Hm-mm. Would that not be true of anybody's candidacy, including that of Senator Hillary Clinton? Once again, the demagogue's statement says a lot more about the demagogue himself than about the object of his attack.

Jesse Peterson, who heads a group called Brotherhood Organization of a New Destiny (BOND), analyzed precisely the reason for the cold shoulder from the so-called black leadership toward Barack Obama—despite Obama's point-by-point, lock-step, parallel liberal positions. "The old style of leadership is: blame, blame, blame, racism, racism, racism. You can't make it in America because you're black. Obama is not quite like that. He gives the message that you *can* make it in America," said Peterson.[33]

After all, from the standpoint of the policy positions adopted by Sharpton and his kind, what's not to like about Obama? Pro gun control? Check. Pro choice? Check. Pro affirmative action? Check. Pro universal health coverage? Check. Anti war in Iraq? Check. Anti education vouchers? Check.[34] And, unlike Senator Clinton, Obama never voted for the authorization of the war since he was elected afterward.

But Harry Belafonte sounded a warning about Obama, "We don't know what he's truly about."[35] Sharpton said, "Right now, we are hearing a lot of media razzle-dazzle. I am not hearing a lot of meat, or a lot of content. I think that when the meat hits the fire, we'll find out if it's just fat or if there is some real meat there."[36] What an interesting analysis, especially coming from someone who failed in his attempt to get elected as mayor, senator, or president. Since neither of these "leaders" care about foreign policy, doesn't Obama's voting record provide some insight into his "meat"? According to the *National Journal*, Obama's voting record in 2005 made him more liberal than 82.5 percent of his fellow senators. Clinton's voting record made her "only" 79.8 percent more liberal than her colleagues.[37]

Black State Senator Robert Ford (D-SC), a state whose Democratic primary consists of 50 percent black voters, flat-out dismissed the viability of Obama's candidacy. Not, mind you, because he dislikes Obama. Indeed, he said, "I love Obama." But in supporting Senator Clinton over Obama, Ford said, "It's a slim possibility for [Obama] to get the nomination, but then everybody else is doomed. Every Democrat running on that ticket next year would lose because he's black and he's top of the ticket. We'd lose the House and the Senate and the governors and everything. I'm a gambling man. I love Obama. But I'm not going to kill myself."[38]

Not exactly "We Shall Overcome." Ford later issued an apology—a most incredible apology: "If I caused anybody—including myself—any pain about the comments I made earlier, then I want to apologize to myself and to Senator Obama and any of his supporters."[39]

So what's the problem with supporting Obama? "Black leaders" are more likely to extract concessions from a white liberal politician than a black liberal politician. Sharpton can play the guilt card against a white politician, like a Hillary Clinton, perhaps dangling a promise of delivering the black vote. How does one use white guilt on a popularly elected black president?

Blacks, one would think, would understand and guard against racism toward others. But often the very people who cry racism practice it against others.

A predominately black ward in Chicago elected Thomas Murphy, a white man, to serve as alderman, the equivalent of a city councilman. Murphy, to better represent interests of his primarily black constituents, wanted to join the city's black caucus. The caucus refused to admit him. "The only reason I was given was that I'm not an African-American elected official," said Murphy. "I believe that the purpose of the caucus was to represent the interests of the black residents of this city. Apparently, they think otherwise."[40]

A similar incident recently happened at the United States House of Representatives. When white Representative Stephen L. Cohen (D-TN), took over black former House member Harold Ford's old seat, Cohen attempted to join the Congressional Black Caucus (CBC). After all, Cohen's district is 60 percent black.[41] But no dice. Congressional Black Caucus chairwoman Representative Carolyn Cheeks Kilpatrick (D-MI) spoke bluntly, "Mr. Cohen asked for admission, and he got his answer. . . . It's time to move on. It's an unwritten rule. It's understood. It's clear."[42]

The bylaws of the Congressional Black Caucus contain no racial exclusion. But tell that to white Representative Pete Stark (D-CA) who, back in 1975, tried to join the CBC. He, too, ran into the "no whites allowed" sign. Stark said, "Half my Democratic constituents were African-American. I felt we had interests in common as far as helping people in poverty. They had a vote, and I lost. They said the issue was that I was white, and they felt it was important that the group be limited to African-Americans."[43] In other words, "No whites allowed."

Black anger does not simply target whites and "sell-out blacks." It also targets liberal blacks if they show insufficient anger. Take Senator Obama. He faces some big problems—attracting black voters.

In 1996, then retired army general and former chairman of the Joint Chiefs of Staff, Colin Powell, considered running for the presidency. At the time, 54 percent of whites said, if given a chance, they would vote for Powell. But among blacks, only 25 percent said Powell would get their vote.[44] Okay, attribute this to Powell's "Republicanism," despite his moderate stances, including his endorsement of affirmative action and his rejection of Newt Gingrich's Contract with America.

But angry Reverend Al Sharpton? He ran for U.S. Senate in New York in 1994, receiving 70 percent of the black vote in the Democratic primary.[45] Sharpton then ran for mayor of New York in 1997. He received 85 percent of the black vote in the primary.[46] Jesse Jackson ran for President in 1984 and in 1988, receiving, in the primaries, 77 percent and 92 percent of the black vote, respectively.[47]

After Barack Obama announced his exploratory committee for the presidency in January 2007, only 28 percent of blacks supported him. CBS News reported that the polls "suggest that certain African-Americans just don't identify with the Ivy League-educated, biracial senator."[48] Around that time, the black monthly magazine *Ebony* featured Obama and his wife on the cover. Both hold law degrees from Harvard, and Obama, a father of two, seems quite happily married and considers his wife his best friend and mentor. Obama shows no sense of anger, does not engage in finger-pointing, and does not play on white guilt. He rejects the victicrat mentality. As a result, he struggles to get the black vote.

Popular black Representative Charlie Rangel uses anger and a sense of grievance as a weapon to influence public opinion. Rangel wants to bring back the military draft, in part because he feels the military exploits the blacks and the poor.

An opponent of the Iraq War, Congressman Rangel says, "This president and this administration would never have invaded Iraq . . . if, indeed, we had a draft and members of Congress and the administration thought that their kids from their communities would be placed in harm's way."[49] In other words, if you're elite or rich or well connected, you're not serving in the military. No, that burden, argues Rangel, is placed on the backs of the poor and the minorities. "A disproportionate number of the poor and members of minority groups make up the enlisted ranks of the military," wrote Rangel in the *New York Times*, "while most privileged Americans are underrepresented or absent."[50]

Rangel put up a similar draft bill in 2003. When Republicans placed Rangel's resolution up for a vote, it went down in the House 402 to 2, with the congressman voting against his own proposal—supposedly to protest Republican procedural meddling.[51] Yet three years later, he's at it again. Is he serious, or just attempting to use race and class to stir up anger and resentment?

Senator John Kerry, a former presidential candidate, also

claims that poor people and minorities serve disproportionately in the military. Kerry told students at California's Pasadena City College, "You know, education, if you make the most of it, if you study hard and you do your homework, and you make an effort to be smart, you can do well. If you don't, you get stuck in Iraq."[52]

Kerry later attempted to dismiss the remark by calling it a "botched joke,"[53] an attempt to take a swipe at President Bush. You know, President Bush equals stupid, equals the United States getting "stuck" in Iraq, but it sure sounded like Kerry considers people in the military stupid, devoid of other options.

But as to Kerry's or Rangel's assertions, what about the facts? Studies show today's average recruit is *more* likely to hold a high school diploma than a nonrecruit. Many officers tout graduate degrees. Bill Carr, acting deputy undersecretary for military personnel policy, said in December 2005 that more than 90 percent of recruits attained at least a high school diploma, compared to 75 percent of civilian youth. And on aptitude tests, says Carr, today's recruit scores much higher average aptitudes than do nonrecruit youths. The Armed Services Vocational Aptitude Battery Test is designed so that the average young person scores at 50 percent. Yet in fiscal 2005, 67 percent of recruits scored above the sixtieth percentile on that test.[54]

Kerry, over thirty years ago, played the race-and-poverty-card in opposing the all-volunteer army. He said that such a force would be "an army of the poor and the black and the brown. We must not repeat the travesty of the inequities present during Vietnam. I also fear having a professional army that views the perpetuation of war crimes as simply 'doing its job.'"[55] Perhaps Kerry didn't realize his insult to the poor, the black, and the brown by suggesting that, were they the bulk of the all-volunteer army, they would happily engage in war crimes as a matter of policy!

Kerry and Rangel are wrong. Young people from the middle class comprise the bulk of today's wartime volunteer army recruits.[56]

Tim Kane, an economics scholar and Air Force Academy

graduate who prepared the report for a 2005 Heritage Foundation study on recruits, said, "We found that recruits tend to come from middle-class areas, with disproportionately fewer from low-income areas." The study found that "on average, recruits in 2003 were from wealthier neighborhoods than were recruits in 1999."[57]

Kerry, Rangel, and others often repeat the lie of "inequities" during the Vietnam War—that minorities died in higher percentages than their numbers in the population. Not true, according to David Horowitz of the Freedom Center. During the Vietnam War draft era, blacks comprised 13.5 percent of the population. Of those who died in Vietnam, 12.5 percent were black, with blacks comprising 12.1 percent of men killed in actual battle.[58]

As for Kerry's claim that only losers serve, he finally apologized to anyone "offended" by his "misinterpreted" words.[59]

Well, maybe the "botched joke" failed to hurt Democrats on election night in 2006, but what about hurting the military?

5.

STUPID BLACK ENTERTAINERS

We are living in terrorism as black people in America. And it has been that way since the dawning of slavery. . . . If we are having problems with finding our own inner souls and dignity to live out a life that is honorable, what is it that has put us in this position? We didn't volunteer for it. And those who have put us here and chosen to keep us here are people who deal in terror.[1]

—HARRY BELAFONTE

Some of the most successful entertainers—who thrive in a brutally competitive field—often scream "racism" the loudest.

Rapper, actress, and host Queen Latifah is, by any standard, a huge Hollywood success. Her star turn in the musical *Chicago* earned her an Oscar nomination for Best Supporting Actress. She recently landed a huge part in the movie *Hairspray* and has a star on the Hollywood Walk of Fame. For a couple of years she hosted a nationally syndicated television show and is a best-selling singer and rapper.

Yet in a July 23, 2007, cover story about Latifah in the black weekly magazine *Jet*, she complains that race remains a problem in entertainment. "Here's what happens in Hollywood: A black guy comes into a studio, does a deal with somebody to produce some movies, takes the money and never does a movie. So, now

I come in. I plan on making movies. I plan on taking their money and using it for the movies, but they're looking at me like, 'Are you going to do what the last black person did?'[2]

"What does it have to do with being black? If the guy is a crook, he's a crook. It has nothing to do with complexion. But we get lumped in together because I'm the next black person coming in.[3]

"That's the kind of stuff I've had to fight through the years— to get people off that ignorant position and get them back focused on 'Let's get this done. Let's make this money.'"[4] So to sum up, racist Hollywood gives blacks money to make films, and the blacks disappear with theirs, making Hollywood reluctant to give the next black person money because the previous black one ran off with it. Given the alleged racism in Hollywood, how does a black guy come in and get "their money" in the first place?

The story of Sean John Combs (Puff Daddy, P. Diddy, and now—as of November 2006—Diddy) simply fascinates. Born in Harlem, New York, Combs became a star rapper and expanded his career portfolio to include a clothing line, Blue Flame advertising company, an MTV show called *Making the Band*, a restaurant chain, and he's branching Bad Boy Entertainment (his record label) into technology, books, and films. Estimates place Combs's net worth at about $350 million.[5]

The concept of voting, however, apparently baffles the entrepreneur.

During the 2004 race, Combs founded an organization called Citizen Change, in an allegedly nonpartisan effort to get out the vote. Their motto was "Vote or Die!" Actually, Combs barely concealed his contempt for the Bush administration, on one occasion even saying at the Rock the Vote Awards: "[We gotta] get Bush's ass up out that office. . . . If you don't agree with me, you got your right to go to the polls and represent him."[6] So much for nonpartisanship.

Combs, just before the 2004 presidential election, appeared on CNN to not only urge young people to get out and vote, but to declare himself a "disenfranchised" voter: "We made them [40 million youth and minority voters] a part of this process, because I'm a part of this community and I'm also a disenfranchised voter. And my first time voting was, like, 2000."[7] Hold the phone. He didn't vote until 2000? When he was about thirty years old? Yet he's disenfranchised.

Cable news anchor Bill Hemmer, appearing a bit confused, tried to offer Combs an escape hatch.

HEMMER: Why do you say you were disenfranchised four years ago?

COMBS: Because politicians, they just didn't pay attention to us. We're part—I call ourselves the forgotten ones, youth and minority voters. Their campaign trails don't come into our communities unless they go to the churches, and they don't stop and speak to us as young men and women, like we have power like veterans do or senior citizens, but that's all about to change.

HEMMER: But let me just try and clear this up. You specifically?

COMBS: Yes, I did. That was my first time voting.

HEMMER: And your vote counted, right?

COMBS: And my vote definitely counted, and I learned from that. And I learned from that, and that helped me to want to get involved in a situation like this.

HEMMER: Okay, just for the sake of our discussion—how were you disenfranchised in 2000?

COMBS: You know, just the candidates not, you know, speaking to my needs, not coming in my community. I'm from Harlem, New York, from an inner-city community, and just going, seeing the school systems there not being taken care of, seeing the people having problems with health care, people having problems getting jobs. And you feel just like nobody cares about you. And your vote doesn't count.[8]

Can someone, somehow, some way, stop this New York resident from voting? Well, actually, no.

Greg Mathis hosts the popular court show, *Judge Mathis*. He came from a troubled background. As a gun-toting teenager growing up in the violent, gang-infested housing projects of Detroit, Mathis appeared well on his way to a life of crime. Mathis dropped out of school and spent time in jail on a variety of charges—purse snatching, breaking and entering, and drug possession. His single mother tried her best to control him and keep him out of the gangs, but she found him incorrigible.

Then one day at the Wayne County Jail, as he awaited trial for yet another crime, he received a visit from his mother that would change his life forever. "She came to visit me and began to talk about all the problems and all the pain I had caused her all her life," says Mathis. "I had hurt her in the eyes of the community, in the eyes of the church, embarrassed her. And she began to cry and she told me that now she's gonna die. She's found out she has cancer and the doctors told her that she has less than a year to live and I'm sitting behind bars once again, embarrassing her. And so it was at that moment that I promised her that I would change. I wanted to make her proud of me before she passed."

Mathis got out of jail and got a high school equivalency diploma (GED). Then he applied for and got admitted to a local university. Mathis describes it as "the proudest moment of my life that I shared with my mother." Despite her death three months later, Mathis persevered. After graduating, he attended and graduated from law school at the University of Detroit, earning a Juris Doctorate degree.[9]

How did he turn his life around? He said he "psychoanalyzed himself," and realized he had to stop pointing fingers, accept responsibility, and take control of his life. He became a lawyer, then a judge—the youngest in Michigan history—before going into television.

So far, so good.

But, like many blacks of influence, he sends a message of

accountability coupled with "blame racism/Republicans/Bush" that practically cancels out the message.

In August 2005, some ten thousand people marched in Atlanta to commemorate the fortieth anniversary of the Voting Rights Act of 1965. Speaker after speaker talked about the vital importance of reauthorizing the Act, while showing their real purpose in assembling—to denounce Bush, the war, the deficit, and almost everything else except the Loch Ness monster. "They all need to be locked up because they are all criminals and they are all thieves," said Judge Greg Mathis. "It is indeed criminal to steal an election and within two years run up a federal deficit of half a trillion dollars, send our young people over to Iraq to die for an unjust war. What they are doing is criminal. . . . [The] Supreme Court . . . was an accomplice to the biggest election crime in history in 2000. And I call it a crime because indeed that is exactly what it was."[10]

The Bush administration somehow became equated with past policies of slavery and segregation, and—according to Mathis— "the enemy of our [black America's] progress." Mathis said, "They shot and missed when they enslaved, segregated, and oppressed our people. They shot and missed when they stole the past two presidential elections. They shot and missed when they denied our right to vote."[11]

Maybe it's time for more psychoanalysis.

Camille Cosby, the wife of entertainer/philanthropist/activist Bill Cosby, once wrote that Congress stood on the brink of taking away the right of blacks to vote. Mrs. Cosby wrote an article for *USA Today*, published the day after a jury convicted her son's murderer. Understanding her grief and anguish, Mrs. Cosby should be given latitude for much of what she expressed. (She said, for example, that America taught her son's killer to hate.)

But she offered this example of "omnipresent and eternalized" racism: "The Voting Rights Act signed by President Lyndon B. Johnson in 1965 will expire in 2007. Congress once again will decide whether African-Americans will be allowed to vote."[12]

Again, with all due sympathy to the Cosbys for their suffering, the problem with Camille Cosby's statement is that a), it's flat-out wrong and b), many blacks believe it. When *USA Today* published the article, given the prestige of her last name, people quickly bought into it.

In fact, the Constitution already guarantees blacks the right to vote under the Thirteenth Amendment, which abolished slavery, and the Fourteenth Amendment, which made newly freed slaves citizens and guaranteed equal protection. The Voting Rights Act of 1965 merely required nine Southern states (and parts of some other states) to have federal monitoring and oversight of elections. The Act requires federal approval of any election law changes in those states, and a later amendment requires that election officials provide voters with material in their own language.

Georgia, for example, wanted to require voters to present photo identification before voting. Because of the Act, the change required federal approval. The feds granted it, but not without accusations against Republicans for allegedly trying to suppress the minority vote. Contrary to what Mrs. Cosby asserted, neither Georgia nor any other state could prevent blacks from voting, even if the Voting Rights Act expired.

What about today's "New South"? With a diverse population, increased minorities, and a more cosmopolitan nature, this is not your grandfather's or your great-grandfather's South. Today the South elects more blacks per capita than any other part of the country. Democrats run many precincts where blacks live, and the kind of blatant, racist tactics used to stop blacks from voting—like poll taxes and literacy tests—are, thankfully, relics of the past. The idea that any politician would attempt to suppress black votes, much less get away with it, borders on lunacy.

The Republican Party stands for states' rights. The Democrats and "black leaders" claim that "states' rights" serves as code language for racism. Still, the "states' rights" Republican Congress, along with President Bush, extended the Voting Rights Act, and federal monitoring remains. But had no action been taken, blacks still had the right to vote, guaranteed by the Constitution.

But the "Republican equals evil" theme never stops playing to this crowd.

Singer/activist Harry Belafonte mans the front lines in this black hatred of Republicans. In October 2002, Belafonte unloaded on then Secretary of State Colin Powell: "There's an old saying, in the days of slavery, there were those slaves who lived on the plantation and were those slaves that lived in the house. You got the privilege of living in the house if you served the master exactly the way the master intended to have you serve him.

"Colin Powell's committed to come into the house of the master. When Colin Powell dares to suggest something other than what the master wants to hear, he will be turned back out to pasture."[13]

When asked about the prominent positions given to blacks, and what this says about the Bush administration, Belafonte told Cybercast News Service, "Hitler had a lot of Jews high up in the hierarchy of the Third Reich." This, of course, is simply not true. But why let the facts get in the way of a good rant?

When asked to explain his comments, Mr. Belafonte asserted, "This was not a personal attack on Colin Powell. However . . . speaking on behalf of so many African-American citizens, I have found Colin Powell to be a tragic failure."[14] Belafonte reserves no love, either, for former national security advisor and current Secretary of State Condoleezza Rice. He attacked Ms. Rice for "abdication of moral responsibility," and likened her to a "Jew" who was "doing things that were anti-Semitic and against the best interests of her people."[15] When asked about the prominent positions given to blacks, and what this says about the Bush administration, Belafonte told Cybercast News Service, "Hitler had a lot of Jews high up in the hierarchy of the Third Reich."[16] This, of course, is simply not true. But why let the facts get in the way of a good rant?

Belafonte even told a Cuban newspaper that the Bush administration used the September 11 terror attacks "to extend its imperialist, economic and political domination all over the planet."[17]

And before a receptive audience at a Martin Luther King Jr. celebration in a Chicago church, Belafonte continued attacking Bush and black members of his administration, accusing the president of thwarting black progress.

Belafonte also said Powell and Rice are hurting the cause of black America: "In fact and practice . . . you are serving those who continue to design our oppression. That is villainy, and I insist you look at it."[18]

Belafonte, in an interview on Finnish television, called members of the Bush Administration *evil*. When asked if he considered leaders of the United States misguided, Belafonte said, "Absolutely. I not only think that they are misguided, but I think they know exactly what they are doing and I think that they are men who are possessed of evil."[16]

Black comic illustrator Aaron McGruder plays the "blacks who are Republicans must be traitors" theme. McGruder, the *Boondocks* comic and TV show creator, called then national security advisor Condoleezza Rice "a murderer." That's right, a murderer. On television's *America's Black Forum*, McGruder said, "I don't like Condoleezza Rice because of her politics. I don't like Condoleezza Rice because she's part of this oil cabal that's now in the White

House. I don't like her because she's a murderer. You know, I'm not bound by the rules of a politician or journalist. So, you know, when I say, 'She's a murderer,' it's because she's a murderer, and that's all that's necessary for me to make those statements."[20] He feels the same way about Colin Powell. Speaking at Emory University, McGruder said of the then Secretary of State, "Let's just say, he's directly killed, not by hand, but he's been the guy who says, 'Those people over there, that whole ethnic group, they gotta go—kill them.' And they just disappear."[21]

Actor Danny Glover said, "We must stand vigilant against Bush in these times and work with the abolitionists. . . . One of the main purveyors of violence in this world has been this country, whether it's been against Nicaragua, Vietnam, or wherever."[22]

Okay, so Glover doesn't like the president. But it takes a tremendous amount of anger to argue that the United States is "one of the main purveyors of violence in this world," while the country mourns the murders of more than three thousand innocent civilians at the hands of terrorists on 9/11.

Glover, in a 2003 interview published by a Brazilian magazine, said, "Yes, [President Bush] is racist. We all knew that, but the world is only finding it out now. As Texas's governor, Bush led a penitentiary system that executed more people than all the other U.S. states together. And most of the people who died from [the] death penalty were Afro-Americans or Hispanics." Glover also complained that Bush has promoted a "conservative program, designed to eliminate everything Americans had accomplished so far in matters of race and equality."[23]

Never mind that President Bush's social spending—which disproportionately goes to blacks—increased at a rate faster than any president since Lyndon Johnson. Bush proposed more aid to Africa—$15 billion over five years for AIDS relief, and $10 billion over three years for economic relief—than any previous president.

Black and nonblack entertainers in Hollywood routinely accuse the Bush administration of racism. Actor Ed Asner, on CNN, said racism motivated Bush's Iraq policy: "I also think that there is a strong streak of racism . . . whenever we engage in foreign adventures. Our whole history in regime change has been of people of different color."[24] Our whole history in regime change? Does this include helping Kuwait or Bosnia? Or, for that matter, what about the war against Hitler?

But for the likes of Belafonte, Glover, et al, they give President Bush no appreciation for appointing the first black national security advisor, and the first and second black secretaries of state. No, a Republican president is an evil racist. Period.

The *New York Post* wrote of actress Whoopi Goldberg's appearance at a 2004 fund-raiser for presidential candidate John F. Kerry: "Waving a bottle of wine, she fired off a stream of vulgar sexual wordplays on Bush's name in a riff about female genitalia."[25] You get the picture. Charming.

Rapper Kanye West, during a live concert fund-raiser for victims of Hurricane Katrina, hosted by NBC, said, "George Bush doesn't care about black people."[26]

Singer Mary J. Blige, despite her success, also repeats the America-is-racist mantra. Blige, in a 2005 interview, complained that her dark skin held her back: "The blacker you are, the worse it is for you. If you're mixed, you've got a shot. If you cater to what white America wants you to do and how they want you to look, you can survive. But if you want to be yourself, and try to do things that fit you, and your skin, nobody cares about that. At the end of the day, white America dominates and rules. And it's racist."[27]

A brief review of Blige's career as of this writing:

- According to *Billboard*, nine of Blige's singles hit number one since 1992.[28]

- She's won three BET awards.[29]

- She's won four American Music Awards (including Favorite Female Soul/R&B Artist).[30]

- She's won ten Billboard Music Awards.[31]

- She's won three Grammys and has been nominated for eight Grammys.[32]

One can only imagine how successful she would have been if only she were lighter skinned!

6.

STUPID BLACKS AND KATRINA

These are American citizens, plus they are the sons and daughters of slaves. Calling them refugees coming from a foreign country does not apply to their status. This shows disdain for them. I'm almost calling this a hate crime.[1]

—REPRESENTATIVE DIANE WATSON (D-CA), DESCRIBING THOSE
SUFFERING FROM HURRICANE KATRINA

For many people, the effects of Hurricane Katrina represented American racism in all its splendor.

But Hurricane Katrina actually represented government sloth and ineptitude at all levels—state, local, and federal. Officials failed to appreciate the severity and gravity of the storm and its aftermath, and they failed to properly evacuate the citizens from New Orleans. The Federal Emergency Management Agency (FEMA) took the brunt of the post-Katrina hostility and blame. But FEMA never pretended to serve as a first responder. In truth, state and local officials deserve the lion's share of the blame.

But somehow this added up to—racism in the Bush administration.

The Congressional Black Caucus's Representative Diane Watson described those suffering as "sons and daughters of slaves."[2]

NAACP attorney Damon Hewitt said, "If the majority of the folks left behind were white individuals, and most of the folks who were able to escape on their own were African-Americans, then I wouldn't be sitting here right now. This is a racial story."[3] Remember rapper Kanye West said the government's poor response to Katrina meant, "George Bush doesn't care about black people."[4]

CNN's grumpy anti-Bush commentator, Jack Cafferty, connected the sluggish response to Katrina to racism. Cafferty spoke to CNN's Wolf Blitzer three days after the hurricane struck New Orleans: "Despite the many angles of this tragedy—and Lord knows there've been a lot of them in New Orleans—there is a great big elephant in the living room that the media seems content to ignore. That would be, until now. . . . [W]e in the media are ignoring the fact that almost all of the victims in New Orleans are black and poor."[5]

Wolf responded, "You simply get chills every time you see these poor individuals, as Jack Cafferty just pointed out, so tragically, so many of these people, almost all of them that we see, are so poor and they are so black, and this is going to raise lots of questions for people who are watching this story unfold."[6] So poor and *so black*. What does that mean? The Katrina victims were, like, really, really dark skinned?

Democratic National Committee Chairman Howard Dean, never missing an opportunity to whip out the Democrats-care-about-you-more-than-Republicans-do race card, said, "We must . . . come to terms with the ugly truth that skin color, age, and economics played a deadly role in who survived and who did not."[7]

Representative Barney Frank (D-MA), five months after Hurricane Katrina struck New Orleans, spoke before a cheering crowd of four hundred Katrina survivors. He blamed the lack of progress in rebuilding New Orleans' poorer areas on the Bush administration's "policy of ethnic cleansing by inaction."[8] Ethnic cleansing by inaction? This inspires comparisons to the horrors of Nazi Germany, or the genocide in Rwanda. The charge is simply outrageous, especially when made by an influential, sitting congressman. But how many newspapers wrote about this slur? One—the *Washington Post.*

Ten months later, Frank, now the new chairman of the House Committee on Financial Services, said the Bush administration's "ethnic cleansing by inaction" was a "calculated . . . policy." "What they recognize," said Frank, "is they're in this happy position for them, where if the federal government does nothing, Louisiana will become whiter and richer. . . . So by simply not doing anything to alleviate this . . . crisis that was so greatly exaggerated by Katrina, they let the hurricane do the ethnic cleansing, and their hands are clean."9

When a right-wing religious "zealot" says something "wacky," newspapers manage to find space to print it. But a Democrat congressman, well . . .

How many newspapers carried Frank's latest charge of "ethnic cleansing"? Again, only one: the *Washington Times.* But a couple of days earlier, when religious broadcaster Pat Robertson made a prediction that a terrorist attack on the United States would occur near the end of 2007, at least thirty newspapers—including the *Chicago Tribune*—ran that story. When a right-wing religious "zealot" says something "wacky," newspapers manage to find space to print it. But a Democrat congressman, well . . .

Representative Frank also said, "There are people who are happy as a result of Louisiana becoming a more right-wing Republican state. If you lose a hundred thousand black voters, you take a state that was marginally Republican, and you've made it solidly Republican." In other words, according to Frank, some of those dastardly Republicans are actually *pleased* by the aftermath of Katrina's destruction. According to the Cybercast News Service, "A spokesman for the NAACP could not be reached for comment."[10] Perhaps even the NAACP was embarrassed by Frank.

Successful black director Spike Lee appeared on the HBO show *Real Time with Bill Maher*. Lee filmed a documentary about the aftermath of Hurricane Katrina, *When the Levees Broke*. Maher, a rabid Bush critic, tried to get Lee to call the government's Katrina failures evidence of today's racism. But this time Lee, a frequent race-card player himself, refused to go along.

Maher told Lee his documentary was "great," that Lee was "a powerful man." Then Maher said he'd seen Hezbollah on the television news, handing out cash on streets after the Israeli strikes in Southern Lebanon, and how Hezbollah "had the sidewalks cleared the next day," and "people were rebuilding their homes." Maher asked, "Who takes care of their people better? FEMA or Hezbollah?" But Lee didn't take the bait, and replied, "I think that's a question for the residents of New Orleans."[11]

Undeterred, Maher talked about black anger, and Kanye West, and that Bush doesn't care about black people, and there's something "deep-rooted" behind it. "I mean," said Maher, "I make a joke out of this all the time that Republicans are bad at sex and that accounts for a lot of our policies. But I think it's actually true and New Orleans, to me, represents everything that right-wingers hate. It's black and it's sexy and it's French and liberated."[12]

Except Maher didn't get the angry-black-man condemnation of Bush and his administration that he was trying to provoke. "But here's the thing, though," said Lee. "It's not just a black/white thing. I think class has a lot to do with it, too. Because, it's funny, I was in Venice when all this was happening. But when I got to New Orleans, I was amazed to see Saint Bernard's Parish got demolished just as much as the Lower Ninth Ward, but they never showed Saint Bernard's Parish on television. You saw black people at the Superdome, black people at the Convention Center, black people lootin'. And that was it. So I got a lot of education, numerous trips I made down there shooting the documentary.[13]

A *Time*/CNN poll showed that white teens consider the country even more racist than do black teens![14] So, even if a black refuses to play the roll of angry victicrat, liberal whites—like Bill Maher—don't want to allow them the option.

Katrina was not about race. While people believe that New Orleans, a predominately black city, endured most of Katrina's fury, Mississippi suffered the brunt of the hurricane. Katrina's most deadly point hit Biloxi in Harrison County, Mississippi, some eighty-five miles east of New Orleans.

But Lee got it right. Katrina was not about race. While people believe that New Orleans, a predominately black city, endured most of Katrina's fury, Mississippi suffered the brunt of the hurricane. Katrina's most deadly point hit Biloxi in Harrison County, Mississippi, some eighty-five miles east of New Orleans.

The devastation included neighboring parishes and Mississippi counties, which were overwhelmingly white. Those hardest hit—besides Orleans Parish—were Saint Bernard Parish (88 percent white, 8 percent black), Jefferson Parish (70 percent white, 23 percent black), Plaquemines Parish (70 percent white, 23 percent black), Saint Tammany Parish (87 percent white, 10 percent black), Hancock County (90 percent white, 7 percent black), Harrison County (73 percent white, 21 percent black), and Jackson County (75 percent white, 21 percent black).[15] So,

Orleans Parish stood as the only hard-hit parish or county with a majority black population.

While the hardest-hit Mississippi counties are more rural than Orleans Parish, all the hardest-hit Louisiana parishes are metropolitan areas. And, pre-Katrina, the population of Jefferson Parish alone almost equaled Orleans Parish, with each having just under half a million residents. Inarguably, most of Katrina's victims were white, not black.

As for Katrina being the smoking gun of Republican racism, the facts fail to square with the rhetoric.

Of the 1,100 bodies recovered in Louisiana after Katrina, over eight hundred were found in New Orleans.[16] But, according to the Louisiana Homeland Security Department, a white person living in New Orleans stood a greater chance of dying than a black person. At the time of Katrina, the Orleans Parish population stood at 484,674 people, 28 percent of whom were white and 67 percent black.[17] Of those who died in New Orleans as a result of Katrina, whites accounted for more than 45 percent, and blacks for almost 51 percent—far above and far below, respectively, their rates in the population. So, statistically speaking, even in New Orleans a white person stood a greater chance of dying in the wake of Katrina than did a black person!

Ray Nagin, New Orleans mayor, is black. His predecessor was black. The last time New Orleans elected a white mayor, Richard Nixon was president. Black mayors have governed New Orleans since 1978.[18] Louisiana's statewide politicians, including governors and senators, generally come from the Democratic Party.

The charge of Bush's "racist" response to Katrina angers Alphonso Jackson, the black secretary of Housing and Urban Development. His agency responded by helping many evacuees, but Jackson points out that the problems in New Orleans are unusual because of the damage by the flood waters. His agency needs to examine whether it's safe to move homes knocked off their foundations, or if it's safe to rebuild. Even so, says Jackson, "We might not want to rebuild the way we did before."[19]

Conditions in the Lower Eighth and Ninth Wards were "not livable" pre-Katrina, says Jackson. "It disturbs me tremendously when people want to say racism played a part in this," Jackson said. "As I reminded the Reverend Jesse Jackson and [NAACP President] Bruce Gordon, for thirty-one years we've had a black mayor in New Orleans; for twenty-five years we've had a predominately black city council in New Orleans, and the quality of life did not change for black people living in the Lower Eighth and Lower Ninth. . . . [T]he quality of life had only gotten worse until the flood came in. . . . My contention is it wasn't race, it was inefficiency and noncompassion."[20]

But the relentless attacks on Bush and his administration had their intended effect. Post-Katrina, Bush's poll numbers, already low at 14 percent among blacks, fell to 2 percent.[21] But perspective, anyone?

Released videotapes also show Democratic Louisiana Governor Kathleen Blanco giving the president false information concerning the condition of the levees in New Orleans. Shortly after noon on August 29, Blanco said, "We keep getting reports in some places that maybe water is coming over the levees. We heard a report unconfirmed, I think, we have not breached the levee. I think we have not breached the levee at this time."[22]

In fact, the National Weather Service had received a report of a levee breach at 9:12 AM and had issued a flash-flood warning. The governor's contradiction of the breach three hours later added to the confusion and failures of response.

And what of the complicity of New Orleans Mayor Nagin? What about the photographs showing more than two hundred New Orleans school buses submerged underwater—buses that officials expected to be used to evacuate imperiled citizens?

Mayor Nagin did point fingers at Governor Blanco and criticized her long delay in asking the feds for help. Nagin said, "I don't want to hear any more promises. I want to see stuff done. And that's why I'm so happy that the president came down here, because I think they were feeding him a line of bull also. And they were telling him things weren't as bad as it was. He came down and saw it, and he put a general on the field. His name is General Honore. And when he hit the field, we started to see action. And what the state was doing, I don't frigging know. But I tell you, I am pissed. It wasn't adequate.

"And then, the president and the governor sat down. We were in Air Force One. . . . I said, 'Mr. President, Madam Governor, you two need to get together on the same page, because of the lack of coordination, people are dying in my city.' . . . They both shook their heads and said yes. I said, 'Great.' I said, 'Everybody in this room . . . we're leaving. These two people need to sit in a room together and make a doggone decision right now.' . . . The President . . . said, 'No, you guys stay here. We're going to another section of the plane, and we're going to make a decision.' He called me in that office after that. And he said, 'Mr. Mayor, I offered two options to the governor.' I said . . . I was ready to move today. The governor said she needed twenty-four hours to make a decision. . . . It would have been great if we could of left Air Force One, walked outside, and told the world that we had this all worked out. It didn't happen, and more people died."[23]

This should have served as a lesson in Government 101—its inefficiencies, bureaucracies, turf-fighting, injection of politics, and scapegoating, while operating in an environment that makes it almost impossible to fire people. Never mind that before 1979, FEMA didn't exist. How did America survive?

In 1871, the "Great Fire" almost completely destroyed Chicago. Citizens, with donations from all over the world, rebuilt Chicago with virtually no government money or assistance. The police, of course, worked to maintain order and try to prevent looting. But the mayor of Chicago put a nonprofit agency, the Chicago Relief and Aid Society, in charge of accepting and distributing the charitable contributions that poured in from all around the country.

The head of the Chicago Relief and Aid Society decreed that every unemployed man, woman, and child capable of physical labor must either work on the rebuilding effort or leave the city. Chicago, in 1871, had a population of 324,000. The fire left 100,000 of them homeless.[24] Today, Chicago ranks as America's third largest city. Somehow, some way, people, approximately 150 years ago, rebuilt that city without a FEMA or a Homeland Security Department.

But for the victims of Katrina the episode serves as evidence of government indifference, if not Republican Party racism.

Bush-bashers point to the Bush administration's pre-Katrina lack of federal funding for Louisiana. "[T]he fact is," wrote *Investor's Business Daily*, "that over the [first] five years of the Bush administration, Louisiana has received more money—$1.9 billion—for Army Corps of Engineers civil works projects than any other state, and more than under any other administration over a similar period. California is a distant second with less than $1.4 billion despite a population more than seven times as large."[25]

And before Katrina hit, several state officials from the Louisiana Office of Homeland Security and Emergency Preparedness found themselves awaiting trial for waste, mismanagement of federal funds, and missing funds. At the time Katrina struck, federal auditors were still trying to find $60 million, funds sent to Louisiana from FEMA, and dating back as early as 1998, that could not be accounted for. Some of the questionable expenditures included $2,400 for sod installation, several thousand dollars for a deputy director's trip to Germany, $1,071 for curtains, $595 for an L. L. Bean parka and briefcase, and unspecified spending for camera equipment, professional dues, and a 2002 Ford Crown Victoria.[26]

But anger ran high after Katrina, and not much seemed to be aimed at state or local officials. Mayor Nagin took some heat, yet was reelected the following year. No, the bulk of the incessant blame—and certainly the nastiest sort of blame—was aimed at the white Republicans at the top.

Katrina served as a metaphor for another classic Democratic gambit—portray Republicans as out of touch, cold, and uncaring.

Former President George Herbert Walker Bush, for example,

once found himself portrayed as an ignorant elitist for reportedly failing to recognize a supermarket grocery scanner. Following the president's campaign stop at a grocer's convention in Orlando, *The New York Times* ran a front-page story with a headline crowing, "Bush Encounters the Supermarket, Amazed."[27]

Turns out, Bush-41 knew about grocery scanners. This particular scanner impressed the then-President, however, because it contained the ability to read *torn* barcode labels. Bob Graham, a systems analyst for the National Grocers Association and the person who showed Bush the scanner, said, "The whole thing is ludicrous. What he was amazed about was the ability of the scanner to take that torn label and reassemble it."[28] Nevertheless, Bush's image as a rich, out-of-touch patrician hurt.

For some reason, the wealth of Democrats does not render them "out of touch." *Roll Call*, the political magazine, annually publishes "The 50 Richest Members of Congress." Certainly, lots of Republicans made the list. But Senator John Kerry checks in at number one, with an estimated net worth of $750 million. Number two is Senator Herb Kohl (D-WI) at $243 mil. In number three comes Senator Jay Rockefeller (D-WV) with $200 million. In fourth position is Representative Jane Harmon (D-CA) at $172 mil. Speaker of the House Nancy Pelosi (D-CA) comes in at a respectable fifteenth place, with a personal fortune of an estimated $14.25 million.[29] Ms. Pelosi and her husband estimated their total combined assets, many in real estate holdings, in a broad range between $25 million and $102 million on disclosure forms in 2003.[30] Yet the Democrats are the "party of the little guy."

Recently, in a positive *New York Times* profile on the leader, she talked about how her hectic schedule allows little time for food. "I had a hamburger last night and it was my breakfast, lunch, and dinner. And I had these strange things. I realized they were french fries," she said, making a spiraling gesture with her finger to demonstrate the strange fries' shape.[31] So Congresswoman Pelosi apparently never heard of curly fries, but it's Bush-41 who gets nailed for his wrongly reported unfamiliarity with a grocery scanner?

And President George W. Bush, during the Katrina crisis, suffered from the out-of-touch, patrician, elitist label. Recall that Black Congressman Charles Rangel, a member of Congress for thirty-six years and chairman of the powerful House Ways and Means Committee, said about Bush's response to Katrina, "George W. Bush is our Bull Connor. And if that doesn't get to you, nothing will be able to get to you, and it's time for us to be able to say that we're sick and tired and we're fired up and we're not going to take it anymore!"[32]

"Bush is our Bull Connor"? In the '60s, Bull Connor, the commissioner of public safety for Birmingham, Alabama, sicced dogs and turned fire hoses on freedom fighters. This spectacle, broadcast on television, shocked America.

"Bush is our Bull Connor. And, if that doesn't get to you, nothing will be able to get to you"? Anger. It's all about the anger. Anger over slavery. Never mind slavery ended in 1865. Anger over Jim Crow laws. Never mind the Supreme Court struck them down, and Congress passed the Civil Rights Act of 1964, the Voting Rights Act of 1965, and the Open Housing Act of 1968. Anger over the wealth gap between whites and blacks. And how does anger close that gap? By conditioning people to consider government the savior, the rescuer, the cure-all?

According to a Pew Research Center survey, 79 percent of Democrats hold government responsible to "take care of people who can't take care of themselves." Fifty-four percent of Republicans agree with that statement.[33] So, a Democrat is far more likely to expect and demand government to redistribute income from person A to person B.

The Republican view toward government, goes the line, makes them care less about the downtrodden. But is that true?

Who Really Cares: The Surprising Truth about Compassionate Conservatism, a book about the charitable habits of Americans, shows that those who believe in a Nanny State give *less* money to charity. Author Arthur Brooks writes that people who believe in limited government give more. Religious people give more than do nonreligious people—and not because the religious give to their own churches. They also give more to nonreligious charities than do secularists. Relative to their income, the working poor are the most generous people in America. But the nonworking poor—those on welfare or other government assistance—are the stingiest group. Conservative households donate 30 percent more money to charity than do liberal households. And it's not just about donating money. If liberals donated blood at the same rate that conservatives do, the blood supply in the United States would increase about 45 percent.[34]

But the Nation of Islam's Minister Louis Farrakhan blamed the Katrina fallout on . . . murder. "I heard from a reliable source," said Farrakhan, "who saw a twenty-five-foot-deep crater under the levee breach. It may have been blown up to destroy the black part of town and keep the white part dry."

Reliance on government induces a mental and emotional dependency. In New Orleans, pre-Katrina, approximately 28 percent lived under the poverty line,[35] with many receiving government assistance. Because of the welfare-induced mind-set that "others will take care of me," many New Orleans residents simply ignored repeated warnings to evacuate. One could argue that the entitlement mentality actually killed people.

But the Nation of Islam's Minister Louis Farrakhan blamed the Katrina fallout on . . . murder. "I heard from a reliable source," said Farrakhan, "who saw a twenty-five-foot-deep crater under the levee breach. It may have been blown up to destroy the black part of town and keep the white part dry."[36] One can only speculate about Farrakhan's "reliable source." But days before Farrakhan made his outrageous comment, the minister met with . . . New Orleans Mayor Nagin. Did Mayor Nagin serve as a "reliable source?" As Dan Rather might have said, "inquiring minds would like to know."

Only wing nuts would buy into such a conspiracy theory, right?

Wrong.

Sadly, Minister Farrakhan and his "reliable sources" were not alone. *Washington Post* reporter Eugene Robinson said on NBC's *Meet the Press*, "I was stunned in New Orleans at how many black New Orleanians would tell me with real conviction that somehow the levee breaks had been engineered in order to save the French Quarter and the Garden District at the expense of the Lower Ninth Ward, which is almost all black. . . . These are not wild-eyed people. These are reasonable, sober people who really believe that."[37] This is reminiscent of the AIDS conspiracy theorists. Black "activist" Steve Cokely said Jewish doctors infected black babies with the virus, and in 1992 even the venerable Bill Cosby said that AIDS "was started by human beings to get after certain people they didn't like."[38]

Others later came forward, insisting that the government intentionally blew up the levees. During Congress's Katrina hearings, Leah Hodges, a black woman from New Orleans, appeared:

> **LEAH HODGES:** I'm sure that race has everything to do with it, as race always has everything to do with the treatment of people of color in America. The fish were evacuated and the people were left to die. The stray animals from the animal shelter—most of whom would have been euthanized—were evacuated two days before the storm and the people were left to die. Buses that could have gotten out people who otherwise could not get out were left to flood and people were left to die. The military which has the great capability of moving entire cities failed to

move in and move out the people the way the dogs and the fish had been moved out and people were left to die— mostly poor, mostly people of color. Race had every- thing to do with the ethnic cleansing and the massacre of predominately African-American people being blamed on Hurricane Katrina.[39]

"Ethnic cleansing." What do you say to that mentality? And how about this exchange with poor Congressman Jeff Miller, Republican from Florida.

HODGES: Jefferson Parish is where the Causeway concen- tration camp was housed, where we experienced the Gestapo-type oppression. . . . We were three minutes away from the airport. They could have taken us to the airport. Those military vehicles could have taken us to any dry, safe city in America. Instead, they dumped us at a dumping ground, sealed us in there, and they backed up all their authority with military M-16s. . . . On the last day we were in there—and let me tell you something—they hand-picked the white people to ride out first. Yes, racism was very much involved. . . . Every day, the crowd got darker and darker and darker until finally there were only—there were 95 percent people of color in that place.
MILLER: Miss Hodges, would you be offended if I re- spectfully asked you not to call the Causeway area a con- centration camp?
HODGES: I am going to call it what it is. If I put a dress on a pig, a pig is still a pig.
MILLER: Are you familiar with the history?
HODGES: Yes, sir, I am. And that is the only thing I could compare what we went through to: a concentration camp. . . . And they stood over us with guns and en- forced their authority, and yes, they tortured us. . . . And yes, I know what a concentration camp is. I'm a college- educated woman.

MILLER: Not a single person was marched into a gas chamber and killed.
HODGES: They died from abject neglect. We left body bags behind. Pregnant women lost their babies.
UNIDENTIFIED WOMAN: That's one of the reasons why some of these people wouldn't come out of those houses, because you was told to come on the street, and when people came out—
HODGES: They were shot—[40]

What can you say? How do you have a conversation with someone with that kind of mentality?

The media watchdog group, Media Research Center, wrote that the mainscream media refused to dismiss these claims.

The Tuesday broadcast network evening newscasts jumped on an inconsequential House hearing, which the AP reported was attended by just seven Members of Congress, where five residents of New Orleans hurled charges that racism limited help after Hurricane Katrina. ABC actually led with the hearing as anchor Elizabeth Vargas teased: "On World News Tonight, *the angry voices from inside the storm. The victims of Katrina tell Congress they're still not getting help because they are poor and black." Vargas trumpeted the charges: "They were brought in front of Congress today so that the voiceless could be heard. Five people whose lives were torn apart by Hurricane Katrina. Five black people who say that when the hurricane came, for so many like them, race did matter." . . .*

CBS anchor Bob Schieffer championed Dyan French Cole, affectionately known to CBS News as "Mama D," as he described her as a "key witness" and reminded viewers that CBS's "John Roberts first reported on her from New Orleans right after the hurricane. And now Congress isn't likely to forget her, either. She gave them an earful today." CBS viewers won't have her wackiest and most insidious charge to forget since in nearly an entire story devoted to her rants, Roberts avoided discrediting her by never mentioning her claim about how the levees were "bombed." Instead, he personally interviewed her and took her allegations seriously: "She came . . . to testify on whether race played a role in the Hurricane Katrina response."

NBC anchor Brian Williams touted how "a special House committee heard emotional testimony from Katrina survivors who insisted racism was a big factor in the government's slow response to the disaster." Kerry Sanders, who showcased Dyan French Cole, also skipped over her levee "bombing" charge, began: "In New Orleans, according to a Gallup poll, six in ten blacks said if most of Katrina's victims were white, the rescues would have come faster."[41]

One Katrina survivor likened the conditions of the New Orleans Convention Center to the experience of slaves: "Imagine being thrown into a dark place, people laying on top of one another, I felt like a slave. Ya see, that's the story they don't want people to know."[42]

Past discrimination, for such people, means present and future discrimination—with Katrina clearly serving as a recent example. End of discussion. Never mind the growing black economy, an all-time high percentage of black homeownership, and a "black GDP"[43] that would make black America the sixteenth wealthiest country in the world.[44] The "black leaders" who fan the flames with their incendiary charges of racism are aided and abetted by a sympathetic, gutless media. This combination does real damage, producing a dangerous, toxic result in the mind-set of many blacks.

More than one year after Hurricane Katrina, Claire McCaskill, then a white Democratic candidate for Missouri's Senate seat, also whipped out the Katrina-is-a-metaphor-for-racism card. But *Meet The Press*'s Tim Russert actually confronted her:

RUSSERT: Let me turn to George W. Bush, because he's become an issue in the campaign. Ms. McCaskill, you were quoted in the pubdef.net giving a speech, which was blogged, saying, "She reminded people that 'George Bush let people die on rooftops in New Orleans because they were poor and because they were black.'" One, why would you say that, and do you believe it?

MCCASKILL: Well, first, I was acknowledging how thousands and millions of Americans felt. The visual that we all saw in Hurricane Katrina was, frankly, something none of us will ever forget. Incompetence turned tragic because the people there were unable to help themselves. This administration—

RUSSERT: But do you think the president let people die because they were poor and black?

MCCASKILL: I do not, I do not believe the president is a racist. I was acknowledging the feelings of many, many Americans that this administration has left the most vulnerable, helpless—this administration has been about Wall Street and not about average Americans.

RUSSERT: But do you apologize for this statement?

MCCASKILL: I, I think if it is misinterpreted that I was calling the president a racist—

RUSSERT: Misinterpreted? "George Bush let people die on rooftops because they were poor and because they were black."

MCCASKILL: That was—I was acknowledging what Americans believed at the time.

RUSSERT: So you stand by it?

MCCASKILL: Absolutely, that's what Americans believed. Now, I don't believe he's a racist, and if that—if people think—and maybe I shouldn't have said it that way, Tim. Maybe I should have said it another way. I probably should have said it another way. But the feelings are real. And by the way, if we had that tragedy, how ready are we for a disaster in this country? After the billions of dollars spent— once again, no accountability—they still are not looking in Congress at how all the money was misspent in Katrina. With all the billions spent on homeland security, our citizens died because we couldn't get them food or water. This is not an administration that is ready to protect us.[45]

Just another example of the willingness of the Democrats to play the race card and bash Republicans, but when they are finally called out on it, they back up. Too late, of course—the damage is already done.

Consider Kia, a recent caller to my radio program when we were discussing Farrakhan's outrageous the-levee-was-blown-up-to-get-blacks statement.

CALLER KIA: I don't know who the reliable source might be, but it's entirely possible that Farrakhan's theory could be true. . . . America is a very extremely racist place and you'd be ignorant not to think it isn't. . . .

LARRY: If America is extremely racist, is there a better place—just for race relations—to live, other than America . . . ?

KIA: It's irrelevant, it's irrelevant, it's irrelevant. . . . We're talkin' about America here and now, and Farrakhan's theory on what might have happened to the levee.

LARRY: You think America is less racist than it used to be?

KIA: No.

LARRY: As racist than when there was slavery?

KIA: I don't know.

LARRY: You don't know? You don't think that being free is better than being a slave?

KIA: Of course, being free is better, but . . . it has nothing to do with his theory on what happened to the levee.

LARRY: Kia, we're changing the subject slightly, and I recognize that we're doing that. . . . If you can handle it, I'd like to ask you a few questions.

KIA: Okay.

LARRY: Thank you. You don't know if conditions for blacks today are better than conditions for blacks during slavery?

KIA: I'm free—so yes, it's better for me, personally. As for a lot of black people that I know, for a lot of them it isn't.

LARRY: I'm sorry—for a lot of people it isn't? Do you know any slaves now?

KIA: For some black people, it isn't. . . .

LARRY: For some black people, it's as bad as slavery? Do you know any black people who would rather live in slavery times than now?

KIA: No, of course not. . . .

LARRY: Earlier you said for some black people it wasn't any better. So now we've qualified that, and it is better for all black people, and not just some, right?

KIA: Okay, we can say that.

LARRY: Kia, you said America is extremely racist, but you also said you were free, so I'm a little confused.

KIA: Well, me and my husband are truck drivers, and we hear on the CB every day people talkin' about "nigger this, nigger that," and "colored" this and that.

LARRY: And therefore you believe that reflects the mainstream view of America?

KIA: It should.

LARRY: Really?

KIA: It has to reflect them, it has to.

LARRY: Kia, I assume you are black?

KIA: Yes.

LARRY: Have you ever gone to a black beauty parlor or a barbershop and heard black people talk about white people?

KIA: Yes.

LARRY: And have you heard some negative and very derogatory things?

KIA: Yes.

LARRY: If a white person were to hear that, should a white person therefore assume that all blacks feel that way?

KIA: It doesn't matter. I don't care. I'm not white.

LARRY: Kia, my point is you've heard some racist talk on the CB, presumably by some white truckers. Do you believe that therefore that reflects how most white people feel? You and I have both agreed that we hear some pretty nasty things at black barbershops and beauty parlors, and if a white person were to hear that, would that white person be justified in assuming that most black people feel that way?

KIA: . . . I guess. [laughs] It's an opinion, I can't speak for them. . . .

LARRY: Do you think most black people are racists?

KIA: Most black people? No. . . .

LARRY: Okay, so most black people are not racist. So if a white person were to hear some people at a black barbershop or a beauty parlor making negative comments about whites, and then assume most black people feel that way, that person would be wrong, correct?

KIA: Correct.

LARRY: Then when you hear some white people using racial epithets on the CB, isn't it entirely possible that they do not reflect how the majority of white people feel, any more than those people in the barbershop reflect how the majority of black people feel?

KIA: Right, that's a true and correct fact. It's true.

LARRY: Well, then what are we arguing about, Kia? Why don't you then at least go with me and say, it is possible that when my husband and I hear these negative comments, that these are some nutballs on the CB talking to each other and we ought *not* conclude, therefore, that it reflects how most white people feel. Why is that such a leap?

KIA: It's not. What you're saying is true and correct, but it's still swaying from the—
LARRY: Okay. Then will you back up on your statement that America is extremely racist?
KIA: No, I can't!
LARRY: All right, Kia. Thank you very much. I don't know what more I can do.[46]

The media and "black leaders" refuse to ask basic questions. What about the responsibility of state and local officials, many of whom are Democrats? What about the damage done by the modern welfare state, helping to create poverty by financially rewarding irresponsible behavior? What about the damage to the black psyche by so-called civil rights leaders who demand not just equal rights, but equal results, helping to create a victicrat-entitlement mentality? Maybe someday one of the news anchors will ask one of these so-called civil rights leaders the following question: Doesn't the demand for race-based preferences, set-asides, private sector antidiscrimination laws, social welfare programs, and social "safety net" programs all conspire to say one thing—"You are not responsible"?

News anchors and black leaders also ignore a far bigger factor than race or class—culture.

Bill Cosby dared to challenge the woe-is-us point of view by demanding personal responsibility on the part of "aggrieved" blacks. Cosby encouraged black youth to learn to speak standard English.

Earlier, at the 2003 Emmy awards, comedian Wanda Sykes wandered up to Cosby, seated in the audience, and tried to banter with him. In an attempt at humor, he ended up lecturing her about the difference between his '80s hit, *The Cosby Show*, and some of the drivel on TV now. "We spoke English," Cosby said.[47]

Cosby now argues that America has, by and large, done its part to live up to its stated goal of equal protection and equal opportunity. Cosby says now we must do *our* part.

Cosby's attitude has a long legacy. In the early 1900s, Nannie Helen Burroughs published a booklet called *The Twelve Things the Negro Must Do for Himself*.

Burroughs was born in 1879. Her mother became widowed and took young Nannie to Washington, D.C., for greater educational opportunities. An excellent student, she graduated with honors, but was denied a teaching job because she was black. She worked as an assistant editor for a Baptist newspaper, and then as a secretary for the Foreign Mission Board of the National Baptist Convention, using her intellect and oratory skill to push for the rights of women within the Baptist church.[48]

Driven to improve the lives of black women, who at the time were mostly limited to low-paying jobs in domestic service or teaching, she wanted to offer professional training to black women so they might be able to command higher salaries. In 1909, she started the National Training School for Women and Girls, offering classes in domestic science, missionary work, social work, home nursing, clerical work, printing, dressmaking, beauty culture, shoe repair, and agriculture. There were also classes in grammar, English literature, Latin, drama, public speaking, music, and physical education. She stressed the three Bs— Bible, Bath, and Broom.[49]

In her booklet, she elaborated on these "twelve Things":

1. *The Negro Must Learn to Put First Things First. The First Things Are: Education; Development of Character Traits; A Trade and Home Ownership: The Negro puts too much of his earning in clothes, in food, in show and in having what he calls "a good time." The Dr. Kelly Miller said, "The Negro buys what he WANTS and begs for what he Needs." Too true!*

2. *The Negro Must Stop Expecting God and White Folk to Do for Him What He Can Do for Himself: It is the "Divine Plan" that the strong shall help the weak, but even God does not do for man what man can do for himself. . . .*

3. *The Negro Must Keep Himself, His Children and His Home Clean and Make The Surroundings in Which He Lives Comfortable and Attractive: He must learn to "run his community up"—not down. We can segregate by law, we integrate only by living. Civilization is not a matter of race, it is a matter of standards. . . .*

4. *The Negro Must Learn to Dress More Appropriately for Work and for Leisure: Knowing what to wear—how to wear it—when to wear it and where to wear it, are earmarks of common sense, culture and also an index to character.*

5. *The Negro Must Make His Religion an Everyday Practice and Not Just a Sunday-Go-to-Meeting Emotional Affair.*

6. *The Negro Must Highly Resolve to Wipe Out Mass Ignorance: The leaders of the race must teach and inspire the masses to become eager and determined to improve mentally, morally and spiritually, and to meet the basic requirements of good citizenship. . . . Ignorance—satisfied ignorance—is a millstone about the neck of the race. It is democracy's greatest burden. Social integration is a relationship attained as a result of the cultivation of kindred social ideals, interests and standards. It is a blending process that requires time, understanding and kindred purposes to achieve. Likes alone and not laws can do it.*

7. *The Negro Must Stop Charging His Failures Up to His "Color" and to White People's Attitude: The truth of the matter is that good service and conduct will make senseless race prejudice fade like mist before the rising sun. . . . Purpose, initiative, ingenuity and industry are the keys that all men use to get what they want. The Negro will have to do the same. He must make himself a workman who is too skilled not to be wanted, and too DEPENDABLE not to be on the job, according to promise or plan. . . .*

8. *The Negro Must Overcome His Bad Job Habits: He must make a brand new reputation for himself in the world of labor. His bad job habits are absenteeism. . . . He also has a bad reputation for conduct on the job—such as petty quarrelling with other help, incessant loud talking about nothing, loafing, carelessness, lack of job pride, insolence, gum chewing and—too often—liquor drinking. Just plain bad job habits!*

9. *He Must Improve His Conduct in Public Places: Taken as a whole, he is entirely too loud and too ill-mannered. There is much talk about wiping out racial segregation and also much talk about achieving integration. Segregation is a physical arrangement by which people are separated in various services. It is definitely up to the Negro to wipe out the apparent justification or excuse for segregation. . . .*

10. *The Negro Must Learn How to Operate Business for People—Not for Negro People, Only.*

11. *The Average So-Called Educated Negro Will Have to Come Down out of The Air. He Is Too Inflated over Nothing. He Needs an Experience Similar to the One That Ezekiel Had—(Ezekiel 3:14–19). And He Must Do What Ezekiel Did: Otherwise, through indifference, as to the plight of the masses, the Negro, who thinks that he has escaped, will lose his own soul. . . . A race rises on its own wings, or is held down by its own weight. True leaders are never "things apart from the people." They are the masses. They simply got to the front ahead of them. Their only business at the front is to inspire the masses by hard work and noble example and challenge them to "Come on!" . . . There must arise within the Negro race a leadership that is not out hunting bargains for itself. . . .*

12. *The Negro Must Stop Forgetting His Friends. "Remember": The*

American Negro has had and still has friends—in the North and in the South. These friends not only pray, speak, write, influence others, but make unbelievable, unpublished sacrifices and contributions for the advancement of the race—for their brothers in bonds. The noblest thing that the Negro can do is to so live and labor that these benefactors will not have given in vain. The Negro must make his heart warm with gratitude, his lips sweet with thanks and his heart and mind resolute with purpose to justify the sacrifices and stand on his feet and go forward. . . . Get to work! That's the answer to everything that hurts us. We talk too much about nothing instead of redeeming the time by working.

R-E-M-E-M-B-E-R

In spite of race prejudice, America is brim full of opportunities. Go after them![50]

A century has passed, yet some people *still* need to read Ms. Burroughs' booklet.

A "lower class" person is not condemned to that social rank in perpetuity. Look at the mid-1800s plight of New York City's Irish underclass. According to "One hundred fifty years ago," wrote William J. Stern in *The Wall Street Journal*, "Manhattan's tens of thousands of Irish seemed mired in poverty and ignorance, destroying themselves through drink, idleness, violence, crime and illegitimacy. . . . An estimated 50,000 Irish prostitutes worked the city in 1850. . . . Illegitimacy soared, tens of thousands of abandoned Irish kids roamed the city's streets. Violent Irish gangs fought each other . . . but primarily they robbed houses and small businesses. More than half the people arrested in New York in the 1840s and 1850s were Irish." The Irish were feared and ridiculed as drunken, depraved criminals.[51]

So many Irish were being arrested that the police vans were dubbed "paddy wagons."[52] Alarmed by the high rate of imprisonment among the Irish, and by the large number of orphaned Irish youths—as many as sixty thousand running in packs—Bishop John Joseph Hughes, known as "Dagger John," took action.

Disgusted by government "charity," Hughes led movements to form non-government-aided Catholic schools and numerous self-help and mutual aid programs. He formed the Society for the Protection of Destitute Catholic Children (also know as the Catholic Protectory). The Protectory's head, Dr. Levi Ives, concerned that the unsupervised children were "exposed to all the horrors of hopeless poverty, to the allurements of vice and crime in every disgusting and debasing form, bringing ruin on themselves and disgrace and obloquy," believed the kids had a chance of living productive lives if they were taught sound values. The Protectory purchased a 114-acre farm . . . , took in boys and girls, and, said Ives, by giving them "proper religious instruction and the teaching of useful trades they could raise the children above their slum environment."[53]

To attack the alcohol problem among the Irish, Bishop Hughes formed a Catholic abstinence society. He labeled sex outside of marriage as sin. His diocese's nuns served as an employment agency for Irish domestics and encouraged women to run boarding houses. He established Catholic schools, which urged religion, moral behavior, and hard work. By the end of his tenure his diocese had more than a hundred schools.[54]

What happened?

Within two generations, writes Stern, "the Irish proportion of arrests for violent crime had dropped to less than 10 percent from 60 percent. Irish children were entering . . . the professions, politics, show business and commerce. In 1890, some 30 percent of the city's teachers were Irish women, and the Irish literacy rate exceeded 90 percent."[55]

Culture changes. Behavior changes. But this requires hope, a belief that effort gets rewarded. Hope dies when authority figures continue to preach helplessness and a lack of options, which conspire to induce a victicrat mentality.

Hope dies when authority figures continue to preach helplessness and a lack of options, which conspire to induce a victicrat mentality.

So while some investigate the failures and breakdowns in Hurricane Katrina, let's hope they put together a commission—privately funded, of course—to investigate another hurricane, the one wrought by the welfare state and the irresponsible use of the race card.

7.

THE CRIMINAL JUSTICE SYSTEM

Too many have sacrificed too much, worked too hard, and come too far, to turn back the clock on that progress.[1]

—SENATOR TED KENNEDY, REFERRING TO EQUAL OPPORTUNITY FOR
ALL AMERICANS

The Supreme Court . . . has repeatedly sought to turn back the clock on civil rights.[2]

—SENATOR TED KENNEDY

Before entrusting Judge John G. Roberts with a lifetime position on the Supreme Court, the Senate must be able to determine . . . whether he will adopt a cramped and contorted view of our Constitution that will turn back the clock.[3]

—SENATOR TED KENNEDY

Because of the disproportionate criminal activity in many black communities, blacks go to jail disproportionately. Ergo, racism. As black actor Charles Dutton said, playing a high school teacher in the movie, *Menace II Society*, "Being a black man in America isn't easy. The hunt is on, and you're the prey."[4] (This from an actor/"prey" who spent seven and a half years in prison for fatally stabbing a man, returning less than two years later for possession of a deadly weapon.)

"Ha, ha, ha, ha, ha, ha. . . . While all of white America weeps, every black person is celebrating. Lordy, Lordy, Lordy, we beat you guys."

On the evening of the verdict in the Michael Jackson trial, in which the prosecution accused the superstar entertainer of child molestation, I came home to receive that e-mail—one of several expressing the same sentiment. Michael Jackson beat the system. Michael Jackson beat "The Man." The race card—never leave home without it.

As with the O. J. Simpson case, polls show a split on the verdict down racial lines. By a two-to-one margin, according to Gallup, whites believe him guilty. By a similar margin, nonwhites believe him not guilty.[5]

After Jackson's acquittal, many people expected him to change his behavior. A glance at Michael Jackson's Web site, MJJsource.com, did not inspire confidence. It pronounced the verdict a milestone in world history, with an intro showing a hand in the "V for victory" position—one of Michael Jackson's trademark gestures. Under an INNOCENT banner were the words, "V is vindication," along with various dates and events. First, "01-15-29, Martin Luther King is born." Next, "11-9-89, Berlin Wall falls." Then "02-11-90, Nelson Mandela is freed." Finally, "06-13-05, Remember this day, for it is a part of history."

Jackson, of all people, played the victim card—an innocent man hounded by a racist criminal justice system.

Many blacks feel the system lies in wait to bring them down. An Associated Press January 2004 "celebrity justice" poll found that in the O. J. Simpson case, 82 percent of whites believe O. J. murdered Ronald Goldman and Nicole Brown, versus 35 percent of nonwhites. In the Kobe Bryant case—by a 76 to 18 margin—whites thought Bryant would get a fair trial. But 43 percent of blacks said he would not. Just prior to Michael Jackson's arraignment, 60 percent of whites thought he would get a fair trial, while only 38 percent of blacks thought he would. But in the case of Martha Stewart, the majority of both blacks and whites, preverdict, considered her guilty.[6] Blacks apparently feel the current justice system works for whites, but not for them.

The "my race, right or wrong" attitude hurts the black community and hurts America. Many black jurors simply refuse to convict black criminal defendants, leading to high inner-city acquittal rates, with bad guys getting off to commit more crimes against the very people who set them free.

This is not the Jim Crow South. Black Harvard sociologist Orlando Patterson said, "The sociological truths are that America, while still flawed in its race relations . . . is now the least racist white-majority society in the world; has a better record of legal protection of minorities than any other society, white or black; offers more opportunities to a greater number of black persons than any other society, including all those of Africa."[7]

The "my race, right or wrong" attitude hurts the black community and hurts America. Many black jurors simply refuse to convict black criminal defendants, leading to high inner-city acquittal rates, with bad guys getting off to commit more crimes against the very people who set them free.

During the O. J. Simpson case, many blacks felt the police planted evidence. But at the time a black man, Willie Williams, ran the Los Angeles Police Department. Because of the accusations of policemen's conduct, Williams conducted an internal review to uncover any evidence, however small, that cops conspired to frame Simpson. He found nothing. But this had no effect whatsoever on how many blacks negatively perceived the police, the investigators, and the prosecution.

After Michael Jackson's arrest for child molestation, brother Jermaine Jackson called it a "modern-day lynching."[8] His father, Joe Jackson, also blamed racism for the charges against his son. A dismissed black jury candidate appeared on *Good Morning America* and warned Jackson about the lack of black jurors, "If I was sitting in his shoes I'd be worried. I just feel that I would want someone there that I could relate to, someone who understood me."[9] Rather amusing to presume that anyone—black or white— could "relate to" and "understand" Michael Jackson. But Joe Jackson said, "I'm sorry that they got rid of the black juror because we needed that juror and it's not fair."[10]

In the waning days before the verdict, however, "spiritual advisors" Jesse Jackson and Al Sharpton downplayed the race card. Why this sudden reversal? As the trial evolved, especially after the cross-examination turned the accuser's mom into a poor witness, many pundits predicted a Jackson acquittal. So, sensing a favorable tide, they jammed the race card back into the pack. Rest assured, they would have whipped it out—and fast— had the verdict gone the other way.

The bottom line is this: Jackson dodged a bullet. Getting a conviction in a child molestation or a rape case is inherently difficult, absent physical evidence. In this case it comes down to "he said, he said." In listening to the jurors, many considered Jackson a child molester, and undoubtedly some even felt Jackson likely molested the accuser. But the prosecutors couldn't overcome the very high burden of proof required in a criminal case.

The jury did its job. Race, quite appropriately, played no role.

Stanley Tookie Williams, convicted multiple murderer and black cofounder of the notorious street gang, the Crips, died via lethal injection at 12:35 AM on December 13, 2005, at San Quentin State Prison. California Governor Arnold Schwarzenegger, only hours before Williams' scheduled execution, refused to grant clemency.[11]

Who was Stanley Tookie Williams, and why did so many people want his life spared?

The Crips became a national—indeed, international—gang, responsible for thousands of deaths since its founding in 1971. In 1981, a jury convicted Williams of murdering four people, and he was sentenced to death.[12] After his conviction—for which he maintained his innocence—Williams partnered with a writer and coauthored several antigang children's books. He renounced his membership in the Crips, urged others to do the same, and apologized for starting an organization that continues to cause death and destruction.

Williams's supporters claim that his conversion saved the lives of many gang members, ex-gang members, and would-be gang members.

But, according to columnist Joseph C. Phillips, Tookie Williams's bestselling children's book, *Gangs and Violence*, has sold a whopping 330 copies. One of his books, *Gangs and Wanting to Belong*, sold two copies.[13] Some impact.

Still, the usual suspects came out in support of Williams's clemency—Hollywood stars and antideath-penalty advocates. So did the National Association for the Advancement of Colored People.

The NAACP took out an ad in the *Los Angeles Times* and started a four-city tour, urging the governor to grant Williams clemency.[14] Bruce S. Gordon, the new president and CEO of the NAACP, called Tookie Williams the organization's "secret weapon" in combating gang violence.[15] Gordon also suggested that race played a part in Williams's conviction, and noted that the criminal justice system "makes mistakes."[16] The NAACP claims to oppose the death penalty on its Web site: "The NAACP has long opposed the death penalty because in many states there has been a disproportionate number of African-Americans sentenced to death, particularly when the crime involves a white victim."[17]

But where was the NAACP's opposition to the death penalty back in 2000? The organization ran an ad during the 2000 presidential campaign of then Governor George W. Bush. The ad, with voiceover of the daughter of James Byrd, the man dragged to death by three men in Jasper, Texas, attacked Bush for not passing enhanced hate-crime legislation. Bird's daughter, in a dramatic voice, said, "[I]t was like my father was killed all over again."[18] But two of three men convicted of killing Byrd had already received the death penalty, with the third, who testified that he attempted to stop the other two from committing the murder, getting life in prison.[19]

The NAACP commercial criticized Bush for allegedly refusing to sign legislation that would have imposed the death penalty for all three. But doesn't the NAACP oppose the death penalty? Apparently, white bigots deserve the death penalty, but a black multimurderer who founded a street gang does not. All clear now?

Williams claimed redemption, but refused to accept responsibility for murdering four innocent people. Williams shot Albert Owens, who worked at a 7-Eleven, twice in the back after Owens pleaded for his life. Williams, eleven days later, gunned down the owners of a small motel, a family of three. According to Governor Schwarzenegger's decision refusing clemency, "Williams . . . robbed a family-operated motel and shot and killed three members of the family: (1) the father, Yen-I Yang, who was shot once in the torso and once in the arm while he was laying [sic] on a sofa; (2) the mother, Tsai-Shai Lin, who was shot once in the abdomen and once in the back; and (3) the daughter, Yee-Chen Lin, who was shot once in her face. For these murders, Williams made away with approximately $100 in cash. Williams also told others about the details of these murders and referred to the victims as 'Buddha-heads.' "[20]

Consider the following hypothetical: David Duke, former Imperial Wizard of the Ku Klux Klan, murders four innocent blacks in cold blood. But wait. While on death row, Duke renounces the Klan and coauthors children's books, urging white kids to reject Klan membership. Yet Duke refuses to accept responsibility for the murder of the four innocent blacks, claiming that an anti-Klan jury convicted him for his reputation, not for the murders. Do you see Snoop Dogg or Jamie Foxx or Ed Asner and the Hollywood crowd organizing a campaign to spare Duke's life? After all, even though this "role model" denies his guilt, he "redeems" himself by urging whites to avoid membership in racist organizations.

Tookie Williams's life inspired the movie *Redemption*, starring Jamie Foxx. But Williams's execution sends a far stronger message: This is what happens. This is where you end up when you think the rules do not apply to you, when anger and rage cause you to kill innocent people.

A truly redeemed Williams would have also added, "I accept responsibility for what I did. I apologize to the family members. I was not a victim of a racist, unfair, criminal justice system, and I urge all criminals to first look into the mirror before blaming the police, the judges, the system. I made choices that put me here. The lesson of my life is, no matter your circumstances, your race, your class, you are responsible for making proper moral decisions. It is your duty to do so."

That's redemption.

Former Atlanta Mayor Bill Campbell, who once claimed, "Everybody who is a person of color in this country has benefited from affirmative action,"[21] later got into trouble when authorities prosecuted him for tax evasion. Whipping out the race card, he cried persecution-of-a-black-man. Allegedly, Campbell accepted payoffs from city contractors that he later used for gambling trips, a mink coat for his mistress, and nice suits for himself.[22]

While acquitted of federal charges for bribery and racketeering, a jury convicted him of tax fraud. He barely escaped the more serious conviction of racketeering because of jurors' confusion over a date in the prosecution's indictment. One juror said, "We got him on three things. But on the corruption, we kind of figured he was guilty, but they couldn't prove it. So we couldn't convict."[23] The judge sentenced him to thirty months in jail with a $6,300 fine and a requirement to pay the government $62,823 in back taxes.[24]

Predictably, Campbell cried selective prosecution, claiming he was the victim of a racist criminal justice system, designed to take down "black leaders." A fed-up *Atlanta Journal Constitution*, with an editorial page run by a black woman, Cynthia Tucker, said enough is enough. Tucker blasted Campbell for the tired, repeated use of the race card in the face of incredible allegations of misconduct:

> *During his tenure, Campbell was combative with critics—flying into a rage, denouncing his enemies, calling for retribution.*
>
> *But his oddest defense was to portray himself as a downtrodden black man being persecuted by powerful white forces—another Kunta Kinte. . . .*
>
> *There is nothing downtrodden about Campbell. He is polished, sophisticated and well-educated, a graduate of Vanderbilt University and the School of Law at Duke University. . . .*
>
> *Before he was elected mayor, he was a federal prosecutor, then an attorney in private practice. He was also elected to the Atlanta City Council. . . .*
>
> *In Atlanta, Campbell lived in a middle-class, predominantly white neighborhood . . . and sent his children to a trendy (and expensive) private school. . . . His lifestyle was redolent of success. . . .*
>
> *But, like so many high-profile criminal defendants before him, Campbell wants observers to believe he is the innocent victim of racist, overzealous prosecutors who won't tolerate successful black men. That defense is almost as dated as wide ties and leisure suits. . . .*
>
> *There is a good reason the oppressed-black-man defense doesn't work the magic that it once did: Times have changed. The federal investigation into Campbell's activities began before former President Bill Clinton left office. At the time, Richard Deane, who is black, was the U.S. attorney in Atlanta, and Theodore Jackson, who is also black, headed the FBI's Atlanta office. They were unlikely figures in any scheme to target black politicians. . . .*
>
> *There is a much more plausible reason for the feds' interest in Campbell than government persecution: He ran the most corrupt*

City Hall in modern Atlanta history. So far, the City Hall investigation has led to convictions or guilty pleas for a dozen people, including several top city officials. . . .

Like all Americans, black or white, Campbell is entitled to a presumption of innocence. . . . But he is not entitled to any special consideration just because he's black.[25]

Speaking of double standards, what about Judge Evelyn Clay, a black circuit judge in Chicago? In a murder trial, she objected to the composition of the jury. Why? The jury contained no blacks. "Folks, you all know I have a rule; I don't seat all white jurors," said Judge Clay while meeting with attorneys in chambers as jurors were being selected for a murder trial. "I try to preside over jury trials in a fair and impartial way—that is always my goal. I carry out all my responsibilities with that goal. . . . I'm telling you folks, I don't know what you intend to do, but I have no intention of seating an all-white jury."[26]

Imagine a Washington, D.C., judge making such a statement. After all, a jury there convicted Oliver North of accepting an illegal gratuity, aiding and abetting in the obstruction of a congressional inquiry, and destruction of documents during the Iran/Contra scandal. How many whites on his jury? Not one.

A D.C. appellate court overturned North's conviction. Among the grounds for appeal, however, North's attorneys *never* argued that he received an unfair trial due to the lack of whites on the jury. Yet a black Chicago judge assumes that a black defendant faces an injustice if convicted by an all-white jury.

Tragically, in July 2005, Los Angeles police killed a nineteen-month-old Hispanic girl, Suzie Marie Peña. Her father, under the influence of drugs and alcohol, earlier threatened to kill a teenage stepdaughter, holding the police at bay for several hours and shooting one officer. After all attempts to negotiate his surrender failed, the gunman used his toddler daughter as a human shield while firing at police. An autopsy would later find traces of cocaine in the little girl's body.

Reverend Al Sharpton came to town to declare solidarity with a grieving community. "If Suzie had been black," said Sharpton, "we'd have been there. If Suzie had been white, someone would have been there."[27] So, to quote Johnnie Cochran, apparently race plays a part of *everything* in America—even the tragic death of a poor little girl whose own father used her body in an attempt to protect himself from bullets while he fired on the police.

Apparently, race plays a part of everything on Capitol Hill— at least according to black Congresswoman Cynthia McKinney (D-GA). The way Ms. McKinney handled her "encounter" with capitol police speaks volumes about the quality of today's "black leadership."

Ms. McKinney, attempting to hurry to a meeting, rushed through a Capitol Hill security checkpoint. Rules allow congresspersons to avoid going through metal detectors, but— although the rules do not require it—many of them wear a congressional ID pin so security can quickly identify them and let them pass through. McKinney admits that she failed to wear her pin.

A capitol police officer failed to recognize McKinney, and as she rushed by the checkpoint, he shouted, "Ma'am, Ma'am!" The police office followed her and grabbed her arm, at which time McKinney turned around and punched him.[28]

At first, McKinney appeared somewhat contrite and put out the following statement:

Earlier today I had an unfortunate confrontation with a Capitol Hill Police Officer. It is traditional protocol that Capitol Hill Police secure 535 Members of Congress, including 100 Senators. It is the expectation of most Members of Congress that Capitol Hill Police officers know who they are. I was urgently trying to get to an important meeting on time to fulfill my obligations to my constituents. Unfortunately, the Police Officer did not recognize me as a Member of Congress and a confrontation ensued. I did not have on my Congressional pin but showed the Police Officer my Congressional ID.

I know that Capitol Hill Police are securing our safety, [and] that of thousand of others, and I appreciate the work that they do. I deeply regret that the incident occurred. I have demonstrated my support for them in the past and I continue to support them now.[29]

Apparently, McKinney somehow cannot get through security checkpoints.

According to the congressional newspaper, *The Hill*:

In 1993, after she complained about being stopped by security guards, Capitol Police posted a photo of her on an office wall so that officers could remember who she was.

In 1995, McKinney reportedly contacted the sergeant at-arms after a white Capitol Police officer asked her to consent to a security check.

In 1996 and 1998, she complained that White House security officials failed to recognize her and did not give her the same treatment as other members of Congress, at one time mistaking her twenty-three-year-old white aide for the congresswoman.[30]

Something happened between McKinney's initial semiapology and her statements a couple of days later. Possibly fearing a charge of assault against a police officer, McKinney went on the offensive and pulled out the race card. She held a press conference, flanked by entertainer/activists Danny "I can't get a cab in New York" Glover, and Harry "Bush is the world's greatest terrorist" Belafonte. "This whole incident," announced McKinney, "was instigated by the inappropriate touching and stopping of me, a female black congresswoman. I deeply regret that this incident occurred and I am certain that after a full review of the facts, I will be exonerated."[31]

Danny Glover said, "We're not here to judge the merits of the case, but here to support our sister."[32]

Belafonte said, "In America and Washington, D.C., issues of race have always been at play and have often been central to justice miscarried. . . . We're here to be sure that this process is handled fairly and it is not rooted in familiar racist behavior, that the outcome of this is going to be done on a very fair and square basis."[33]

McKinney's lawyer said, "Like thousands of average Americans across this country, [she] is too a victim of the excessive use of force by law enforcement officials because of how she looks and the color of her skin. Ms. McKinney is just a victim of being in Congress while black."[34]

Now *she* became the victim, and the officer the perpetrator, although, with some fourteen black female members of Congress, one wonders how the others somehow, some way, managed to get through security.

One day before McKinney's slugfest, *U.S.A. Today* ran a cover story about a "stop snitching" campaign among minorities in the inner city: "The slogan appeared in Baltimore about two years ago as the title of an underground DVD featuring threatening, gun-wielding drug dealers and a brief appearance by NBA star and Baltimore native Carmelo Anthony. Anthony, who later said he didn't know the video's theme, told *ESPN The Magazine* that the dealer-turned-informer excoriated in the DVD 'ran our neighborhood. Now he's working with the state and the feds. You can't do that. He turned his back on the 'hood.' "[35]

Prosecutors say that primarily because of witness fear and intimidation, and also because of some sort of street code of honor, they face difficulties in obtaining convictions. In an attempted murder case in Pittsburgh, prosecutors wanted to put on the stand—as their star witness—the intended victim, a man named Rayco "War" Saunders. What happened?

The "star witness" showed up in court to give his testimony wearing a "Stop Snitching" T-shirt and hat. The prosecutor asked him to turn the T-shirt around and take his cap off. Instead, victim/witness Saunders stormed out, never taking the stand. The case collapsed.

Crimes go unsolved because people like Saunders feel it is better to allow guilty criminals to prey on others than to cooperate with "the man." Some refuse to step forward because of fear due to witness intimidation. The ones who pay the price are the majority of hard-working, law-abiding, inner-city residents.

Congresswoman McKinney helps to set this example by displaying hostility and antagonism toward police officers who are simply attempting to do their jobs in our post–9/11 world. After all, in 1998, a gunman broke into the Capitol and murdered two officers, one of them right outside then Majority Whip Tom Delay's office. What do we want the capitol police to do? Allow people to go around checkpoints even when the police fail to recognize them, just because that person happens to be black—possibly exposing the officer to a charge of "racial profiling"?

Apparently, McKinney thinks that, as a black woman in 2006, her life should be completely devoid of problems or inconveniences. But if something negative does happens to her, it must be because of race! And if she has some sort of exchange with a police officer, well, obviously that officer deserves condemnation.

Many black academicians reinforce this view. Some appeared in the 2002 cable documentary, *OJ: A Study in Black and White*, Todd Boyd, a professor from USC, said his white colleagues were dismayed when the O. J. Simpson verdict came down. At that moment, said Boyd, he never felt so black in his life. What does that mean? UCLA and Columbia law professor Kimberle Crenshaw said, "Usually, you could roll out a Fuhrman, and not have to worry about it. But [Simpson] is a guy who's got major bank, and if they try to do that stuff that they usually do to us, they're gonna be caught up short."

Black USC law professor Jody Armour wrote in the *Los Angeles Times* about the "indignities" he endured, just being questioned by the police while in his "German car" in one of the nicer areas of South Central Los Angeles, which he described as "aggressively policed."[36]

The late Johnnie Cochran, famed O. J. Simpson defense attorney, once had this exchange with Bill O'Reilly on *The O'Reilly Factor*:

COCHRAN: I believe that it—there's overpolicing, and I don't think in fairness—

O'REILLY: Overpolicing?

COCHRAN: Yes, I think it's overpolicing. I think—

O'REILLY: Have you been to South Central L.A. lately?

COCHRAN: I've been to—

O'REILLY: Do you think there's overpolicing down there?

COCHRAN: Oh, yes. Well, I think it's overpolicing with regard to some of these drug cases. . . .

O'REILLY: Yes, I don't think there's enough cops in there. I want more cops in there.

COCHRAN: Well, listen, more cops don't always solve the problem. I think we need to look at some of the other root causes.[37]

So these upper-middle-class blacks lament the damage done by "excessive policing." As one cop told me, you fish where the fish are. Police departments *should* deploy cops in areas with the greatest rates of crime. That's just common sense.

Nationally, the murder rate (incidents per 100,000 people) for 2005 was 6.9. The robbery rate was 195.4 and the rate for aggravated assault was 340.1.[38] While the national rates include rural areas and small towns, known for their lower crime rates, some larger cities have rates below the national average. San Jose, California, for example, has almost one million residents. Its murder rate was 2.9, robbery was 97.1, and aggravated assault was 254.7.[39] San Jose's population is 3.5 percent black and 30 percent Hispanic.[40]

What about cities with predominately minority populations? Washington, D.C., which is 60 percent black and 8 percent Hispanic,[41] had a murder rate of 35.4, robbery was 636.1, and aggravated assault was 700.1.[42] Newark, New Jersey, at 54 percent black and 30 percent Hispanic,[43] had a 34.5 percent murder rate, 444.7 for robbery, and 494.9 for aggravated assault.[44] Cleveland, Ohio, with a population 51 percent black and 7 percent Hispanic,[45] had a murder rate of 23.8, robbery of

815.7, and aggravated assault of 454.6.[46] Compton, California, 40 percent black and 57 percent Hispanic,[47] had a murder rate of 67.1, a robbery rate of 489.3, and an aggravated assault rate of 1189.2.[48]

In inner-city schools, more than half of young black men fail to finish high school.[49] By 2004, 21 percent of black men who did not attend college were in prison, and 72 percent of black male high school dropouts in their twenties were unemployed—either unable to find a job, not looking for a job, or incarcerated.[50] There is a problem here.

The NBA held their 2007 All-Star Game in Las Vegas. While no NBA player got into trouble, the All-Star Game attracted a crowd that reportedly included some rather rowdy folks. Some establishments briefly shut down because of disruptive behavior. "All-Star Weekend revelers," according to one black sports-writer who attended the event, "have transformed the league's midseason exhibition into the new millennium Freaknik, an out-of-control street party that features gunplay, violence, non-stop weed smoke, and general mayhem.

"Word of all the criminal activity that transpired during All-Star Weekend has been slowly leaking out on Las Vegas radio shows and TV newscasts and on Internet blogs the past 24 hours.

" 'It was filled with an element of violence,' Teresa Frey, general manager for Coco's restaurant, told klastv.com. 'They don't want to pay their bills. They don't want to respect us or each other.'

"Things got so bad that she closed the 24-hour restaurant from 2 AM to 4 AM.

" 'I have been spit on. I have had food thrown at me,' she said. 'I have lost two servers out of fear. I have locked my door out of the fear of violence.'

" . . . [T]here were multiple brawls, at least two shootings, more than 350 arrests and a lot of terror in Vegas over the week-end. . . . There were so many fights and so many gangbangers and one parking-lot shootout at the MGM Grand that people lit-erally fled the hotel in fear for their safety. . . . There are reports of a brawl between rappers and police at the Wynn Hotel. Vegas police were simply overwhelmed along The Strip."[51]

J. A. Adande, a *Los Angeles Times* sportswriter who also attended the event, wrote, "Unfortunately, there's still a segment of the African-American population that thinks the All-Star game is an acceptable time and place to smoke weed wherever and whenever, walk around drinking Patron out of bottles with two-foot straws, pick up women by demeaning them, and set a franchise record for use of the n-word."[52]

Crash, three time Oscar-winning film in 2006, became a metaphor for poor "race relations." Set in Los Angeles, the movie interwove the lives of a dozen people over a thirty-six-hour period.

One of the principal themes is the deep-seated racial feelings and biases that—so argues the film—we all carry.

Where have we heard *that* before?

In *Crash*, Matt Dillon plays a racist police officer who takes advantage of a black couple he stopped by fondling the man's wife. *Crash* "exposes," among other things, the alleged poor relations between blacks and the police. But the stats show that regular people—blacks and whites—appreciate and respect the police. Unlike these black lawyers and academicians—and the writers and producers of *Crash*—most blacks do not accept the idea of institutional police brutality. The black community, as a whole, needs the police and respects what they do.

In 1999, the *Los Angeles Times* reported a federal study asking people whether they support the police in their own neighborhoods. Nationwide, 85 percent of all respondents agreed. They broke the survey down city by city. In cities like Knoxville, Tennessee, and Chicago, Illinois, there was a disparity between the way whites and blacks perceived the police. In Knoxville, 91 percent of whites were satisfied with the police and only 63 percent of blacks. In Chicago, 89 percent of whites were satisfied as opposed to 69 percent for blacks. But in many other cities, the numbers were nearly equal. San Diego, California, had the second highest rate of satisfaction, at 95 percent of whites and 89 percent of blacks (a close second to Madison, Wisconsin).[53]

What about Los Angeles, the cauldron of racial tensions that served as a setting for *Crash?*

According to the study, 86 percent of all Angelinos support the police. Whites support the police at 89 percent. And blacks? They support the police at 82 percent. The reason is not so complicated. In the inner city, blacks get targeted for crime at twice the rate as do whites.[54] Thus, people living in the inner city need cops more than do people living in the suburbs.

A friend, a captain in the National Guard, received orders to mobilize on the eve of the second Rodney King trial. Recall that the first trial resulted in mostly acquittal verdicts, and spawned several days of riots that left fifty four people dead, more than three thousand stores destroyed by fires or looting, and an estimated total damage of $1 billion-plus.[55] Local authorities feared a rerun, so they dispatched the National Guard. My captain friend told me that black men and women came pouring out of their homes and walked up to my friend in his camouflage fatigues. "Where have you been?" "What's taken you so long?" "Why does it take something like a trial to have you guys come out?" "We need your help."

No, most blacks, as opposed to some loudmouth "black leaders," do not hate the police. They know the police represent the line between *their* side—hardworking, taxpaying, decent citizens—versus the minority of thugs that seeks to maim, hurt, and debase culture and property. Most blacks want a police presence. Most blacks condemn crime and violence, and want to be able to leave homes, go to school, and go to and from work without incident. Yet, cities constantly run budget deficits in order to fund social programs—health care, welfare—while ignoring the most fundamental of duties—protecting the citizens.

> No, most blacks, as opposed to some loudmouth "black leaders," do not hate the police. They know the police represent the line between *their* side—hardworking, taxpaying, decent citizens—versus the minority of thugs that seeks to maim, hurt, and debase culture and property.

But instead of encouraging young minorities to join the police and to serve their communities, "black leaders" like McKinney consider the police a hostile occupying force, decreasing the possibility of citizen police cooperation and increasing the possibility of crimes going unsolved.

Nice work, Congresswoman.

In 2002, during the weeks-long sniper investigation in the Washington, D.C., area, black police chief Charles Moose became the public face of multijurisdictional law enforcement on the nightly news.

Moose—thrust into the national spotlight after just three years as chief—never intended to be a cop. "I was going to be a defense attorney," said Moose, "because, as an African-American male in 1975, I really didn't like the police. I was pretty sure the police made up the things that they did so that they could be mean . . . to African-Americans in particular. So by being a police officer for a couple of years, I would have some tremendous insight about how they did that, how they thought, and then I would be a very good defense attorney."[56]

Just one problem with his plan. As a young cop, Moose made a lot of arrests and talked to a lot of victims. And a funny thing happened on his way to becoming a defense attorney. He learned that the cops—at least the ones he worked with—did not plant evidence, did not lie to convict otherwise innocent people. So Moose abandoned his law school plans and remained a police officer, rising through the ranks.

Contrast Moose's opinion of police officers with that of, say, an Al Sharpton. One is a formerly distrustful young man who spent decades on the inside, working with the badge. The other has spent decades on the outside, full of fury and accusations. Question: Who to believe?

In May 2006, Malik Zulu Shabazz, a leader of the New Black Panthers, traveled to Durham, North Carolina, to blast the "racist" criminal justice system. Prosecutors had charged three young, white, male members of the Duke University lacrosse team with rape. The alleged victim, a black woman, worked as a stripper. Shabazz immediately pronounced the whites guilty. "We don't care if our sister was stripping or not. We say that that was only a temporary condition of circumstance. But to us she is a righteous and divine woman by nature," said Shabazz.[57]

"We will defend our black women. [The] New Black Panther Party and black men is not going to stand by, idly by, and let our black women be raped," said Nigi Muhammed, another Panther member.[58] Also showing up to "defend" the alleged Duke rape victim were members of the Nation of Islam. As with the New Black Panther Party, these members of the Nation of Islam demanded justice for the alleged victim.

Quite a different position from the one that the leader of the Nation of Islam took when beauty queen and high school class valedictorian, Desiree Washington, claimed that the heavyweight champion, Mike Tyson, raped her in 1991. A multiethnic jury found him guilty, and Tyson served three and a half years.

Apparently, the Nation of Islam adamantly believes the alleged Duke rape victim. Before Tyson's conviction, however, its leader took an entirely different position. Although Mike Tyson's accuser is black, just like the Duke Lacrosse team accuser, Louis Farrakhan dismissed her charges in a vulgar and sexist way: "You bring a hawk into the chicken yard and wonder why the chicken got eaten up. You bring Mike to a beauty contest and all these fine foxes just parading in front of Mike. Mike's eyes begin to dance like a hungry man looking at a Wendy's beef burger or something. She said, 'No, Mike, no.' How many times, sisters, have you said 'No' when you meant 'Yes'?"[59]

So if a black alleged rape victim accuses a white person of rape, string him up, trial to follow. But if a black alleged rape victim accuses a rich and famous black man of rape, she's guilty of playing a "deceitful game." Different rules.

Durham District Attorney Mike Nifong, the white prosecutor in the Duke case won his 2006 reelection in a virtual landslide, thanks in large part to the almost monolithic support he received from the black community. Why did blacks rally behind him? Credit Nifong's unwavering, rabid, and outspoken promises to prosecute the three Duke University lacrosse players for the alleged rape of a black woman. Nifong, preelection, publicly maligned the lacrosse players, making statements even though he was aware of potentially exculpatory evidence.

So if a black alleged rape victim accuses a white person of rape, string him up, trial to follow. But if a black alleged rape victim accuses a rich and famous black man of rape, she's guilty of playing a "deceitful game." Different rules.

The district attorney repeatedly stated that he believed the alleged victim even though it turned out that neither he nor anyone in his office spoke to the woman about the events of that night until much later. Flaunting a total disregard for police procedure and state guidelines, authorities showed the accuser a photo lineup *only* of the forty-six white Duke lacrosse players. Normal police protocol requires, for every suspect photo, the inclusion of at least seven nonsuspect photos. But at the time of the photo lineup, based on the accuser's claim, all the lacrosse players at the party were potential suspects.[60]

The case appeared shaky from the very beginning. Video of the dancers' "performance" during the lacrosse players' party shows the accuser weaving, stumbling, and, at times, apparently unable to stand. Witnesses reported seeing her drinking that night, and the alleged victim admitted taking Flexeril, a powerful muscle relaxant, not to be combined with alcohol.[61]

The second exotic dancer at the party that night, Kim Roberts, promptly contradicted the alleged victim's version of events, and claimed that the alleged victim asked her to mark up the victim's body on the night in question![62]

Nifong hired Dr. Brian Meehan to conduct DNA testing sortly after the alleged rape was committed. Not until after Nifong's re-election did Meehan admit that the DNA he found in the rape kit and on the accuser's underwear belonged to at least four other unidentified men—none of it from *any* of the lacrosse players. Yet Meehan's report failed to mention finding other men's DNA, an omission that he later called "an error in judgment."

Did Nifong, the Durham DA, ask Meehan to exclude the information? Meehan said, "Well, it was my decision based on my understanding of what was asked in this case from when the case began." Meehan testified that he and Nifong had agreed to limit the written report to "just the stuff that matched" the Duke players or three of the accuser's friends. Meehan says that when he found there was DNA evidence from other unidentified men, he gave that information to Nifong verbally—in person and on the phone—before he completed his report.[63]

Nifong knew the accused players' semen was not found in the rape kit. The accuser told her hospital examiners that no condoms were used in her alleged rape. So how do three men brutally gang-rape a woman without condoms and sanitize the area in such a way as to leave not a single speck of their own DNA, yet still preserve other DNA from previous sexual encounters? Well, despite initially stating that DNA tests would "immediately rule out any innocent person," Nifong did an abrupt U-turn, publicly speculating that no DNA from the lacrosse players was present because the players might have used condoms—even though the alleged victim claimed no condoms were used.[64]

Nifong proclaimed that the hospital's examining nurse found symptoms consistent with sexual assault, and that he had "no doubt" a rape occurred, but the actual rape exam indicated only that "diffuse" swelling was present, which can be caused by normal sexual activity.[65]

During the three days prior to the lacrosse party, a friend of the accuser's regular escort service driver told police he drove the accuser to half-hour and hour-long jobs at different hotels every day, although the accuser denies she engaged in sexual activity with those clients. She did admit to police that she used a vibrator in one performance, and, by some accounts, the accuser had sex with two men the week prior to the lacrosse party.[66]

The accuser's various accounts of the night have varied from rape to groping and back to rape again, with the number of perpetrators ranging from two men to twenty men. At one time, she even accused her fellow dancer of participating in the rape. Also, the accuser claimed she was strangled during the attack, but the examining nurse found no physical evidence of strangulation.[67]

The attorney for one of the accused, Reade Seligmann, produced alibi evidence including records, receipts, and witnesses that have Seligmann placing six phone calls to his girlfriend during the mere fifteen-minute window in which it appears the rape could have occurred, and then hopping in a cab, going to an ATM, and back to his dorm. Yet when Seligmann's attorney tried to bring this exculpatory evidence to Nifong in an attempt to stave off the indictment, Nifong refused to review the evidence.[68]

Nifong accused the players of stonewalling him and the police. Yet the co-captains, who rented the house where the party was held, not only quickly agreed to come with the police to the station for questions, but they didn't even try to get a lawyer and offered to take a polygraph. Later, when Nifong ordered DNA samples for all forty-six players, their attorney was meeting with the students and telling them how they could appeal it. Instead, the players abruptly left the meeting, got in their cars, and drove to the police station to offer their DNA.[69]

H. P. Thomas, a former security manager at the accuser's strip club, told the *Raleigh News and Observer* that the alleged victim told him—four days after the rape supposedly occurred—that she was going to get money from boys at a Duke party who hadn't paid her, but never mentioned being hurt or injured. "She basically said, 'I'm going to get paid by the white boys,'" said Thomas. "I said, 'Whatever,' because no one takes her seriously." Thomas said he gave a sworn statement to the DA's office a month before the election. The story, unfortunately, ran only a couple days before the election—not that more time would have made a difference in the outcome.[70]

Following his I-feel-your-pain exhortations to the black community and his evidence-be-damned attitude, Nifong easily won reelection. According to Brooklyn College history professor KC Johnson, eight of Durham County's election precincts have a more than 90 percent black electorate. In his re election, Nifong received between 91.2 and 96 percent of the vote in those eight precincts.[71]

Then, a month after his reelection, Nifong decided to drop the rape charges against the lacrosse players. About a week later, the North Carolina bar filed ethics charges against Nifong, citing forty-one quotations he made to the press, which amounted to "improper commentary about the character, credibility, and reputation of the accused."[72] Among the quotations:

Nifong referred to the lacrosse players as "a bunch of hooligans."[73]

He declared: "I am convinced there was a rape, yes, sir."[74]

He told ESPN: "One would wonder why one needs an attorney if one was not charged and had not done anything wrong."[75]

He told *The New York Times*: "I'm disappointed that no one has been enough of a man to come forward. And if they would have spoken up at the time, this may never have happened."[76]

The North Carolina bar accused Nifong of breaking the rule against "dishonesty, fraud, deceit, and misrepresentation" when, after DNA tests failed to produce any evidence, Nifong told a reporter that the players might have used a condom. The bar charges that Nifong knew his assertion was misleading, since he had the emergency room nurse's report in which the accuser said her attackers did *not* use a condom.[77]

The law requires a district attorney to turn over to the defense any information that tends to exonerate the accused. Although Nifong had been told that the accuser's rape kit and underwear produced DNA from four unidentified men, Nifong didn't inform the defense until a judge ordered him to do so—a full six months later. Even worse, prior to the judge's order, Nifong stated in court that he was "not aware of any additional information" that might be exculpatory.[78]

Can you imagine a prosecutor doing these things to a black defendant? No justice, no peace!

Nifong likely thought of himself as Gregory Peck's Atticus Finch in *To Kill a Mockingbird*—the gallant white man risking the wrath of the community while standing tall on behalf of an oppressed, downtrodden black victim. Nifong's former campaign manager said, "He got caught up in the media, and he got addicted to it." Facing ethics charges and growing scrutiny, Nifong finally recused himself from the case,[79] resigned as DA a few months later and, following an ethics hearing, was disbarred by the state.[80]

While the mainscream media extensively covered the Duke lacrosse case, they ignored a nearby, similar case. Less than two months before the alleged rape at Duke, four black students from the historically black Virginia Union University were accused of raping a white coed from the more upscale University of Richmond, after they had all attended a campus party. Two of the accused had ties to their school's football team. One was a star quarterback as a freshman.[81] No outcry, no national coverage. The case quietly went to trial, where two of the men were convicted, one pled guilty to lesser charges, and charges against the fourth man were dismissed.[82] And, in this case, race was never considered as an issue.

In January 2007, a railroad worker found a twenty-three-year-old white man's body, shot and burned and dumped along railroad tracks in Knoxville, Tennessee. Two days later, police found the body of the dead man's missing girlfriend in a trash can. Allegedly, both were sexually assaulted, with household cleaner poured in the woman's mouth to remove evidence. Within days, police arrested four black men—and later, one black woman—with the heinous crimes. This story received almost no national media coverage, presumably because the crime lacked evidence of racial animus.[83] How, then, does one explain the lack of coverage in a black-perps/white-victims case in Long Beach, California—a case of *clear* racial animus?

On Halloween night, 2006, a mob of thirty to forty teens and a few adults—mostly black—beat three young white women in Long Beach just outside Los Angeles. Without provocation, the mob brutally kicked, punched, and pummeled the white women, slamming them to the ground, ripping earrings from their lobes, and beating them with a skateboard. One of the victims had twelve fractures in her face that may require multiple surgeries, as well as damage to her teeth and her eyesight. The women also suffered internal injuries and concussions. But for the efforts of a black Good Samaritan, who waded into the crowd to help the girls, they might well be dead.[84]

Yet, within a week of the attack, an Internet search showed that only two newspapers, the *Long Beach Press Telegram* and the *Los Angeles Times*, bothered to write about it. And in the case of the *Los Angeles Times*, the newspaper wrote the article a full week after the attack!

According to witnesses, during the rampage the mob yelled, "We hate white people, f—— whites!" But when authorities first charged ten of the youths with felony assault a week later, they declined to file hate-crime charges.[85] A full three weeks after the attack, when the authorities finally filed hate-crime charges against eight of the youths, the local NAACP branch said, "[W]e do not have sufficient information to determine whether this is a true hate crime and we just have to monitor this."[86] Yet the NAACP didn't have to "monitor" the situation or wait for "sufficient information to determine" that the Rodney King beating was a hate crime. One of the defendant's uncles, Karl Rowe, published a pamphlet explaining that "white bitches"—another of the epithets allegedly hurled at the white victims—is an acceptable phrase in some urban environments.[87]

National Public Radio, almost a month after the attack, finally got around to discussing it. On a program called *News and Notes*, moderator Farai Chideya put the following question to her guests: "[S]ome people say black folks cannot be racist because the root of the issue is power. So what do you make of this crime where you've got twelve- to seventeen-year-olds and, you know, black people attacking whites? Is this a traditional hate crime? Should it be prosecuted as such? People in the community are kind of divided about that."[88] Perhaps Chideya might ask the young white female victims whether they felt their black attackers lacked "power." Talk about an insane double standard.

Remember when Reverend Al Sharpton came to Los Angeles to declare solidarity with a grieving community over the death of a nineteen-month-old Hispanic girl? He said, "If Suzie (the nineteen-month-old girl justifiably shot by the police) had been black," said Sharpton, "we'd have been there. If Suzie had been white, someone would have been there."[89] But in this case, Reverend Sharpton was nowhere to be found.

Also around Halloween, a twenty-second video tape of two Los Angeles police officers attempting to subdue William Cardenas was played on TV news stations across the country. One of the officers appears to have his knee on Cardenas's neck, and Cardenas is punched in the face about a half dozen times. According to one of the officers, the struggle lasted for five to ten minutes, yet only these few seconds of video have shown up. The officers also testified that they had recognized Cardenas as a

known gang member with an outstanding warrant for possession of a stolen gun, and that they had chased him after Cardenas threw a heavy object at them and ran. The police officers say
they tackled him, that Cardenas hit one of the cops in the face,
and that the suspect twisted to avoid the handcuffs and tugged at
one of the officer's gun belts. The officers assumed that Cardenas
was attempting to grab one of their guns, and this, according to
the officers, prompted the punches.[90]

It turned out that more speeders were black than white, justifying why cops pulled over black motorists so often.

Virtually no media coverage of a white victim allegedly raped
by blacks, or the beating of white victims by black perpetrators.
But it's stop-the-presses time when the victim is black or Hispanic, especially if the "perpetrator" is a white cop.

Many blacks cite Driving While Black (DWB) as a prime example of racism in America. But, again, the facts get in the way.

Numerous complaints of DWB were filed by blacks driving
on the New Jersey Turnpike. So the state entered into a consent
decree, agreed to federal monitoring, and put their officers
through "sensitivity training," among other things. New Jersey
commissioned a study, checking motorists' speed with laser
guns and photographing drivers of vehicles going fifteen miles
per hour or more over the speed limit.[91]

The result?

It turned out that more speeders were black than white, jus-
tifying why cops pulled over black motorists so often. The U.S.
Justice Department, which requested the study, did not want the
results released to the public. Instead, they accused the researchers

of using a "flawed methodology."[92] Why shelve a report that disproves racism? Isn't it good news that Jersey Troopers do not willy-nilly pull blacks over? Would this not improve race relations in New Jersey? No, the facts did not fit the script.

The next year, state police "stop data" showed that, on the southern part of the turnpike, 30 percent of the drivers pulled over were minority—almost twice the 16 percent rate of minority stops elsewhere on the turnpike.[93] So, amid new allegations that cops were targeting minorities, and to correct the "flawed methodology" of the previous researchers, New Jersey Attorney General Peter Harvey commissioned another study.[94] The result? Again, it turned out a disproportionately higher percentage of drivers on that stretch of highway were black, *and* that blacks were more likely to drive eighty miles per hour or faster.[95] Again, less than a day after this report was released, critics were complaining its methodology was "flawed."[96]

So when you don't like the message, shoot the messenger. And if you don't like the study, blame the data.

8.

AFFIRMATIVE ACTION

I confess that I do not envy the white boy as I once did. I have learned that success is to be measured not so much by the position that one has reached in life as by the obstacles which he has overcome while trying to succeed. Looked at from this standpoint, I almost reached the conclusion that often the Negro boy's birth and connection with an unpopular race is an advantage, so far as real life is concerned. With few exceptions, the Negro youth must work harder and must perform his tasks even better than a white youth in order to secure recognition. But out of the hard and unusual struggle through which he is compelled to pass, he gets a strength, a confidence, that one misses whose pathway is comparatively smooth by reason of birth and race.[1]

—BOOKER T. WASHINGTON, *UP FROM SLAVERY* (1901)

When did opposition to affirmative action become "I want minorities to fail"? And when did support of affirmative action become synonymous with justice and fair play?

The U.S. Supreme Court, on June 23, 2003, ruled five to four in favor of the University of Michigan law school's use of race in considering admissions. The Court said that colleges and universities may consider an applicant's race, but the justices also restricted the extent to which race-based factors can influence the selection of students.

Supreme Court Justice Sandra Day O'Conner wrote the majority opinion in the University of Michigan law school case. How do color-blind admissions keep blacks down? It yet again provides excuses for "underrepresentation," yet a black person unqualified for admission to "School A" could certainly meet the admission requirements for "School B." But O'Connor wrote that the law school's "holistic" and "individualized" consideration of race in admissions was necessary for at least the next twenty-five years.[2] So, the clock is ticking.

During a luncheon at the Rainbow/PUSH organization's thirty-second annual convention, actor Danny Glover gave the just announced Supreme Court's affirmative action decision his grudging and qualified support. "It's a very temporary victory," said Glover to reporters. "There is still a lot of work to do. If we are ever going to create the kind of world, the kind of America that [the Founders] envisioned, then we are going to have to have affirmative action in the full sense of the word."[3] Hm-mm. I've read the Constitution, the Bill of Rights, the Federalist Papers, and many other writings by our Founding Fathers, yet I don't recall ever seeing a mention of "special treatment for *some* of the people." But maybe Glover's a better historical scholar than I am.

Black Representative Barbara Lee (D-CA) gave the keynote speech at the luncheon. While she praised the Supreme Court decision, Lee accused the Bush administration of pursuing "white supremacist" policies in America. "This administration and allies in Congress are rolling back advances in racial equality, economic opportunity, and gender equity," said Lee. She also accused the administration of endorsing racially segregationist policies pushed by the late Senator Strom Thurmond during his failed 1948 presidential campaign on the Dixiecrat ticket. "Believe me," said Lee, the Bush administration's "policies are taking us back to those days nonetheless."[4]

Lee said she attended oral arguments at the Supreme Court when the University of Michigan's attorneys argued their case, and was offended by the comments of the Bush administration's Solicitor General Ted Olson. "Sitting there, I thought, 'How sad,' and I felt how horrible it is to witness our own government arguing against the interests of so many of its people."⁵

Lee blasted Supreme Court Justice Antonin Scalia for his comments during the court case. "[Scalia] said that [the University of Michigan] could either be an elite, first-rate school or it could lower its standards and pursue racial diversity—that is what he said," Lee noted. "How sinister. How wrong can he get? . . . Justice Scalia was in fact offering a false dichotomy. In reality, you cannot be a top-flight university without diversity."⁶

Really?

The *Detroit News* found that, in the push for diversity, the racial preferences policies of seven Michigan colleges and universities resulted in a disturbing pattern. Many minority students dropped out at a much higher rate, presumably because of lowered standards for admission. "Among black students," reported the *Detroit News*, "who were freshmen in 1994, just 40 percent got their diplomas after six years, compared to 61 percent of white students and 74 percent of Asians. . . . The state's universities have special programs aimed at helping black students meet financial, social and academic challenges, but graduation rates for blacks haven't improved consistently over the past decade, the *News* found. . . . Universities knowingly admit students who have a high chance of failing."⁷ This is the sports equivalent of athletes who bypass the minor leagues, where they could perform well, and go straight to the major leagues, where they struggle and ultimately flunk out.

Affirmative action, carried to its logical extreme, can kill. For example, hospitals in the Western Cape province of South Africa cancel as many as ten scheduled operations a day. Why? By adhering to a so-called equity policy, the hospitals reject well-qualified white and Indian doctors who apply, leaving vital posts vacant and causing two-year-long patient wait lists. Meanwhile, hospitals wait in vain for black candidates to apply. "The biggest losers," according to an article in the *South African Sunday Times*, "are disadvantaged patients who already have to wait months, or even years, for surgery. The equity policy that gives preference to black candidates has been labeled 'playing racial politics with patients' lives.' "[8]

When you get on a 747 and notice a black pilot, do you want someone who represents company diversity or a guy who aced the flight academy?

Preferences lower standards to achieve racial diversity, thus discriminating against the more qualified applicants. Laws and policies that punish merit, however well-intended, ultimately hurt everybody. When you get on a 747 and notice a black pilot, do you want someone who represents company diversity or a guy who aced the flight academy? When your mother has a heart attack and they wheel her on a gurney into the OR, do you want a "diverse" group of doctors, nurses, and paraprofessionals, or do you want the best and most competent people you can afford?

Research shows that by 1969, blacks and whites who came from the same socioeconomic background and had similar educations showed no difference in their average incomes. This was a few years after passage of the Civil Rights Act, and affirmative action programs had not been in place long enough to affect the education and employment history of working blacks. The accomplishment of black women was even more remarkable. In 1950, black female college graduates were making 91 percent as much as white women with the same education. One decade later, by 1960, four years *before* the 1964 Civil Rights Act was passed, black women were earning 2 percent *more* than the whites.[9]

Yet former Atlanta Mayor Bill Campbell, before his conviction for tax fraud, said: "There's not been anybody [of color] who has gotten into college on their own, nobody who's gotten a job on their own, no one who's prospered as a businessman or business-woman on their own without affirmative action."[10] *No one?* Talk about insulting legions of black men and women, most of whom got ahead without someone tipping the scale in their favor.

Nobody owes you a job.

How does Mr. Campbell explain the success of black immigrants? Economist Thomas Sowell found that in 1969, when American-born blacks were making 62 percent of the average income of all Americans, black immigrants from the West Indies were earning 94 percent. Even more striking, children of immigrants from the West Indies were earning 15 percent *more* than the average American. How, then, to explain the attitude of Bill Campbell and other victicrats, who ignore the successes of hard-working black men and women while blaming failures on racism? Sowell says, "There is a positive hostility to analyses of black success if they suggest that racism may not be the cause of black failure."[11]

Nobody owes you a job. Our knowledge-based economy makes losers out of those who refuse to invest in themselves. Equal rights and equal results are two different things. Here's a suggestion for people who are feeling down: Rent the film *Pursuit of Happyness* starring Will Smith. It depicts the true-life story of a black man who, through hustle, determination, and grit, became a top stockbroker who eventually started his own firm.

In a *Chicago Sun-Times* article called "Color Us Hypocrites"[12] we learn the following:

According to a recent study by Richard Lapchick of the Institute for Diversity and Ethics in Sport, the percentages of whites at newspapers in the United States and Canada are as follows:

> *Sports editors: 95 percent.*
> *Assistant sports editors: 87 percent.*
> *Columnists: 90 percent.*
> *Reporters: 87.5 percent.*

Okay, therefore what? Affirmative action for sportswriters? Affirmative action for editors? Whom should they fire to open a seat for persons of color?

Did the researcher who came up with the report, entitled the "Racial and Gender Report Card," offer to voluntarily step down in favor of a black researcher to head his organization? Of the current sports writers, how many consider themselves un-qualified for their jobs and therefore express a willingness to give up the seat for a "more qualified, more sensitive" minority?

And what constitutes an "imbalance," anyway? Should one assume that because blacks comprise 65 percent of the NFL,[13] they should therefore comprise 65 percent of sports writers covering it? Or, since the WNBA is 100 percent women, only women should cover it? Should women be equally represented as ditch diggers, firefighters, and steel builders? Should only white teachers teach white students, and black teachers black students?

In other words, studies like the "Racial and Gender Report Card" are saying that, whatever the percentage of the population—whether apportioned by race or gender—the percentage of people covering, reporting on, or editing their activities should be the same.

There's only one relevant question: Did racism and dis-crimination prevent *otherwise qualified* applicants from succeed-ing? Even if the answer is yes, private-sector companies should be able to hire and fire as they wish. If stupid team owners re-fuse to hire the most qualified athletes and front-office mem-bers, expect the product on the field to suffer. The World Series–winning Chicago White Sox has a black general man-ager, Kenny Williams. Williams's blackness, however, did not mean he avoided a contentious relationship with their former black slugger, Frank Thomas. About Thomas's departure from the Sox, Williams said, "He's an idiot. He's selfish. . . . We don't miss his attitude. We don't miss the whining. . . . Good riddance. See you later."[14]

Yet, once again we see the phenomenon of people in a very liberal profession, such as journalism, essentially being called bigots.

This is not exactly a smoking gun for institutional racism. For starters, journalism schools—which turn out many of the hirees in places like *The New York Times*—consist of only 7.9 percent blacks in journalism and mass communication masters' programs.[15] Of those graduates, many find themselves highly desirable recruits and can thus pick the plum from an array of choices. Does anyone really believe that the liberal *New York Times* has a "don't recruit, don't hire" policy for blacks?

In 1998, according to the American Society of Newspaper Editors, 5.4 percent of newsroom employees were black.[16] In 2006, the percentage is 5.6 percent.[17] In broadcast news, blacks are 9.5 percent of the workforce.[18] And on television, according to the Radio and Television News Directors Association, women comprise 57 percent of all anchor jobs.[19] Is this the result of the National Organization for Women pushing for gender-based hiring? No. Maybe television takes a business-oriented approach, recognizing that a large percentage of disposable-income people watching their news are men, who generally enjoy looking at attractive women. Or maybe female viewers like watching other women, even if—in some cases—only to criticize them. Or maybe . . . who knows?

No one owes you a job.

9.

STUPID BLACK MEN AND SPORTS

The way for a young man to rise, is to improve himself every way he can, never suspecting that any body wishes to hinder him.[1]

—ABRAHAM LINCOLN

Because of their celebrity and achievement, athletes command our attention. Their words make news—even when they say things that are stupid, demoralizing, or even racist.

Charles Barkley, the former NBA star turned television analyst, alternately entertains and leaves you scratching your head. Sometimes he shows common sense, as when he disputed the notion of athletes as role models and properly proclaimed that raising children is the job of the parents. But sometimes he recklessly ventures into the victicrat mentality and makes wild and stupid accusations of racism.

For example, Barkley accused the Masters Golf Tournament of intentionally lengthening Augusta National's course to diminish the possibility of a win by Tiger Woods. "They're lengthening the course for one reason, to hurt Tiger," says Barkley, adding, "What they're doing to Tiger is blatant racism."[2] Fortunately, ESPN sportscaster Dan Patrick had the cashews to challenge him.

PATRICK: Charles, I don't agree with you at all on these comments.

BARKLEY: So?

PATRICK: You know what? There's enough racism, and how many conversations have we had—

BARKLEY: You know what, you're right. There is enough racism.

PATRICK: But this isn't racism.

BARKLEY: But I'm just gonna tell you this. You're right, there is enough racism. It's about time that black men in positions of power start standing up for it. As far as the thing at Augusta . . . Hootie Johnson, I think that's his name, he reassured Mr. Woods recently that it wasn't racism. And I'm tryin' to figure to myself, why would he have to go to Tiger, or Tiger have to go to him, and have this conversation? Why do you think they had this conversation, Dan?

PATRICK: I think there's a sensitivity level that racism did exist and probably does on more of a covert operation at Augusta . . .

BARKLEY: Well, first of all, golf is probably the most racist sport in the world. I mean, I don't think Augusta really gives rat-ass what Tiger thinks or what Tiger wants.

PATRICK: I don't know that. I asked Tiger about that, he said—

BARKLEY: Well, first of all, Tiger can't say that.

PATRICK: Well, okay. Let me tell you what *he* said, "All I can do is—"

BARKLEY: . . . He can't say anything against the golf establishment. He cannot say—

PATRICK: You are right.

BARKLEY: So, please. I mean, hey, Tiger's my brother, and I love him. But I understand he's in a very awkward situation. He can't—first of all, he's the only black guy on the tour, number one. It is a lily-white sport. Every tournament he goes to, he's the only black pro. There are no—most of the courses he plays, there's probably only one black member—that's just so they can hold tournaments there. So Tiger is obviously in a unique situation. He can't say the truth.

PATRICK: Lengthening the course at Augusta wipes out about thirty more players from winning. That's why it's not racism. If anything, this *helps* Tiger. Because of his swing—

BARKLEY: Tiger's gonna win, regardless.

PATRICK: Okay, then why would you say it's racism? It makes it easier for him to win if it's longer. You know what? You want to make this tougher for him, make the course shorter, and make the fairways very narrow, and then you bring everybody into the mix. That way—

BARKLEY: You sayin' he can't hit fairways now?

PATRICK: I'm saying that it brings everybody in, Charles. *You* said that I'm saying he couldn't hit fairways. I'm saying this brings everybody in. By lengthening it, you know what? You just took out thirty golfers who hit the ball 280 yards off the tee. Now, is that racism? Is that—

BARKLEY: You can take it how you want to, Dan, and you can disagree with me. But I said what I wanted to say. Those designs are made as a blatant attempt—those attempts are made to influence Tiger's game.[3]

Poor Dan. Barkley wouldn't listen. Woods, especially then, drove the ball longer than almost anybody else. Therefore, a longer court provides Woods with an *advantage*. Indeed, the other, less powerful golfers suffer. A cynic might even argue that, given Woods's ability to deliver higher television ratings, the Masters folks *wanted* to see Tiger in contention. But Barkley nevertheless accused the Masters of racism against the PGA's most popular, money-generating player.

Baseball star Barry Bonds reportedly admitted he "unknowingly" took steroids. Enter actor/activist Danny Glover. "The issue with race," explained Glover, "is that it's always there, but people feel as if they're afraid to talk about it. So they can cloud it up and say, hey, the cat used steroids."[4] So all the media frenzy, the public interest, and the ensuing debate had nothing to do with Bonds's amazing stats, what part steroids might have played in his achievements, and whether his alleged steroid use may have been accidental or purposeful. Nope—it was all about taking a black man down.

KNBR sportscaster Larry Krueger criticized the play of the San Francisco Giants. The Giants, coming off two superb seasons, entered 2005 Barry Bonds-less, and, at the time of the incident involving Krueger—in early August—the team's record stood at forty-five wins, sixty-one losses.

After two difficult losses to the lowly Colorado Rockies, Krueger, a sports commentator at the station for over eight years, teed off: "I cannot watch this brand of baseball any longer. A truly awful, pathetic old team that only promises to be worse two years from now. It's just awful and bad to watch. Brain-dead Caribbean hitters hacking at slop nightly."[5]

Felipe Alou, the Dodger's manager from the Dominican Republic, in his playing days starred as an outfielder with the San Francisco Giants. Now seventy, he entered the 2004 season as a third-year manager for the Giants. After hearing about Krueger's comments, Alou simply went ballistic on ESPN's *Outside the Lines.* Alou called Krueger "this messenger of Satan, as I call this guy now . . . and I believe there is no forgiveness for Satan."[6] Hold the phone.

Can we agree to distinguish between ham-handed remarks and racism? After all, whites can be inarticulate, too. Everyone says something stupid at some time, uttering words they later regret. Sometimes we say them in a moment of emotion, or we just speak thoughtlessly and without malevolent intent.

Can we agree to distinguish between ham-handed remarks and racism?

Did Krueger's comment warrant the accusation of "messenger of Satan"? After all, he quickly apologized and attempted to personally apologize to Alou, who refused to give him an audience.

KNBR promptly suspended Krueger without pay for one week, promising to reinstate him. But, over the next several days, Alou continued to fan the flames and then others weighed in.

Ozzie Guillen, from Venezuela, manages the then high-flying Chicago White Sox. After reporters asked Guillen about Krueger's comments, Guillen lit into him: "That's just ignorant, man. The thing that made me mad is to talk about a guy [Alou] who worked very hard to be where he is, and then some idiot makes some comment and don't know what he's talking about. It's ignorant. It's just ignorant. You have someone dealing with the media, dealing with people, to say something like that, that's ignorant, man."[7]

Ozzie Guillen giving a lecture on civility is tantamount to Michael Jackson opening up a daycare center. In April of 2005, Guillen angrily criticized a former White Sox player, Magglio Ordoñez—like Guillen, a Venezuelan—and said, "He's a piece of (expletive). He's a (expletive), that's what he is. He's another Venezuelan (expletive). (Expletive) him. He has an enemy. Now he has a big one. He knows I can (expletive) him a lot of different ways. He better shut the (expletive) up and play for the Detroit Tigers."[8] What action did baseball take? Nothing.

And get this. Less than a minute following his tee-off on Krueger, Guillen greets a man, apparently a friend, and with reporters still questioning him, shouts, "Hey, everybody, this guy's a homosexual! He's a child molester."[9] The friend took no offense, but after the holier-than-thou demolition of Krueger, Guillen, in front of others, jokingly likens homosexuality to child molestation? Again, Guillen did not intend any malice, but talk about political incorrectness. Imagine the reaction of the fans in San Francisco if manager Alou even jokingly referring to an old friend by saying, "He's a homosexual . . . a child molester." A year later, however, we learn that apparently there is a line even Guillen shouldn't cross. After calling a *Chicago Sun-Times* reporter a "fag," Major League Baseball fined Guillen an undisclosed amount and ordered him to undergo sensitivity training.[10]

When managing the Chicago Cubs, Dusty Baker, a black man, gave a curious explanation as to why his black and Latin ballplayers play better in the sun than do whites: "It's easier for most Latin guys and it's easier for most minority people because most of us come from heat. You don't find too many brothers in New Hampshire and Maine, right? We were brought over here for the heat. Isn't that history? . . . [Black] skin color is more conducive to heat than it is to lighter-skinned people."[11]

Chicago sportswriter Rick Morrissey wrote in the *Chicago Tribune*, "Thank goodness Baker is black and not white. In 1987, Dodgers general manager Al Campanis said blacks lacked the 'necessities' to be baseball managers or general managers. The next year, CBS personality Jimmy 'the Greek' Snyder said blacks were better athletes than whites because they were bred that way. 'This goes all the way back to the Civil War, when a slave owner would breed his big black to his big woman so that he could have a big black kid, see,' he said. The careers of both men were ruined."[12]

Baseball took no action against Dusty Baker for suggesting that white players can't perform well in the sun and, presumably—by logical extension—black players flop in places like Maine or New Hampshire.

But poor KNBR's Krueger. Not only did his employer suspend him for seven days without pay, but a week later they fired him. Why? Well, a few days after the station suspended Krueger, the morning team ridiculed Alou's comparison of Krueger to a "messenger of Satan" on ESPN the previous evening, playing bits about Satan from the irreverent Comedy Central show *South Park*. Krueger, the morning show producer, and the programming director were all canned. Remember, the station suspended Krueger a few days earlier, and Krueger was not even around when his morning show colleagues ran the parody of Alou.

Why? Because Alou continued his attack. "[Caribbeans and others] were offended by that idiot. This guy offended hundreds of millions of Caribbeans."[13]

KNBR's general manager issued this statement:

[L]ate on August 3, Sportsphone 680 Host Larry Krueger made regrettable comments about Caribbean baseball players in lamenting the Giants' loss to the Colorado Rockies. In the heat of describing his disappointment with the Giants' season, Krueger characterized some of the players by their nationality and made a wholly inappropriate analogy. . . . On August 5, KNBR suspended Krueger for one week without pay, while weighing the gravity of his offense.

On August 9, the KNBR Morning Show *opened with a discussion of Felipe Alou's related comments on ESPN's* Outside the Lines, *which aired the previous evening. The segment, featuring inappropriate comedy sound bytes, demonstrated an utter lack of regard for the sensitivity of the issues involved and a premeditated intent to ridicule Felipe Alou's commentary.*

KNBR will not tolerate such behavior and has taken decisive action against the individuals responsible for these unfortunate events. Effective August 10, Program Manager Bob Agnew, Morning Show *Producer Tony Rhein and* Sportsphone 680 *Host Larry Krueger are no longer employed by KNBR. . . .*

We would like to express our deepest apologies to Felipe Alou,

his players and the Giants organization for this offense to the Ca-
ribbean community.[14]

But is there any factual basis for Krueger's remarks? Many people within baseball circles say that Latin ballplayers *do* lack discipline at the plate, and frequently swing at outside pitches. Latino slugger Sammy Sosa once admitted, "It's not easy for a Latin player to take one hundred walks." Sosa said that if he'd learned earlier in his career to take more pitches and be more relaxed, "I would have put up even better numbers."[15] Omar Minaya, the Texas Rangers scout who discovered then sixteen-year-old Sosa in the Dominican Republic, explains, "You've got to understand something about Latin players when they're young. . . . They know the only way to make money is by putting up offensive numbers"[16]—meaning hits, home runs, and RBIs. This is undoubtedly what Krueger meant when he referred to "brain-dead Caribbean hitters hacking at slop."

Moreover, in Krueger's nine-minute rant that day, he criticized not just Caribbean players, but Tony Torcato (a white guy from California), Justin Knoedler (a white guy from Illinois), and Adam Shabala (another white guy from Illinois). He also berated General Manager Brian Sabean for "calling up guys who will be moving pianos in two years," and also told off owner Peter Magowan, saying he should go on vacation to Hawaii and fumigate the Giants' executive offices.[17] Furthermore, although Krueger did say Alou's mind had turned to "Cream of Wheat" during his rant, he also called Alou a "brilliant tactician," and said Alou's job was practically impossible with the personnel decisions made by management.[18]

Alou, however, following the "insult," held a meeting with the Caribbean ball players. He warned them to watch out and be on alert for further verbal abuse.

Why not recommend that his players read Hank Aaron's book, *I Had a Hammer,* and hear the stories of the abuse experienced by baseball pioneers during the Jackie Robinson era? Or listen to the stories experienced by the Hall of Fame ball players like Frank Robinson as they battled discrimination in the minor and major leagues?

Now, however, the number of African-American Major League Baseball players has declined from 27 percent in the mid-1970s to 8.3 percent on 2007's opening day rosters.[19] A problem? Some think so. Cleveland Indian starting pitcher C. C. Sabathia—the only black on last season's twenty-five-man Indians roster—says, "There aren't very many African-American players, and it's not just in [Cleveland], it's everywhere. It's not just a problem—it's a crisis."[20]

"Crisis?" What about the "crisis" of the "overrepresentation" of blacks in football and basketball? Sabathia also seems to see something nefarious about the relatively small number of American-born blacks in baseball, "[I]t's an issue for the whole country. I think Major League Baseball should do something about it. I don't know exactly what they could be doing, but I know it's not enough."[21] Why, by all means, call for a congressional investigation!

Some sports writers happily go along with the blacks-in-sports-as-victims theme. Sports writer Bill Plaschke, for example, a columnist for the *Los Angeles Times*, feels blacks' pain. According to Plaschke, fewer American-born blacks play on Major League Baseball teams because they "prefer to play another sport. . . . [C]ompared to baseball, other major sports provide the average player more quick money. More status. More education. More of the things sadly lacking in inner cities everywhere."[22] Somebody, quick, do something! Encourage inner-city kids to trade in algebra and science books for baseball bats and gloves.

Sports, more so than almost any other field, depends on ability—the fastest, the quickest, the strongest, the most agile succeed. Frequently these skills can be quantified. Either a sprinter runs the hundred meters faster than somebody else, or he doesn't—not a whole lot of room for subjectivity.

Is the lack of American-born black baseball players *really* a problem? If the number of blacks who want to play baseball

declines, should we call out the National Guard? The important question is whether discrimination bars blacks from playing baseball. It doesn't. Players of color—from Asian countries,
Latin countries, and the United States—now comprise about
40 percent of the roster,[23] verses 0 percent pre-Jackie Robinson. Talent, drive, character, self-confidence are what count—
and of all those characteristics, drive is the most important.

If lack of facilities and opportunities prevents inner-city
blacks from playing baseball, how does one explain the large
number of players coming from dirt-poor places in the Caribbean? Many players come from the impoverished Dominican Republic. This area has produced more than its share of great
shortstops: Albert Pujols, Angel Berroa, Juan Uribe, and Alex Ro-
driguez.

All-Star Cesar Izturis and his brother Maicer Izturis respectively play for the L.A. Dodgers and the Los Angeles Angels of
Anaheim. When they were growing up in Venezuela, their father struggled. He barely made enough to buy food for his wife
and six children by delivering fruits and vegetable in an old
pickup truck. Young Cesar and Maicer played baseball in the
street, using makeshift balls and borrowing the gloves of other
players. After a player hit, the boys returned the hitter's glove
and borrowed the one of the next player to hit.[24]

"I felt bad," said their father, Cesar senior, "because I was
their father. They didn't have what the other kids had. . . . My
kids were always the worst-dressed kids. It was agonizing." But
his sons showed real talent. So, what did he do? He sold his
truck for sixty dollars in order to buy baseball gloves and shoes
with cleats for his promising sons, both nine years old at the
time.[25]

Sixteen years later, both sons still remember that day, when
they no longer had to borrow other kids' gloves. "That smell,"
said young Cesar. "It was new." Maicer remembers thinking,
"Now we can catch at the same time other kids practice." But
their father says, "The real payoff was not that they made it to

the big leagues. The real payoff was that day. Even if they never made it, I'd do it again."[26]

Woe to the psyche of the small number of blacks playing at the minor league and college levels. A *Los Angeles Times* columnist wrote about a black college player named Bobby Andrews. His lament? Only a handful of blacks play baseball at the college level. Andrews recounts an early-spring, out-of-town game, when a man shouted from the stands. Although the man didn't point at anyone, or call anyone by name, Andrews says he knew—because he was the only black on the team—that the man had to be talking to him. "He was telling me to go back to where I came from," Andrews said. "He was telling me to go back to Africa."[27] Andrews immediately saw racism. Hey, maybe the guy was telling him to go back to his California college town.

Andrews, mind you, acknowledges that his teammates of three seasons—including the Latino ball players—welcomed and embraced him. Still, he complained, "In this sport, if you are black, you stand out more, people expect more of you. Sometimes I think you have to do something better just because you are black." And if he sees a black player on the opposing team, he goes up to him after the game. "I'll give him a longer handshake, tell him 'good game' more than anybody else," Andrews said. "I let him know I support him. We're different. I have to."[28]

Andrews apparently has no clue about what people like the barrier-breaking Jackie Robinson went through. Do opposing players, as they did to Jackie Robinson, attempt to spike Andrews as he slides into the base? I recently met Hall of Famer Robin Roberts, who pitched many years for the Philadelphia Phillies. Roberts, in the late 1940s, saw his manager say to Robinson, "Jackie, you're a hell of a player. But you're still a nigger." Robinson, according to Roberts, just smiled and walked right by.

In the NBA, approximately 80 percent of the players are

black. Should white kids feel intimidated, insecure, or oppressed because of the lack of people in the locker room who "look like them"?

Notre Dame, in 2001, sought a new football coach. Reverend Jesse Jackson urged the school to hire a man of color because, as Jackson put it, "If a school like Notre Dame makes that breakthrough, it changes the whole mental construct of the issue."[29] Mental construct? In other words, without a black Notre Dame football coach, blacks feel mentally ill-equipped and incapable?

Notre Dame did indeed hire a black man: Tyrone Willingham, a coach formerly with Stanford. After an excellent first season, going 10-3, Willingham's team fell 5-7 in his second season, and after a 6-5 third season Notre Dame canned him with two years left on Willingham's contract.[30] So, is the reverse true? Does it also change the whole mental construct? Should blacks now feel mentally inadequate because coach Willingham failed at Notre Dame?

Black tennis superstars Venus and Serena Williams came from the working-class community of Compton, California, where their father, Richard Williams, invested in property. The Williams' parents saw the potential in their daughters at a young age, and through hard work and focus, Venus and Serena achieved the peak of the tennis world.

Venus and Serena's other sisters are also quite accomplished. One works as an actor and singer, another as a lawyer, and a third was a registered nurse and business owner.

Does the success of his children, in the mind of father Richard, show the declining factor of race in the success of blacks? Apparently not.

On Fox's *The Best Damn Sports Show*, Richard Williams complained, "In America, black peoples [sic] doesn't [sic] really have an opportunity in nothin'. They [sic] not even considered what we call second-class citizen or third-class citizen. They [sic] not even considered a citizen at all. And the reason for that, I really

believe is that the Caucasian peoples [*sic*] in America haven't really realized the damage that they have done to the black race.
It's kinda bad bein' black in America. Actually, I been treated
better in the grave—I haven't gone to the grave yet."

Host Tom Arnold, sensing the tension, attempted to lighten
the moment, "I agree, I hate white people. I'm with you
there. . . . But do Serena and Venus still have to deal—even
at their level, up *here*—do they still have to deal with the racists,
the racism?"

"Yes they do," said Williams. "And what peoples [*sic*] try to
act like, that they are not. I think racism should be talked about,
like what we doin' like right now. And just really talk about it. I
remember the time in the field you was [*sic*] in, like Bill Russell,
and Bill Russell came along, Cascy Jones and all those guys.
Hell, well we had had [*sic*] the same problems today. Does [*sic*]
Venus and Serena had [*sic*] the same problems today? Heck,
yeah. Most people would act superficial with the idea, and present that, 'Oh, I really like you.' In all reality you [*sic*] just a per-
sona non grata to that person. In our reality I think that the dog
is a little more important than some of the figures we been
talkin' 'bout here—tennis—but Venus and Serena's well accepted."

"But there is racism still on the tour?" asked Arnold.

"Yes, there's a lot of racism on the WTA tour," said
Williams. "The WTA tour will act like it's not any there, and try
to hide it, and so on. Right now, actually, we're interviewin'
a lady who told me that—some of the things she told is too
embarassin' to even talk about it, have to walk away. But yes,
there's a lot a racism out there. Matter of fact, when I first came
out there, they tried to bring that against me. Talkin' 'bout, 'You
can't do this! And you can't do this! And since we let you guys
come here, you should really be happy.' I said, 'What the
hell?' . . . So you gotta go with an attitude out there on the tour,
and so on. But you see a lot a racism."

"You look very Mike Tyson right now," said Arnold.

Despite his daughters' success, huge marketing deals, and uptick in television ratings when they appear, Daddy Williams still easily uncovers "evidence" of ... racism. In 2001, Venus Williams withdrew from a match in Indian Wells, California, against her sister, Serena, with four minutes' notice. Venus cited a previously unmentioned knee injury. A disappointed crowd apparently booed the announcement.

Richard Williams claims that the crowd wildly denounced him and his daughters, using threats and racial epithets—notably the "n-word." Serena Williams said that she herself did not hear the "n-word." Venus declined to state that she actually heard the epithets, but supported her father, saying, "I heard what he heard." When asked exactly what words she and her father heard, Venus did not elaborate. According to reports, no one else at Indian Wells heard threats or racial name-calling.

This did not deter Mr. Williams, who called the Indian Wells incident "the worst act of prejudice in America *since the assassination of Martin Luther King* [emphasis added]."[31]

Despite his daughters' success, huge marketing deals, and uptick in television ratings when they appear, Daddy Williams still easily uncovers "evidence" of . . . racism.

How bad is it for black athletes in America? The Davie Brown Index ranks 350 active and retired athletes on their appeal, consumer awareness, influence, and degree of trust—in other words, all the attributes an advertiser is looking for in a product pitchman. The index's Web site calls its approach the new standard for celebrity ratings: "DBI is an index that determines a celebrity's ability to influence brand affinity, consumer buying behavior and purchase intent. . . . DBI represents the un-biased view of the consumer perspective on celebrities."[32]

So next time Charles Barkley or Danny Glover or Richard Williams whines about America's racism toward black athletes, ask them to explain why the top six of seven spots on this index are occupied by nonwhites.

Which athletes top the list? Tiger Woods checks in at number one, with Michael Jordan at number two and Muhammad Ali at number three. Boxer/pitchman George Foreman came in at number four, one slot above cyclist Lance Armstrong. Former basketball player-turned-businessman Magic Johnson occupies the number six spot, with Shaquille O'Neal at number seven.[33]

Notice anything? Only one white guy made it into the top seven. One. Six of the top seven athletes that American consumers like, trust, respect, and listen to are black.

So next time Charles Barkley or Danny Glover or Richard Williams whines about America's racism toward black athletes, ask them to explain why the top six of seven spots on this index are occupied by nonwhites.

10.

EDUCATION

Ladies and gentlemen, the lower economic people are not holding up their end of this deal. These people are not parenting. They are buying things for kids—$500 sneakers for what? And won't spend $250 for "Hooked on Phonics."[1]

—BILL COSBY

You need only do three things to avoid poverty in this country," said UCLA public policy professor emeritus James Q. Wilson. "Finish high school, marry before having a child, and produce the child after the age of twenty. Only 8 percent of families who do this are poor; 79 percent of those who fail to do this are poor."[2] But in many black communities, pursuing academics means "acting white." Incredible.

Former heavyweight champion Lennox Lewis sponsors a Memphis, Tennessee, elementary school chess team, comprised of mostly black youths from an impoverished area.

Lennox came to Memphis years ago to promote his boxing match against Mike Tyson. Lewis, an avid chess player, was invited to meet the local chess club at Oakhaven Elementary School. After a little chess talk and a demonstration game, Lewis promised to keep in touch. Their fledgling chess program desperately needed money for supplies and travel, and they soon received a $14,000 check from the champion. He didn't leave them high and dry; he continued sending money year after year.[3]

With a state championship already under their belts, the next year, the team won the U.S. Chess Federation K-8 national championship. They've also won several state and regional titles. "We were lucky to get connected to him," says math teacher and team founder Jeff Bulington, who started the program to challenge the kids' minds, keep them focused, and keep them off the dangerous neighborhood streets. "It was lashing on to a giant whale that goes by. You get further than you ever would on your own. When the parents of our kids, who were poor, saw them competing successfully against affluent kids, it said something not only about kids, but about the parents themselves and what's possible."[4]

But several of the kids on the team were West African, and their Muslim parents initially balked at allowing their kids to play because they considered chess a form of gambling, and their faith prohibits gambling and images like carved chess pieces. The cross on the king chess piece especially disturbed the parents. But one father, the leader of a local mosque, reluctantly accompanied his kids to a tournament where he saw hundreds of kids competing. The father began to cry. "I asked him where he was going," said Bulington, "and he said, 'I have to pray to God to ask what I did to get this opportunity for my children.'" His son was later accepted at Tennessee Tech with a half scholarship in chess.[5]

The money helped. But Lennox Lewis's belief in them, coupled with the kids' parental support, produced these results. Attitude matters. A positive outlook from a role model—a teacher, a mentor, a parent—matters a *lot*. Focus, hard work, and believing in yourself—all combine to open a world of possibilities for kids.

Students, parents, and teachers marvel at the dedication that Lewis, now retired and no longer needing self-promotion or photo ops, gives to their chess program. "If you start something," says Lewis, "it's important you stay with it. I knew from the beginning what I wanted to do. I wanted to help these kids with their chess and I wanted to help them develop as people."[6]

Oprah Winfrey built a $40 million school for poor black girls in South Africa. Why South Africa? Why not in America? "I became so frustrated with visiting inner-city schools that I just stopped going. The sense that you need to learn just isn't there," she says. She doesn't think American students appreciate the free education offered to them, unlike African students, who have to pay for the privilege of schooling. "If you ask [American] kids what they want or need," says Oprah, "they will say an iPod or some sneakers. In South Africa, they don't ask for money or toys. They ask for uniforms so they can go to school."[7]

Winfrey, in essence, complained about the values of American inner-city kids—values that come from parents who fail to instill an interest and enthusiasm for education. Why? Credit a lifetime of hearing that no matter how hard you work, the white man keeps you down.

Again, money helps, as Lewis and Winfrey show. But students' attitudes determine success or failure. Many educrats, when addressing underperforming schools, say, "If only we had more money." But money without values won't achieve anything.

Federal Judge Russell Clark failed to understand this. In 1985 Clark held the state of Missouri and the Kansas City school district liable for sanctioning a segregated—and inferior—education for urban black kids. Finding that the Kansas City schools engaged in this historical discrimination, which supposedly caused the performance gap between black and white kids, Judge Clark ordered the government to spend billions.[8]

Instead of desegregating by busing black students to suburban schools, Kansas City decided to build fabulous facilities in the inner city, to lure the white kids there. The judge's court order forced the state to pick up 75 percent of the tab, and the school district launched an enormous spending spree.[9]

The district built fifteen new schools. Then it equipped dozens of magnet schools with equipment and personnel for state-of-the-art academic, athletic, and arts programs. One elementary school offered private Suzuki violin lessons for every student. A middle school hired ten "resource teachers" to develop projects in specialty subjects. Kansas City added a Montessori kindergarten and a first-grade Spanish immersion program. Some teachers got raises, while others received reduced workloads. And still they kept spending. . . .[10]

One high school boasts nine hundred top-of-the-line computers, an Olympic-sized swimming pool complete with six diving boards, a padded wrestling room, a classical Greek theater, an eight-lane indoor track, and a professionally equipped gymnastics center.[11] Other renovations included a robotics lab, TV studios, a zoo, a planetarium, and a wildlife sanctuary. Instead of using buses to bring white kids in to the schools, the district hired 120 taxis.[12]

The result? After fifteen years and $2 billion, the Kansas City school district failed all of Missouri's eleven academic performance standards and became the first big-city school district to lose its academic accreditation. All that spending managed to attract several hundred white suburban students in the early 1990s, but many later left. Today, the district is as segregated as ever, with 72 percent black and 8 percent Hispanic students. Test scores remained largely stagnant, and the scoring gap between black and white students has not narrowed.[13]

Kansas City per-pupil spending rocketed to $11,700.[14] So, now what?

Kansas City's local J. S. Chick elementary school came up with another idea. According to *The Christian Science Monitor*, "The court-ordered approach in Kansas City focused on trying to attract white students by creating magnet schools with top-notch facilities and themes ranging from technology to Latin. Meanwhile, African-American teachers and families at Chick, then a neighborhood school, decided to take academic improvement into their own hands."[15] True, educators call it an "African-centered" school. But most likely the results reflect something quite simple. When teachers, students and—most of all—parents commit themselves to high standards, good things happen. Writes the *Monitor*, "On the Missouri Assessment Program (MAP) fourth-grade math test in 2005, 48 percent of Chick students scored at the proficient or advanced level. Statewide, only 24 percent of black students and 36 percent of white students scored that high."[16]

Similarly, a "Latino-themed school" seems to show some slight improvement of grades. Principal Marcos Aguilar of Los Angeles public charter school La Academia Semillas del Pueblo, who, in an interview said about white culture, "We don't necessarily want to go to white schools. What we want to do is teach ourselves, teach our children the way we have of teaching. We don't want to drink from a white water fountain, we have our own wells and our natural reservoirs and our way of collecting rain in our aqueducts. We don't need a white water fountain. So the whole issue of segregation and the whole issue of the civil rights movement is all within the box of white culture and white supremacy."[17]

In an interview on NPR, Aguilar said: "Nowhere in the Constitution of the United States or in the Declaration of Independence does it say that because you come here, you now have to become an American. The United States is who is the immigrants here, not us."[18]

The students, who came out of horribly performing schools, achieved higher marks on test scores. But while Principal Aguilar attributes the success to the Latino-themed nature of the school, the reason likely rests elsewhere. As with Kansas City's J. S. Chick school, La Academia Semillas del Pueblo requires parental involvement. The school holds parents to high standards just as they do with children. Again, when a committed, caring parent emphasizes education and convinces children of its value, good things happen.

Did the emphasis on Latino or African-American self-esteem help? Studies show that black kids actually score at least as high if not higher on self-esteem tests as do whites. A University of North Carolina at Chapel Hill study found that "the average black young person's self-esteem falls at about the fifty-sixth percentile of self-esteem for white children and adolescents."[19] In other words, a full six points above the average white kids' percentile.

Ultimately, improved self-esteem comes from achievement, not the other way around. Sooner or later, upwardly mobile students enter a competitive world where results are dictated by hard work and talent, and not by a "you owe me" sense of entitlement.

But so-called black leaders don't understand the simple truth that what a person earns—what a person has to pay for, has to fight for—is always more valued than what is given to a person. In an NPR interview in January 2003, Al Sharpton said, "I believe in public education, do not believe in going into privatization, whether that be through vouchers or other schemes."[20] He's not alone. The Democratic Party, the NAACP, and many "black leaders" reject the notion of school vouchers, despite the fact that many inner-city parents are begging for them.

Ultimately, improved self-esteem comes from achievement, not the other way around.

In 1993, surveys found that up to 88 percent of blacks favored school choice.[21] That year, California's Education Vouchers Initiative, or Proposition 174, lost statewide but drew its strongest support from blacks, conservatives, and private school parents.[22] To show their support for Proposition 174 and school vouchers, a group of blacks rallied at the Capitol in Sacramento. "I can think for myself. I can make choices for myself," said Pastor S. C. Carthen, "African-Americans can be diverse. I can decide where my child goes to school." Another black said, "We need something like Proposition 174 to act as a vehicle to help uplift ourselves." And finally, Pastor Phillip Godeaux said, "The issue is: What are we getting for our taxpayer dollars?"[23] The proposition failed that November, but not for lack of support among blacks.

According to the Joint Center for Political and Economic Studies, support for school vouchers among all blacks stands, as of 2000, at 60 percent.[24] A 1999 National Opinion Poll conducted for the Center found that a whopping 87 percent of black parents, ages twenty-six to thirty-five, want vouchers.[25] Many high-profile Democrats in Washington, D.C., send their own kids to private schools, presumably for a better education. Yet "black leaders" and Democrats—strongly supported by teachers' unions—routinely block voucher efforts.

Indeed, poll after poll finds vouchers the most popular among people who most wish to opt out of the command and control of the government's school system—inner-city parents. In Oakland, where administrators pushed "Ebonics" in the late '90s, the average black kid checked in with a D-plus grade point average. Yet Asian and white students at the same schools maintained a B average.[26] In Los Angeles, a recent study showed that only 44 percent of high school students received a high school diploma.[27] (The study did not take into consideration students who dropped out or who were getting their GEDs.)

Do kids get a better education at private schools? Nationwide, 22.5 percent of parents who are also public school teachers send their own kids to private schools, compared to 17.5 percent of parents who are not teachers. And the numbers go up dramatically in major urban school systems, according to a 2000 census by the Fordham Institute. In Baltimore, 35.1 percent of households with a teacher send their kids to private school, versus 20.9 percent for nonteacher parents. In Chicago, it's 38.7

Kwame Kilpatrick, the mayor of Detroit, agreed—at least initially.

Enter the teachers' union and their customary resistance to anything that jeopardizes the status quo—their jobs, their security, their pay. The union balked and began talking of a "takeover" by outsiders. Soon, they whipped out—you guessed it—the race card! The mayor grew wobbly. Suddenly, he too expressed concern over the encroaching, looming, nefarious, evil cloud of privatization. Detroit's unionized public school teachers staged a one-day walkout and demonstration at the state capitol. The mayor withdrew his support, and the deal collapsed.[40] "You've got a lot of poison in the air," said Mayor Kilpatrick, "People here are sensitive about white people bossing them around."[41]

Thompson tried again, this time teaming up with the Skillman Foundation—a black nonprofit with a long history of working with Detroit schools—and former Detroit Piston's basketball star Dave Bing. For Bing's efforts, a group called the Call 'Em Out Coalition gave the basketball star the "Sambo Sell-Out Award." Democratic City Councilwoman Sharon McPhail, at the group's annual dinner, handed out the award.[42] Lovely.

The black de-emphasis on education appears to be a fairly recent phenomenon. During slavery, laws criminalized anyone who taught a slave to read and write. Yet within just a few decades after emancipation, more than 70 percent of blacks could read and write.

Economist Thomas Sowell writes about the excellent all-black schools he attended growing up in New York: "The test scores in ordinary Harlem schools in the 1940s were quite comparable to the test scores in the white working-class neighborhoods on New York's Lower East Side. Sometimes the Harlem schools scored a little higher and sometimes the Lower East Side schools scored a little higher, but there were no such glaring racial disparities as we have become used to in urban schools in recent years."[43]

Today, many blacks openly tease other blacks for "sounding white" and attacking those with high aspirations as "thinking you're better than somebody else."

Marva Collins, the woman who founded the celebrated Westside Preparatory School in inner-city Chicago in 1975, believes some of the keys to improving education are holding children up to high standards and getting the parents involved. Every school day begins with recitation of the Marva Collins Creed, which includes lines such as, "I promise that each day shall be gained, not lost; used, not thrown away." The students are taught that they own—and are responsible for—their education.[44]

Today, many blacks openly tease other blacks for "sounding white" and attacking those with high aspirations as "thinking you're better than somebody else."

Marva Collins's schools also reject any need for a "culturally relevant" curriculum. They use the Socratic method of teaching, with questions, answers, and logical analysis, to develop kids' reasoning skills, and to enable them to truly understand the material. The students study classical literature because "the content of classical literature is challenging and helps to enhance vocabulary skills and provides profound writing topics for our students."[45]

In San Bernardino County, California, however, the school board is going in an entirely different direction. In 2005 they adopted a program for Ebonics.

Cal State San Bernardino sociology professor Mary Texeira says, "Ebonics is a different language, it's not slang as many believe. For many of these students Ebonics is their language, and it should be considered a foreign language. These students should be taught like other students who speak a foreign language."[46] A foreign language?

Call this the "Ebonicization of education." This mirrors the philosophy of a Los Angeles English teacher who wrote "Man vs. Ho" on his classroom's white board, to get his students to learn by discussing the lyrics of the late rapper Tupac Shakur: "Blaze up, gettin' with hos through my pager." This teacher is not alone, according to the *Los Angeles Times*, "Teachers nationwide are using rap—the street-savvy, pop-locking, rhyming creations of Shakur, Geto Boys, Run-DMC and others—to teach history and English. Some colleges even train future educators to weave rap into high school lessons."[47] Rap classes probably won't be found at Beverly Hills High or private college prep schools, though. Isn't it condescending to think that poor, black, inner-city students "need" to be taught in rap before they can master standard English?

Shelby Steele, a research fellow at the Hoover Institution, a public policy center at Stanford, and a political essayist who taught college English for nearly 25 years, is appalled. Steele, a black man, said, "I would be outraged to find out my child is being subjected to Tupac Shakur in an academic classroom." Steele says kids can learn rap lyrics on their own time. Like Marva Collins, Steele says that in school "they need to be taught great literature."[48]

Ebonics is *not* "black English." David H. Fischer, in his book, *Albion Seed*, calls Ebonics a bastardization of Standard English from Britain. British immigrants to Virginia brought over a pre-Revolutionary War dialect that later spread throughout the South. Where Northerners would say, "I am," "you are," "she isn't" and "I haven't," Virginians said, "I be," "you be," "she ain't, and "I hain't." Southerners tended to embellish vowels and soften consonants, thus "pretty" became "puriddy" and "with" became "wid." According to Fischer, these speech patterns were regional dialects spoken throughout the south and west of England during the seventeenth century, although, under pressure by fellow Englishmen to speak "proper English," these speech patterns began to disappear in England. "In the twentieth century," says Fischer, "words like 'dis' or 'dat' were rarely heard in any part of rural

England, but they persisted among poor whites and blacks in the American South." Over the years a few African-origin words fell in, but, says Fischer, "The major features of the Virginia accent . . . were established before African slaves could possibly have had much impact on language."[49]

Low standards and lower expectations plague schools all across America. Yes, the American economy remains the world's most productive, with American workers, on a per capita basis, producing more than anybody else. But our declining educational standards, K through 12, threaten that prosperity. Recent studies show American students underperforming in important subjects compared to Asian and many European students.

Public schools find it difficult to attract quality teachers in math and sciences. Blame the lockstep pay schedule, which pays an English teacher as much as a hard-to-find teacher in math, chemistry, or biology. Prospective math and science teachers can choose from many options, including lucrative opportunities in the private sector. But teachers' unions oppose merit pay, or adjusting pay schedules to reflect supply and demand. Why should scarce physics teachers and plentiful English teachers earn the same money? Credentialing also shuts out potential teachers. Most states require some sort of "certification," a process that excludes competition and bolsters job security for "credentialed" teachers.

The unions also protect incompetent teachers, in some estimates numbering as high as nearly 10 percent of all teachers. School districts, wary of the high cost and legal battle of fighting the union when trying to fire a teacher, try different approaches. Economist Tom Sowell writes that teachers are often offered a lump sum, in addition to their pension, to retire early. Or the district transfers the incompetent teacher to another school where parents are less likely to complain. And if do they complain, the incompetent teacher is transferred again. Sowell calls this the "dance of the lemons." Schools with parents who are affluent and well-educated are more likely to transfer bad teachers. Schools where parents are not as in-volved, influential, or articulate are most likely to get stuck with the worst teachers.[50]

The reverse happens, too. Good, hardworking, disciplined teachers, and others who expect students to meet certain stan-dards of behavior, often fail to get support from the administra-tion. One school bus driver in Santa Clara, California, trying to maintain order after a fight between two black students, made two dozen black students sit at the front of the bus where he could keep a better eye on them. The result? Charges of segrega-tion, racism, and an investigation by the school district and the NAACP.[51]

Consider the plight of Scott Phelps, a teacher at Muir High School in Pasadena, California, for twelve years. Phelps posted an e-mail in a school district chat room—later distributing it to his fellow teachers—discussing recent scores of the school's stu-dents on the Academic Performance Index. He committed the politically incorrect sin of wondering why low socioeconomic African-American students, as a group, have historically scored lower on standardized tests, and why many seemed to lack aca-demic focus. "If you look at their scores and track them over the years you will see that they're horrible," said Phelps. "I'm not singling out a group. I'm not saying that low test scores are caused by low socioeconomic students, I'm saying that low scores and low socioeconomic students are directly related."[52]

Further, Phelps audaciously suggested that, of the students who engage in disruptive behavior, black students are dispro-portionately involved. "Overwhelmingly," Phelps wrote, "the students whose behavior makes the hallways deafening, who yell out for the teacher and demand immediate attention in class, who cannot seem to stop chatting and are fascinated by each other and relationships but not with academics, in short, whose behavior saps the strength and energy of us that are at the front lines, are African-American. . . . Eventually, someone in power will have the courage to say this publicly. . . . Class is something they do between passing periods, lunch or nutrition break, when they chase each other in the hallways, into class-rooms, yelling at the top of their lungs."[53]

The resulting uproar got Phelps suspended. But at town hall meetings parents and even some black students and teachers demanded that the popular and widely respected teacher return. Kitty McKnight, a black teacher for forty years who graduated from Muir and sent her two sons there, literally leaped up from her seat to defend Phelps. "I cannot sit and listen to this!" she shouted. "Our boys are out of control. We have to do something. We are losing our boys!" She later admitted feeling guilty for her past inaction, "Having been a teacher all these years, I never made it a point. But it's true. You talk to another black teacher about the behavior of black students and they know exactly what you mean. I feel like I'm at fault for not addressing it sooner."[54] The school board reinstated Phelps.

Things didn't work out so well for Josh Kaplowitz, who, fresh out of Yale, turned his back on lucrative career options—Wall Street or a profession in corporate America. He wanted instead to participate in President Clinton's Teach For America (TFA) program. He felt strongly about raising educational standards for black kids, and accepted a position at an inner-city elementary school. He shortly realized that he was in a system where hard work, good intentions, and desire only carry you so far. When he submitted his students' first report cards in November, most of them received Ds because their numerous quizzes and tests showed they fell far below the expected standards at their grade level. He explained to all the parents that their kids' grades would improve once they started behaving and the students did their assigned lessons. Kaplowitz believed he was making real progress. Did the school support him?[55]

The principal called him in and demanded that he raise the grades. Kaplowitz explained that the grades were what the students deserved and offered to show the principal the students' portfolios. Kaplowitz was cited for insubordination, and then told that he would be transferred to a second-grade class because he "would be able to control younger students more effectively."[56]

One day, Kaplowitz tried to quiet a particularly disruptive boy. Frustrated, Kaplowitz escorted the child toward the door, with his hand on the small of the kid's back, then nudged the kid into the hall and closed the door, turning his attention back to the rest of his students. The kid's mother—who happened to be in the school at the time to discuss placing her son in a class for emotionally disturbed children—called the cops. She claimed that Kaplowitz physically abused her son, and accused him of violently shoving her son in the chest, causing injuries to his head and back. The police arrested Kaplowitz, and he spent a night in jail. (Normally, this was not police practice, but, as luck would have it, Kaplowitz got arrested on September 11, 2001, and the preoccupied department kept Kaplowitz locked up for the entire night.)[57]

Kaplowitz was acquitted at his criminal trial, but the school district settled a $20 million lawsuit for $75,000. Kaplowitz, who started out anxious and enthusiastic, learned a horrible lesson about the workings of the inner-city public school system. "I know for sure that inner-city schools don't have to be hellholes . . . ," says Kaplowitz, "with their poor administration and lack of parental support, their misguided focus on children's rights, their antiwhite racism, and their lawsuit-crazed culture. Some of my closest TFA friends . . . went on to teach at charter schools, where they really can make a difference in underprivileged children's lives."[58]

Despite the underperformance of many inner-city blacks, many public schools still focus the kids' attention on . . . racism.

The Seattle public school system put out a paper called *Delivering on the Dream: Academic Achievement for Every Student in Every School*. Under "Equity and Race Relations," they include several definitions of racism taken from an educator's sourcebook called *Teaching for Diversity and Social Justice*:

Racism: The systematic subordination of members of targeted racial groups who have relatively little social power in the United

States (Blacks, Latino/as, Native Americans, and Asians), by the members of the agent racial group who have relatively more social power (Whites). The subordination is supported by the actions of individuals, cultural norms and values, and the institutional structures and practices of society.

Individual Racism: The beliefs, attitudes, and actions of individuals that support or perpetuate racism. Individual racism can occur at both an unconscious and conscious level, and can be both active and passive. Examples include telling a racist joke, using a racial epithet, or believing in the inherent superiority of whites.

Active Racism: Actions which have as their stated or explicit goal the maintenance of the system of racism and the oppression of those in the targeted racial groups. People who participate in active racism advocate the continued subjugation of members of the targeted groups and protection of "the rights" of members of the agent group. These goals are often supported by a belief in the inferiority of people of color and the superiority of white people, culture and values.

Passive Racism: Beliefs, attitudes, and actions that contribute to the maintenance of racism, without openly advocating violence or oppression. The conscious or unconscious maintenance of attitudes, beliefs, and behaviors that support the system of racism, racial prejudice and racial dominance.

Cultural Racism: Those aspects of society that overtly and covertly attribute value and normality to white people and Whiteness, and devalue, stereotype, and label people of color as "other," different, less than, or render them invisible. Examples of these norms include defining white skin tones as nude or flesh colored, having a future time orientation, emphasizing individualism as opposed to a more collective ideology, defining one form of English as standard, and identifying only Whites as great writers or composers.

Institutional Racism: The network of institutional structures, policies, and practices that create advantages and benefits for

Whites, and discrimination, oppression, and disadvantages for peo-
ple from targeted racial groups. The advantages created for Whites
are often invisible to them, or are considered "rights" available to
everyone as opposed to "privileges" awarded to only some individu-
als and groups.[59]

Kind of makes you long for the good old days, when there
was just one kind of racism. It was bad, but at least it was easy to
spot. Thankfully, the Seattle schools removed this page from
their Web site for "revision," due to the strong, angry reaction.

Never mind that blacks have an easier time getting into college than whites.

But a recent "Black Youth Project" study, conducted by researchers at the University of Chicago, shows widespread psychological defeatism among blacks. The survey examined the
attitudes of 1,590 blacks age fifteen to twenty-five. Sixty-one
percent believe "it is hard for young black people to get ahead
because of discrimination,"[60] yet 48 percent say "they were dis-
criminated against *rarely or never* because of their race."[61] Sixty-
eight percent believe "the government would do more to find a
cure for AIDS if more white people had the disease."[62] Lessons
like the one the Seattle school system sought to teach—that
"the system" holds blacks back—have already been delivered.

Never mind that blacks have an easier time getting into college than whites. In one study of twenty-eight elite colleges and
universities, only one in four whites with SAT scores between
1,250 and 1,300 out of a possible 1,600 got admitted. For blacks
scoring between 1,250 and 1,300, three out of four received ac-
ceptance notices.[63] Blacks need to understand that the educational system is not rigged against them.

When blacks fail to match the aptitude test scores of whites, some attribute this to "cultural bias." Of college-bound seniors in 2006, whites averaged a score of 527 on the critical reading portion of their SAT. Blacks averaged 434. For the writing section, whites averaged 519, blacks 428. For mathematics, whites averaged 536, and blacks averaged 429.[64] Some educators attribute this to cultural bias. Cultural bias? What's biased about two plus two equaling four?

And if the test is culturally biased, how to explain the superior performance of Asian and Pacific Island students? Many Asian students attend the same inner-city schools attended by blacks, and English is not the primary language in some Asian homes. Yet Asian and Pacific Islanders received average scores of 510 on reading, 512 on writing, and 578 on math.[65] So much for cultural bias.

For real "cultural bias," look how the Duke faculty responded after three of their lacrosse players were accused of raping the black stripper. About three weeks after the alleged incident at the lacrosse team party, a full-page ad appeared in Duke's student-run newspaper, *The Chronicle*. Headlined with a large font, "What Does a Social Disaster Sound Like?" included students' anonymous quotes sandwiched between an introduction and conclusion.

The ad began, "Regardless of the results of the police investigation, what is apparent everyday now is the anger and fear of many students who know themselves to be objects of racism and sexism." The students' quotes included: "We go to school with racist classmates, we go to gym with people who are racists." Another read: "Being a big, black man, it's hard to walk anywhere at night, and not have a campus police car slowly drive by me." And another: "I was talking to a white woman student who was asking me, 'Why do people—and she meant black people—make race such a big issue?' They don't see race. They just don't see it." The ad concluded: "We're turning up the volume in a moment when some of the most vulnerable among us are being asked to quiet down while we wait. To the students speaking individually and to the protestors making collective noise, thank you for not waiting and for making yourselves heard."[66]

It was signed by Duke faculty, which came to be known as the "Group of 88." For many months, the ad was maintained on a Web page hosted by the Department of African and African-American Studies.[67]

Then—after the truth about the DNA evidence came out, after the district attorney was under ethics investigations and he recused himself, after Duke's president invited the accused lacrosse players to return to school—a full ten months after the original incident, a new "open letter to the Duke community," signed by eighty-seven "concerned faculty" members, was posted. This new letter said the original ad "has been broadly, and often intentionally, misread. . . . The disaster is the atmosphere that allows sexism, racism, and sexual violence to be so prevalent on campus. The ad's statement that the problem 'won't end with what the police say or the court decides' is as clearly true now as it was then." The letter did offer one minor retraction from the original ad: "We do not endorse every demonstration that took place at the time." But then the new letter continued: "We appreciate the efforts of those who used the attention the incident generated to raise issues of discrimination and violence. . . . We stand by the claim that issues of race and sexual violence on campus are real."[68]

Immediately, the left-leaning faculty used this incident to propagate their world-view that racism remains problem number one in America. But even after all that later transpired, they barely back down. They're not even embarrassed. They still don't get it. And they remain perpetually angry victicrats.

Dr. James Sherley, a black professor of biological engineering at MIT, attributes his denial of tenure because of "racist attitudes" at MIT. He vowed to go on a hunger strike until granted tenure: "I will either see the Provost resign and my hard-earned tenure granted at MIT, or I will die defiantly right outside his office," Sherley writes. "This is the strength of my conviction that racism in America must end." MIT says they followed "well-established procedures" for tenure, and "are confident it was followed with integrity in this case."[69] Perhaps, just perhaps, Sherley's colleagues consider him not quite good enough. Or, perhaps, they take offense at offering lifetime jobs to those who threaten hunger strikes if they fail to get their own way.

Or how about the always peeved black professor Cornel West, a professor of religion at Princeton University? Before his current position, he taught at Harvard. West left Harvard in a huff because Harvard's then new president, Lawrence H. Summers, former Treasury secretary under Clinton, dared to chastise West for grade inflation (90 percent of students in his Introduction to African-American Studies course received As),[70] and for not producing scholarly work. What was West doing instead of the expected professorial pursuits? Among other endeavors, he served as campaign advisor to then presidential hopeful Al Sharpton. West also cut a rap CD with lyrics like this:

> *From the heights of rich African humanity,*
> *to the depth of sick American barbarity,*
> *in the whirlwinds of white supremacy,*
> *black people preserved their sanity and dignity. . . .*
> *No other people in the modern world have had*
> *such unprecedented levels of unregulated violence*
> *against them.*[71]

West considered it "racist" that Summers dismissed his rap CD and the time he spent advising Al Sharpton as "nonscholarly." So off he trucked to Princeton, where the school welcomed him with open arms.

Professor West also accompanied Harry Belafonte and Danny Glover to Venezuela in 2006, where their delegation met with president Hugo Chavez for six hours, and Belafonte assured Chavez, "No matter what the greatest tyrant in the world, the greatest terrorist in the world, George W. Bush, says, we're here to tell you: Not hundreds, not thousands, but millions of the American people . . . support your revolution."[72]

According to Peter Schweizer in *Do As I Say (Not As I Do): Profiles in Liberal Hypocrisy*, West, a self-proclaimed Marxist, believes that "without socialism, 'we are simply headed toward Armageddon. I mean race war.' . . . Moreover," writes Schweizer, "blacks who try to escape urban poverty by starting their own business or otherwise striving upward are condemned as race traitors and sellouts. . . . With the fire and brimstone of a preacher, he attacks middle-class blacks who are 'preoccupied with getting over—with acquiring pleasure, property and power.' West despises middle-class blacks who have embraced the 'culture of consumption' and want to send their kids to Ivy League colleges so they can 'get a better job (for direct selfish reasons).'"[73]

West often lectures students against the perils of materialism. West talks the talk, but fails to walk the walk, as Peter Schweizer writes:

> *West is himself the consummate entrepreneurial capitalist. With an appetite for expensive cars, thousand-dollar suits, and million-dollar homes, the question isn't whether he's willing to die for the cause, but whether he is willing to take a meager pay cut.[74]*
>
> *[T]he Marxist critic was famous for cruising around town in his "plush Cadillac Sedan de Ville."[75]*
>
> *Privately, this socialist paragon revealed his true colors when he bought homes in two of Boston's best neighborhoods. According to real estate records, he bought a condominium valued at $820,000 on Boylston Street, while his primary home on Commonwealth Avenue in Newton cost him more than a million. . . . Naturally, the Wests also hired a maid.[76]*
>
> *West has repeatedly lambasted other upwardly mobile blacks for abandoning the inner city and moving into white neighborhoods. . . . [H]e called middle-class blacks "decadent" for abandoning their "brothers and sisters" and fleeing to the suburbs and their*

shopping malls. For those who may be wondering about West's fla-vor of choice, the black population in Newton is only 2 percent.[77]

So West walks a fine line. Successful, a life of hard work cou-pled with drive and talent, he still doesn't say, "Hot damn, I busted my butt and made it. Maybe if you bust your butt you, too, can make it." So, he makes a different pitch—I made it, but The Man holds everybody else back. He manages to pull this off while living high, probably, as a tenured professor, working only a few hours a week, all without fear of losing his job.

11.

BLACK MUSLIMS IN AMERICA

[A]mong all Negroes the black convict is the most perfectly preconditioned to hear the words, "the white man is the devil."[1]

—MALCOLM X, AS TOLD TO ALEX HALEY

In *Because They Hate*, Christian Lebanese writer Brigitte Gabriel describes the genesis of the hostility toward the "infidels." Simply put, many Muslims grow up hating Christians, Jews, and any other non-Muslim. They learn this from parents, and from the moment they enter school. And Islamofascists want to call black American Muslims to jihad.

Why target American blacks for recruitment? Al Qaeda, writes *Investor's Business Daily*, "seeks to lower its Arab profile for future attacks. Savvy about U.S. politics, the terror group knows law enforcement wouldn't dare profile African-Americans. And recently, al-Qaeda has tailored its recruiting directly to blacks living here.

"In a videotaped message aired last year, for example, an al-Qaeda operative known as Azzam the American invited blacks to convert to Islam and take revenge against a nation that enslaved their ancestors. . . . There are an estimated two million black Muslims in America, and that segment of the Muslim population is growing fastest—outstripping Muslim immigration from the Mideast and Pakistan."[2]

In May 2007, al Qaeda's Ayman al-Zawahri likened the struggle against "infidels" to the struggle against racism, and openly encouraged American blacks to spill their blood in al Qaeda's jihad against the "injustice" of the American "oppressors." Al-Zawahri repeatedly invoked the name of the "struggler and martyr" Malcolm X. "I want blacks in America to know that when we wage jihad in Allah's path, we aren't waging jihad to lift oppression from the Muslims only," al-Zawahri said. "We are waging jihad to lift oppression from all mankind."[3]

Mark Silverberg, author of The Quartermasters of Terror: Saudi Arabia and the Global Islamic Jihad, writes, "In 2005, Robert Mueller, Director of the F.B.I., told the Senate Intelligence Committee that 'prisons continue to be fertile ground for extremists who exploit both a prisoner's conversion to Islam while still in prison, as well as their socioeconomic status and placement in the community upon their release.' According to published reports, radical Islamists have put a high priority on reaching disaffected inmates and recruiting them for their own deadly purposes. . . . The conversion program is funded with Saudi money through the National Islamic Prison Foundation, an organization that underwrites 'prison outreach' but whose real goal is the conversion of large numbers of inmates (primarily African-American) . . . not only to Wahhabism, but to its radical Islamist agenda . . . and the effort is both successful and, for the most part, hidden from public view."[4]

Captured al Qaeda training manuals make it clear they seek to covert imprisoned blacks to Islam, in hopes that they might induce some to attack America. According to The Washington Times:

Recruiting new operatives takes up several pages of the al Qaeda training manual, which describes recruiting as "the most dangerous task that an enlisted brother can perform."

The manual lists as "candidates" for recruitment those persons "disenchanted with their country's policies"; convicted criminals, especially smugglers; adventurers; workers at coffee shops, restaurants and hotels; security personnel at borders, airports and seaports; and "people in need."

A key area of recruitment, the sources said, are U.S. prisons and jails, where al Qaeda and other organizations have found men who have already been convicted of violent crimes and have little or no loyalty to the United States.

"It's literally a captive audience, and many inmates are anxious to hear how they can attack the institutions of America," said one federal corrections official.[5]

Dr. Walid Phares, a senior fellow at the Foundation for Defense of Democracies in Washington, D.C., wrote a book called *Future Jihad*. Phares specializes in analyzing the ideologies and strategies of Islamoterrorists, and their role in regional, local, and Western Jihadic groups. He sees a surge of these movements in the Middle East, as well as in the West, Africa, and South Asia. He testifies, advises, and conducts briefings in Congress, the State Department, the Department of Justice, Homeland Security, the European Parliament, the UN Security Council, and other foreign ministries. In short, when Phares talks, people listen—or at least, they should.

"[T]he Mohammed Atta type of terrorist," writes Phares, "is not in the majority anymore. Today, 2006–2007, the new *Jihadists* are mostly U.S.-born, speak the language well, are educated and operate within the system. And more importantly, they benefit from a militant political shield, which protects them as they grow ideologically and organizationally. In the past few months, more evidence is emerging on the deep influence the pro-*Jihadist* groups have developed inside the country. The wall protecting the spread of the Wahhabi-Salafi, and even Khomeinist ideologies in America has become close to being legal, after it has thickened politically.

"The mutation of Jihadism *inside the US is the single most important challenge the country will face in this decade and maybe beyond* [emphasis added]. The incapacitation of the US Government in its counter *Jihadist* efforts has become the central breach in national security."[6]

A "Khomeinist" follows the practices and preachings of the radical Ayatollah Khomeini of Iran. Wahhabism—or, as its practitioners prefer, Salafism—is the predominate form of Islam practiced in Saudi Arabia, birthplace of Osama bin Laden. "As a teen-ager," according to a post–9/11 article on the al Qaeda head in *Forbes* magazine, "bin Laden joined the ultraconservative *Wahhabi* sect of Islam and served with the police enforcing *sharia* laws. (The Wahhabi movement is supported by the Saudi monarchy, among others, and today is one of the fastest growing tendencies in the Islamic world; it is ultra-puritanical and anti-modern; in things like avoiding contact with women or nonbelievers.)"[7]

Dr. Michael Waller—an expert on foreign propaganda—in his October 2003 Senate testimony, called the Islamic Society of North America (ISNA) a powerful Saudi-supported Islamic educational organization. It certifies Wahhabi-trained chaplains to the U.S. Bureau of Prisons. The ISNA seeks to impose Wahhabi religious conformity on American Islam.[8] Dr. Waller argues that the National Islamic Prison Foundation wants to convert American inmates to Wahhabism.[9]

"The FBI," writes *Investor's Business Daily*, "says black Americans have become al-Qaida's top recruiting target since 9-11. It wants to use terrorists who are non-Arab Muslims—preferably hip, English-speaking Americans—to lower the group's profile and avoid suspicion in carrying out strikes on America. Black Americans are less likely to attract the same level of scrutiny at security checkpoints, especially given law enforcement's fear of being accused of racially profiling blacks.

"Al-Qaida's recruiting ground of choice in America, surpassing hard-line mosques, is now prisons. Islam is the fastest-growing religion in U.S. prisons and military brigs, and the ranks of Muslim inmates at state and federal facilities have swelled to an estimated 200,000. Most happen to be black men."[10]

The total number of Muslims in America is estimated to be over 4.5 million.[11] Many of them are black converts. Some of them belong to the Nation of Islam, a separatist, anti-Semitic group that consistently condemns America. The number of Nation of Islam members is unknown, with estimates ranging from ten thousand to one hundred thousand.

The Nation of Islam (NOI) makes no secret about its separatist agenda. Its Web site lists its ten-point "Muslim Program." The list includes demands for freedom, equality, and justice, and calls for the release of all those serving death sentences in state or federal prisons who believe in the Nation of Islam. NOI wants no taxation for all blacks, separate taxpayer-supported Muslim schools for blacks, and calls for women to receive education in colleges and universities specifically for women. The Nation prohibits "intermarriage and race-mixing."[12]

"We want our people in America," continues the list of demands, "whose parents or grandparents were descendants from slaves, to be allowed to establish a separate state or territory of their own—either on this continent or elsewhere. We believe that our former slave masters are obligated to provide such land and that the area must be fertile and minerally rich. We believe that our former slave masters are obligated to maintain and supply our needs in this separate territory for the next twenty to twenty-five years—until we are able to produce and supply our own needs."[13]

For further insight, consider NOI's leader, Minister Louis Farrakhan, and a few of his discerning comments:

"These false Jews promote the filth of Hollywood that is seeding the American people and the people of the world and bringing you down in moral strength. . . . It's the wicked Jews, the false Jews that are promoting lesbianism, homosexuality. It's wicked Jews, false Jews that make it a crime for you to preach the word of God, then they call you homophobic!"—Farrakhan at Saviours' Day, Chicago, Illinois, February 26, 2006[14]

"The war in Iraq is not your war; that's Israel's war. . . . The rudder that is turning America is not your elected officials; it's that small influential group of neo-conservatives that are using America's power to destroy the enemies of Israel."—Farrakhan at 12th Annual Pre-Kwanzaa Festival held by Cops Against Police Brutality, Newark, New Jersey, December 11, 2004[15]

"White people are potential humans . . . they haven't evolved yet."—Farrakhan quoted in *Philadelphia Inquirer*, March 18, 2000[16]

"It is not accidental that the Black male is in the condition he is in . . ." This is because of a "conspiracy of our government against the Black male" along with "our [Blacks'] failure to accept responsibility for our actions"—Farrakhan on *Meet the Press*, October 12, 1997[17]

"German Jews financed Hitler right here in America. . . . International bankers financed Hitler and poor Jews died while big Jews were at the root of what you call the Holocaust. . . . Little Jews died while big Jews made money. Little Jews [were] being turned into soap while big Jews washed themselves with it. Jews [were] playing violin, Jews [were] playing music, while other Jews [were] marching into the gas chambers"—Farrakhan at Mosque Maryam, Chicago, March 19, 1995.[18]

"I'm warning you, America. You better get rid of them neocons. That's the synagogue of Satan. They have made America weak. You're a weak nation now, and your country has been taken from you by the synagogue of Satan. They own Congress. That's why the Congress ain't right."—Farrakhan at Saviours' Day, Chicago, Illinois, February 26, 2006[19]

"A decree of death has been passed on America. The judgment of God has been rendered and she must be destroyed." —Louis Farrakhan to followers, August 9, 1997[20]

Followers of Farrakhan give the minister a pass for his acknowledged role in the assassination of black activist Malcolm

X. Malcolm X renounced his affiliation with the Nation of Islam, forming another organization called Muslim Mosque, Inc.[21] After Malcolm visited Mecca and saw that people of all colors, including whites, worshipped side by side, he reconsidered the Nation of Islam's mantra of calling all whites "white devils."[22]

He returned to America with a more open, humanist philosophy. Months later, as Malcolm X delivered a lecture, several people in the audience opened fire, killing Malcolm in front of his wife and children.

A jury convicted three men with ties to the Nation of Islam and they were sentenced to life in prison. Years later, one of Malcolm X's daughters, Qubilah Bahiyah Shabazz, as an act of revenge, planned to kill Minister Farrakhan. Authorities arrested her, charging her with hiring a hit man to kill Farrakhan. (The charges were later dropped).

Two months before Malcolm X's assassination, Louis Farrakhan said, "The die is cast. Such a man is worthy of death."[23] Farrakhan later reconciled with Malcolm X's widow, Betty Shabazz, and apologized for having "helped create the atmosphere"[24] that led to Malcolm's death. Again, Farrakhan followers and other sympathizers give Farrakhan a pass for his role in the assassination.

The Nation of Islam uses anger and resentment as a tool for recruitment and indoctrination. In *The Autobiography of Malcolm X*, as told to Alex Haley, Malcolm X—the separatist turned humanist—told Haley about Muslim recruiters who found angry young black inmates ripe for conversion:

> *When one was ripe—and I could tell—then away from the rest, I'd drop it on him, what Mr. [Elijah] Muhammad taught: "The white man is the devil." . . .*
>
> *That would shock many of them—until they started thinking about it. This is probably as big a single worry as the American prison system has today—the way the Muslim teachings, circulated among all Negroes in the country, are converting new Muslims among black men in prison. . . .*

"[T]he white man is the devil." You tell that to any Negro. Except for those relatively few "integration"-mad so-called "intellectuals," and those black men who are otherwise fat, happy, and deaf, dumb, and blinded, with their crumbs from the white man's rich table, you have struck a nerve center in the American black man. He may take a day to react, a month, a year; he may never respond, openly; but of one thing you can be sure—when he thinks about his own life, he is going to see where, to him, personally, the white man sure has acted like a devil. . . .

That's why black prisoners become Muslims so fast when Elijah Muhammad's teachings filter into their cages by way of other Muslim convicts. "The white man is the devil" is a perfect echo of that black convict's lifelong experience.[25]

Forty years later, today's Islamic prison clerics offer an even more hostile message. Black former convict Warith Deen Umar calls the 9-11 killers "martyrs," and argues that large numbers of American Muslims "secretly admire and applaud" the September 11 terrorists. "Without justice," says Umar, "there will be warfare, and it can come to this country, too."[26] Umar, a convert to Islam and former prison chaplain, now visits American prisons in order to convert convicts to Islam. After 9-11, he predicted that the next large attack on America would be carried out by black American Muslim converts.[27]

Umar may be correct.

British "shoe bomber" Richard Reid, the son of Jamaican immigrants, converted to Islam while in prison.[28] In late 2001, Reid boarded American Airlines flight 63, bound for Miami from Paris. Reid tried to light a fuse connected to explosives in his shoe. His attempted bombing was foiled by crew and passengers.

One year after 9-11, Gulf War veteran and sniper John Muhammad and his young black acolyte, Lee Malvo, terrorized the Washington, D.C., area as part of a prolonged terror campaign against the country he once served. The plans for their horrendous campaign included the bombing of children's hospitals and school buses.[29] Muhammad, the so-called "Beltway sniper," was a member of the Nation of Islam, the organization that refers to whites as devils and advocates a separate state for blacks.

One year later another Gulf War vet and Muslim convert, Sergeant Hammad Abdur-Raheem, along with several other young Muslim men in Virginia, were arrested for their participation in what prosecutors called an attempted "jihad" in America.[30]

Around the same time, the "Lackawanna 6"—all U.S. citizens of Yemini descent—were arrested. The six men from the Buffalo area, according to prosecutors, intended to engage in suicide missions. Authorities found a document that said, "Martyrdom or self-sacrifice operations are those performed by one or more people against enemies far outstripping them in numbers and equipment. . . . The form this usually takes nowadays is to wire up one's body, or a vehicle or suitcase with explosives, and then to enter into a conglomeration of the enemy, or in their vital facilities, and to detonate in an appropriate place there in order to cause the maximum losses in enemy ranks."[31]

In Torrance, California, in 2005, several black Muslims were arrested for plotting to attack military recruiting stations and synagogues in the state. The ringleader, Kevin James, founded and promoted am'iyyat Ul-Islam Is-Saheeh (JIS), a radical militant Muslim group, while serving time in a California state prison in 1997. According to the 2005 indictment, James "preached the duty of JIS members to target for violent attack any enemies of Islam or 'infidels,' including the United States Government and Jewish and non-Jewish supporters of Israel."[32] Jim Kouri, vice president of the National Association of Chiefs of Police, says, "The indictment alleges that James recruited fellow prison inmates to join JIS. . . . James allegedly distributed a document in prison that justified the killing of 'infidels,' and made members take an oath not to talk about the existence of JIS. He also allegedly sought to establish groups or 'cells' of JIS members outside of prison to carry out violent attacks against 'perceived infidels,' including the U.S. government, the government of Israel and Jewish people."[33]

The Miami 7—all young black men who converted to Islam in the Miami projects—were arrested in June 2006 for conspiring to blow up Chicago's Sears Tower and FBI offices across the country. Unaware that they were dealing with an undercover FBI agent in a sting operation, the seven men, five of them American citizens, allegedly swore allegiance to al Qaeda and trained to raise an "Islamic army" to "wage jihad" against America.[34]

Derrick Shareef, a twenty-two-year-old black Muslim convert, was arrested in December 2006 for allegedly plotting to set off hand grenades inside a Rockford, Illinois, shopping mall. Shareef told a friend "he wanted to commit acts of violent jihad against targets in the United States," and planned to commit his barbaric act on December 22, the Friday before Christmas, figuring he could kill and injure the most shoppers because the mall would be very crowded.[35] Luckily, according to the indictment, Shareef disclosed his plans and even tried to purchase the grenades from a government informant and an undercover agent, and he was apprehended.[36]

"Black Muslim ex-cons," writes *Investor's Business Daily*, ". . . may be attracted to al-Qaida because they share the global terror network's hostility toward the U.S."[37] The hostility of many black Americans is, no doubt, in large part bred, fed, and nurtured by "black leaders'" incessant cries of racism, then further inflamed by a compliant, sympathetic media—a media that consider racism, sexism, homophobia and global-warming denial a bigger problem than the fight against Islamofascists.

Other converts find Islam outside of prison walls. Christopher Paul converted to Islam in college. Paul, born in 1964 as Paul Kenyatta Laws, was one of the few black kids in nearly all-white Worthington, Ohio, where he grew up. He was arrested in

April 2007 at his home in Columbus, Ohio, for providing mate-rial support to terrorists and conspiring to use weapons of mass destruction.[38]

According to polls, an astounding 70 percent of black Muslims consider American Middle East policy the primary cause of the 9/11 attacks!

After his conversion, Paul traveled to Pakistan and Afghani-stan in 1990 for the purpose of "obtaining military-type training at a terrorist training camp and to further the purpose of violent jihad," according to his indictment. Changing his name several times, Paul allegedly trained his fellow al Qaeda members to carry out bombings in the United States and Europe, including tourist resorts and military bases.[39]

Paul's indictment detailed the tools of terrorism in Paul's home and that of his father, including a night vision scope, a laser range finder, a remote-controlled boat, and books on bomb-making and booby-traps. "The indictment of Christo-pher Paul," said Assistant Attorney General Kenneth Wain-stein, "paints a disturbing picture of an American who traveled overseas to train as a violent jihadist, joined the ranks of al Qaeda, and provided military instruction and support to radical cohorts both here and abroad."[40] Disturbing picture, indeed.

According to polls, an astounding 70 percent of black Mus-lims consider American Middle East policy the primary cause of the 9/11 attacks! When asked, "Is the United States 'immoral'?" 57 percent of black Muslims say yes.[41]

I grew up with a childhood friend named John. His parents

divorced, and John seemed to grow angrier and angrier after his dad moved out. John began to routinely defy authority. A gifted athlete, and the best player on the basketball team, John nevertheless frequently cursed out his coach. Under pressure to win games, the coach still allowed John to start and play. During football season, John became the starting quarterback, and he also made both the baseball and tennis teams.

But when the UCLAs and Notre Dames came around, inquiring about John's attitude and "head," John's coaches, concerned about their own reputations, told the big colleges about John's disruptive, surly, and uncooperative attitude. So bye-bye Bruins, so long Fighting Irish, and hello to an undistinguished local school with an even more undistinguished basketball program.

John began doing drugs and launching into diatribes against the "white man" and the "white man's system," and how he refused to yield to the "establishment." He changed his name and professed allegiance to the religion of Islam—not enough to renounce drugs, booze, and women, mind you. But Christianity had become the "white man's religion." Today he sits in his mother's home, a self-pitying man in his midfifties, blaming the racists who sabotaged his life.

America pays a price when so-called black leaders, the Democratic Party, and the sympathetic we-feel-your-pain media exaggerate the impact of racism. America pays a price when this same group blames a "lack of access to capital" for perpetuating black poverty. A 50 percent drop-out rate? Blame a racist disparity in funding between urban and suburban school districts. The country suffers when people cry racism to explain, for example, black-versus-white differences in access to health care.

It's not just the monolithic black vote that this kind of victicrat mentality creates. We also run the real risk of producing homicide bombers—born out of a culture of anger, hostility, and rage.

Al Qaeda and other Islamofascist groups hope that this kind of anger creates a generation of jihadists to take up arms against their own country.

We create victims, at their own—and at our nation's—peril.

12.

THREE THINGS THAT NEED TO BE SAID TO STUPID BLACK PEOPLE: "GROW UP, GROW UP, GROW UP"

Ninety-nine percent of the failures come from people who have the habit of making excuses.[1]

—GEORGE WASHINGTON CARVER

Most people, in their daily lives, simply ignore angry people. But sometimes people need a wakeup call. It is not racist to stand your ground. Sometimes little acts of courage—by calmly explaining why race had nothing to do with the complaint—can go a long way toward moving this country in a cohesive, positive direction.

One of my former interns, Stephen, told me of his five-week trip to Italy. Steve, a white college student, accompanied a handful of other American college students for this summer sabbatical. A female black student in his group constantly complained about racism. She turned a discussion of poverty into race. She turned a discussion about the War on Terror into race. She turned a discussion about Paris Hilton into race. Increasingly, the others in the group found her thin-skinned, hypersensitive, and obnoxious. But nobody said anything.

Stephen, however, angered at being called "racist" one too many times, finally said to her, "Here's the deal. I'm the furthest from a racist you've ever seen. You don't know me. But you've turned everything into race and you've turned everybody off. Everybody in this room feels this way, but nobody except me has the guts to say it. It's not about ideology, it's not about race, it's about *you*."

Refusing to call blacks "racist" for unfairly applying that term to others simply perpetuates more racism.

Think about it. If you're a white person, how many times did you make a joke, only to have a black person take offence? How many times did you make an innocent remark, or perhaps even offer a compliment, only to be denounced as a "bigot" or "insensitive?" How many times have you innocently said things like, "Why does the NAACP have the word 'colored' in it?" only to get attacked for possessing "Klanlike sensibilities."

Give me a break!

After Steve's "harsh" comment, the woman seemed absolutely stunned—as if this were the first time she had ever heard anything like this. She looked around, and no one in the room made eye contact. Their silence said it all.

Refusing to call blacks "racist" for unfairly applying that term to others simply perpetuates more racism. How dare Reverend Al Sharpton call the Central Park Jogger a "whore" and announce, "The boyfriend did it!" Imagine a leader from the so-called religious right calling a savagely beaten black rape victim "a whore," and saying her boyfriend did it. That would end his career, and no mountain of apologies could overcome the nondenominational, transnational, multiethnic condemnation.

Some blacks consider poor service in restaurants "Exhibit A" for racism. A couple years ago, a black friend and I went to a restaurant in the Korean section of Los Angeles. We walked into the nearly empty restaurant with tables in the center and booths on each side. I requested a booth, but the rather cold Korean hostess frowned and said, "The booths are for three or more people." I glanced around the room. "What about those two sitting in that booth over there?" I pointed out that there were several booths occupied by only two people and again insisted that my friend and I preferred a booth.

Embarrassed, she sighed, then seated us at a booth. When she left, my friend said to me, "These Koreans can't stand blacks."

"Maybe," I said to my friend, "this lady has had bad experiences with blacks. Who knows? But I don't think it's fair to call her racist just because of what happened. Why don't we wait and see? My dad used to run a restaurant, and people generally know that the more pleasant they are, the greater the tip."

Like my friend, many blacks complain about the "coldness" of Korean owners of convenience stores. A few years ago in Los Angeles, a Korean storeowner shot and killed a teenage black girl whom she suspected of stealing. It's become a big issue in Los Angeles, with many Korean storeowners and Korean associations vowing to improve race relations between blacks and Koreans.

The waitress came back. I smiled, and we rather expertly ordered a variety of things. The waitress recognized that I knew my Korean food, and she finally smiled.

"Her initial coldness," I told my friend, "could be the result of a lot of things. Maybe that's just how she is. Maybe she's had bad experiences. And maybe she resents the poor tipping habits of blacks."

"Poor tipping habits?" my friend said.

"Sure," I said. "Waitresses and waiters tell me that blacks tip like crap."

"Bull——,"said my friend.

"No, really," I told him. "Someone actually sat down and re-searched this. Studies show that blacks tip poorly, and are often, according to disgruntled waiters, quite demanding."

Professor Michael Lynn of Cornell University School of Hotel Administration published a paper called *Ethnic Differences in Tipping: A Matter of Familiarity with Tipping Norms*. His conclusion—blacks were lousy tippers.[2]

Lynn and his researchers wrote, "This black-white difference in tipping is not due to income or other demographic differences between the two ethnic groups, because that difference remained both sizable and statistically significant after controlling for sex, age, education, income, and household size. Nor can this difference in tipping be attributed to discrimination in service delivery, because it remained significant after controlling for service quality. In one of the studies, black restaurant patrons actually rated the service slightly higher than did white patrons, but the black patrons still tipped less."[3]

Why so? Lynch offered a number of reasons, but the most likely is pretty straightforward. The failure to leave a 15 to 20 percent tip comes from simple ignorance of what custom deems fair and appropriate. Black servers also expect smaller tips from their black customers. Like their white counterparts, in some cases they try to avoid serving black customers for fear of getting smaller tips. Lynn also found that many waiters and waitresses consider black patrons rude and demanding, "Not only am I not treated well when waiting on them, but I am not tipped well,"[4] said one of the servers.

Is it possible that when some black customers get less-than-attentive service, the server resents working hard for a small tip and an apparent lack of appreciation? So this becomes a self-fulfilling prophecy.

"Poor-tipping blacks," I told my friend, "in order to get better service, need to get rid of the attitude, 'Hey, they get paid enough already. Why should I give them more?' "

Our food began to arrive. With each dish our server brought, her smile grew broader and then she began engaging in small talk.

She even brought a free side order, as well as two complimentary desserts. My friend, who dined at this restaurant often, said he'd never seen a reaction like that. I left our waitress a handsome tip.

My parents taught me that pleasant attracts pleasant. I recently stopped at an inner-city seafood/soul food restaurant. I had never been there and I wanted to pick up some food for my family. As I walked in, I saw that the place was nice and well maintained. I understand that I am precious cargo and that 10 to 15 percent of people in the inner city want me dead, so I chose a place that didn't have a lot of people loitering around outside.

A polite, young black woman stood behind the counter. I placed my order with the woman and, as I talked with her, I saw a frowning black man, maybe sixty-five to seventy years old, leaning forward to listen.

LARRY: May I ask you where you went to high school?
WOMAN: I went to Hamilton High School.
LARRY: Hamilton was in the same conference that I was in when I went to Crenshaw High, but they're not anymore. And when I was there, Hamilton was about 99 percent white. In fact, I went to all the track meets and there was only one black guy on the team and he was their best guy. What is the racial composition now? *[I was assuming she just graduated.]*
WOMAN: Well, I don't know what it is now, but when I went there it was still majority white.
LARRY: It still is, right? I mean, you just graduated.
WOMAN: Oh no, I'm a lot older than I think you think I am.
LARRY: May I ask how old are you?
WOMAN: Twenty-eight.
LARRY: Well, after you graduated from Hamilton High School what did you do?
WOMAN: I didn't do much of anything.
LARRY: What do you mean, you didn't do much of anything?

WOMAN: I got pregnant.
LARRY: Did you get married?
WOMAN: No, *[smiling]* but I'm thinking about it.

I sat down to wait for my food to arrive. The older gentle-
man turned to me and said:

MAN: So, how you doin', Mr. Elder?
LARRY: *[reaching to shake his hand]* Your name?
MAN: Flemming.
LARRY: Mr. Flemming.
MAN: May I tell you something? I do a lot of activism in
the streets and try to do what I can to prevent violence.
About ten years ago, I was pepper-sprayed and pushed
around by the police. It took me a long time to settle the
case, and we finally settled it, but it was a long, hard
struggle.
LARRY: I know why you're telling me this, because
you're familiar with my show and you think I am a little
too unsympathetic with how rough it is in the streets,
and the police really are far more brutal than everyone
thinks. Man, sometimes I think you just don't understand. I don't doubt your story. Cops are human beings.
It's a rough, tough job. You put on a flak jacket in the
morning. Why? Because somebody could shoot you. And
they could still shoot you in the head. And you go
through that every single moment of the day. Imagine
that. Then you stop people, and by definition, you're
only stopping bad people. And they give you lip. I don't
know the percentage, but they do. Sometimes, by the
way, it's 100 degrees outside and you're wearing your
flak jacket, which means it's like 120 degrees. There's a
lot of crime in the inner city, that's why they're here.
And they're being proactive. Tell me, were you standing
around with some other people?
MAN: Yes, I was.

LARRY: Were they younger, kind of thug-like?

MAN: Yes, they were, but I wasn't.

LARRY: I know you weren't. But the cops had a negative assumption. And they probably said something and you said something back and you resented the way they treated you. I am not saying that what happened to you should have happened, but for crying out loud, put yourself in their position. That guy that got beaten up in New Orleans, that old man they showed a lot on the news? A sixty-four-year-old teacher who was minding his own business. The cops said he was intoxicated, but he was a recovering alcoholic who hadn't had a drink in fifteen years, and everybody knew him. Those two cops beat him up. And your response is, "Horrible, horrible, no justification." I am not defending them, but I am explaining something. These cops were working eighteen hour shifts, sleeping four or five hours, and doing it again. They walk down the street and tell somebody to move and they think that the guy gave him lip. They were wrong. They are human beings. They're not Nazis. They're your brothers and your fathers and your sisters and the same people from the same neighborhood who decided to become a cop because they wanted to help. Every cop I know became a cop because he wanted to help. They didn't say, "I wanted to become a cop because I wanted to go out and get niggers." There's no perspective in that mentality, "It's us against them. Cop pulls me over and it's my time to prove how macho I am. I am not going to let him tell me what to do."

[Everyone in the place, at this point, is listening to what I am saying to this man.]

LARRY: You know that Tony Muhammad guy, the local head of the Nation of Islam? He's supposed to be involved in stopping gang violence? They are having a candlelight vigil because of black-on-black crime, and he is double-parked. The cops ask him to move his SUV.

He says, "Make me, make me." The cops ask again and get the same response and a big scuffle. And this is the guy who is supposed to be telling young people how to deal with violence? There's a problem here! Do you want fewer cops? Do you want them not to be here? Do you want them to be less aggressive? What do you want? That's what's goin' on here. And there's no perspective whatsoever. You got Jesse or Al and Farrakhan saying cops are bad, cops are evil, the white man is out to get you. And you are surprised these black kids have attitudes. I am tired of it. My dad is behind burglar bars in his house, along with every other house on the block, and it's not because of Mark Furhman. This is not a *game*. *[The man just took it, listening intently.]*
MAN: *[smiling for the first time]* I hear what you're saying, Mr. Elder.

Later that day, I took my ninety-year-old dad to his barbershop. Dad goes to the same barbershop that my brothers and I went to when we were growing up. Different people now own the shop, and I hadn't set foot in there in probably thirty-five years. Is it, I asked dad, still the same Afrocentric, trash-talking joint I remember? "Yes," he sighs. At one time, posters of Malcolm X, Elijah Mohammad, and Marcus Garvey stared at you from the walls. The two barbers talked the same kind of smack that barbers talked when I sat in that chair decades ago. The white man this, the white man that.

When we got there, it was packed. Two barbers were cutting hair, with about six or seven people waiting.

But as soon as my dad and I walk in, one of the barbers recognized me.

BARBER: Mr. Larry Elder, how you doin'?
LARRY: Hi, this is my dad.
BARBER: I had no idea that was your father.

LARRY: How many ahead of him?
BARBER: Two.

The barber offered to take my dad right away, cutting in front of others, but Dad and I quickly refused.

As we waited, the barber decided to, as he put it, "Get real."

BARBER: I understand you benefited from affirmative action.
LARRY: Have you ever heard my show?
BARBER: No.
LARRY: I've been on the radio thirteen years and you've never heard my show?
BARBER: No, but I know all about you, from other people.
LARRY: How can you possibly know all about me if you've never heard my show? You don't have a clue what I'm all about. Did I benefit from affirmative action? Do you mean, was it easier to get into certain schools because I'm black? Yes. But do I believe that, if it wasn't for affirmative action, I'd be driving a truck? I don't think so. *[Everyone starts laughing.]*
LARRY: If I hadn't gone into school A, I would have gone to school B.
BARBER: But you did benefit?
LARRY: If I did benefit, why are we having this conversation? (Everybody laughs again.) I'm fifty-four years old and I'm having a conversation with you about my resume—all because I "benefited from affirmative action."
[Now another man who had been listening, clearly disagreeing, could take it no longer.]
MAN: But you have to admit, Elder, that the playing field is not level. White people have more money and more property than we do.
LARRY: *[turning to him]* Okay, let's say I'm white, and I got money. *[More laughter]* Either I worked for it, or my dad

worked for it or my grandfather worked for it, and I in-
herited it. That's *your* problem! I'm not givin' my money
to you! I'm sorry about Rodney King. I'm sorry about
Emmett Till, I'm sorry about Rosa Parks. I'm sorry they
turned water hoses and dogs on Martin Luther King. I'm
sorry about Jim Crow. I'm sorry about slavery. But *I*
didn't do it. I never owned a slave, and I don't use the
"n-word." I'm *not* giving you my money. Now what are
you gonna do about it? Try and take it from me? I believe
in the Second Amendment. I own a gun. *[Laughter]* You
try and take it from me politically, I'm gonna vote Republican. *[More laughter]* Now I ask you again, what do
you intend to do about it? Bitch? Moan? Whine? Sit
around and say, "You owe me, give me a set-aside program, give me a jobs-training program, give me a whatever"? I'm sorry about Tookie. I'm sorry about the
Tuskeegee Experiment. I'm sorry about Rosewood. I'm
not giving you my money, and I don't feel guilty about
keeping it. Now what do you intend to do about it?

Most of the young men in the barbershop now listened at-
tentively.

LARRY: These kids come in here every two weeks, listen
to you guys *[pointing to the barbers]* talking all this nonsense. Some kids don't have fathers in the home, and
many kids don't attend church on a regular basis. Where
they do come on a regular basis is here, and listen to
what? "The white man's out to get you. Woe is me, I'm a
victim." If more people said to kids what I'm sayin' now,
maybe things would be a whole lot better. Invest in
yourself. *[I pointed to my dad.]* When I grew up, my dad
was a janitor. He served in the war, and came out and
worked two jobs, cooking for a family on the weekends.
He went to night school to get his GED. He grew up in
the Depression when the unemployment rate for black

adults was 50 percent. He does not know who his biological father is, and his mother—for reasons we won't get into—kicked him out of the house when he was thirteen years old. Where was *his* program? And *he* votes Republican.

Both barbers now laughed.

LARRY: When can we blacks get to the point where you and I can have a disagreement without somebody being a sell-out or an Uncle Tom? Is that at all possible? Am I asking too much?
BARBER: [*smiling*] I'm feelin' you.

My dad just watched the "debate" unfold. He and I caught each other's eye from time to time and smiled. What did my dad think? No need to wonder; he's the one who taught me.

When we got home, my dad said, "That was something, Larry."

I said, "No, Dad, *you* are something."

Dad understood. I was just standing my ground . . . saying what needed to be said.

13.

CHANGE IN THE AIR: THE MARCH OF PERSONAL RESPONSIBILITY

The civil rights movement was over 50-something years ago. Many people know nothing of it other than a recitation [during Black History] month. People are tired of that. They want to see more relatively. The worst mistake one can make, in my judgment, is to try to tailor a message to a group and to say: 'I am the person for your group.' He should be the person for the American people.[1]

—DOUGLAS L. WILDER, DEMOCRATIC BLACK MAYOR OF RICHMOND, VIRGINIA, AND FIRST ELECTED BLACK GOVERNOR, ON BARACK OBAMA

M any people see through the nonsense—the stupid things said and done by those who are blind or intentionally oblivious to this country's wonderful opportunities. Even though the headlines go to the yellers and screamers, a growing chorus condemns the shameless antics of those who irresponsibly cry racism, saying, "We've had it with the whining and the failure to see the obvious progress."

There's hope—a lot of it.

I was on the set of one of my television shows around the time that Jesse Jackson and others blamed racism for Hollywood's alleged failure to hire blacks. A black man came up to me and told me about his behind-the-camera job, which he'd held for almost thirty years. "Nobody marched to get me my job," he said. "This is a tough, competitive business. And you need to be tough and competitive to succeed." He was rightfully proud of his accomplishments.

Even though the headlines go to the yellers and screamers, a growing chorus condemns the shameless antics of those who irresponsibly cry racism.

Shelby Steele, in his book *White Guilt*, explains how whites' liberal guilt paralyzes them from taking pride in the accomplishments of Western civilization. After all, white Western civilization became the moving force behind notions like inalienable human and civil rights, which devolves from a power higher than government. Western civilization stands on concepts like rule of law, respect for private property, religious tolerance, and equal rights for men and women and people of all races.

As former Italian Prime Minister Silvio Berlusconi said, "We should be conscious of the superiority of our civilization, which consists of a' value system that has given people widespread prosperity in those countries that embrace it, and guarantees respect for human rights and religion. This respect certainly does not exist in the Islamic countries."[2] Berlusconi also said Western civilization is superior because it "has at its core, as its greatest value, freedom, which is not the heritage of Islamic culture."[3]

As Shelby Steele might have predicted, multiculturalists attacked Berlusconi and considered his remarks to reflect the chauvinism of Western civilization. Berlusconi promptly apologized, not wanting his remarks to be interpreted as "racist."

But in America, the evidence against the notion that racism holds blacks back is overwhelming. In the debate over the extent of racism, whites, especially Southern whites, feel as guilty about slavery as Germans feel about the Holocaust.

Black fisherman Ish Monroe climbed to the top in the mostly all-white sport of bass fishing. He caught his first fish at age two, and has been addicted to fishing ever since. Monroe, in this extremely competitive field, now yearly earns six figures.

One of his white competitors said race is not an issue. "Our sport does not discriminate," said Rick Clunn, a four-time winner of the Bassmaster Classic—the "Super Bowl" of the sport. "It does not matter if you're blue, green, black, or yellow. It's how you can handle a rod and reel."[4]

As Ish worked his way up the fishing ladder, driving from event to event—many held in the Deep South—he says cops often pulled him over for "routine checks." He says one time the police took him to jail, and another time he was asked to step aside for a canine unit to sniff his rig. But times change. He finds cops now stop him because they are fans. "It's funny," says Monroe. "I'll be driving down and they'll throw their lights on and I'm like, 'You've got to be kidding me.' And they're like, 'Ish, we just wanted to get your autograph.' "[5]

But Monroe says that in many areas he sees the Confederate flag: "[T]he Confederate flag still flies in some places, and that's just wrong."[6]

Is the Confederate flag, however, automatically synonymous with racism?

Black former Congressman Harold Ford (D-TN), while campaigning for Senate in 2006, saw a Confederate flag hanging outside a bar and grill. Reluctantly, Ford walked in to do some hand-shaking. The woman behind the bar greeted him with outstretched arms, "Baby, we've been waiting to see you."[7]

Maybe some Southerners, in fact, perceive the Confederate flag as a symbol of Southern pride, not as a relic of black subjugation. The restaurateur who greeted Ford with graciousness and hospitality apparently held that view. Things have changed.

Republican National Committee Chairman Ken Mehlman, on July 14, 2005, apologized to NAACP members at their annual convention for the GOP's decades-long dismissal of the black vote. "By the '70s and into the '80s and '90s," said Mehlman, "the Democrat Party solidified its support in the African-American community, and we Republicans did not effectively reach out. Some Republicans gave up on winning the African-American vote, looking the other way or trying to benefit politically from racial polarization. I come here as Republican chairman to tell you we were wrong."[8]

Even Al Gore's black former campaign manager, Donna Brazile, complemented Mehlman on his speech. In an appearance on CNN's *Inside Politics*, Brazile said, "Well, I'm an African-American. I believe that both political parties should woo blacks. Blacks should be treated as swing voters, not base voters, and blacks should not be taken for granted, like other voters in this country. So, I say that as an American, and I'm proud that Ken made that speech today."[9]

Wow. This from Ms. Brazile, who once referred to Republicans as "white boys," saying, "A white-boy attitude is 'I must exclude, denigrate and leave behind.'"[10] She also said, "Republicans bring out Colin Powell and J. C. Watts because they have no program, no policy. They play that game because they have no love and no joy. They'd rather take pictures with black children than feed them."[11] Yet now she's applauding the RNC chairman. And she sounds almost . . . reasonable.

Young blacks seem less willing to buy into the notion of "Democrats good, Republicans evil." While blacks overwhelmingly vote for Democrats, young black adults appear to be more skeptical than their parents about the Democratic Party.

According to the Joint Center for Political and Economic Studies, a 2000 National Opinion Poll showed that only 51 percent of young blacks (ages eighteen to twenty-five) considered themselves Democrat, 36 percent identified as Independent and 9 percent as Republican.[12] True, a growing number of young blacks identify themselves as Independents rather than Republicans, but this may provide an opening for the Republican Party, provided blacks obsess less about racism and more about policies and principals that lead to progress and prosperity.

More and more, I receive letters like the following:

Dear Larry:

I've been listening to you since your first couple of weeks on the air in Los Angeles. . . .

I'm black, a former pro athlete, and have been working with at-risk youth since 1991 as a mentor, coach, program director, event planner, etc. At first I used to argue with you all the time! I used to say, "Why is Larry always putting down black folks? Why is he trying to kiss white peoples' behinds all the time?" Then my cousin (who is in the news business) came out to cover the anniversary of the L.A. riots. I was never in love with Jesse Jackson and his inability to speak clearly, and I did resent how he was portrayed as the black leader. My cousin was interviewing local leaders and those affected by the riots and recovery efforts. He told me when Jesse saw the cameras, he simply injected himself into the scenario. My cousin, being a consummate professional, rolled with it and interviewed Jesse. When they were finished, Jesse asked my cousin where they were going and my cousin mentioned that they were touring all of the hot spots of the riots. Well, like the media whore that he is, Jesse insisted on tagging along even though he had nothing to say nor add to the coverage. My cousin said he was so transparent and acting like a little boy with nothing else to do!

It was at that point that I began to question my stance on a lot of "black" and social issues. You see, my family has a tradition of community activism and my grandparents and father had dinner at the White House with Presidents Kennedy, Johnson, and Carter for their efforts in the community, and my mother consults with a number of national nonprofit and leadership organizations. I began to see more clearly that people like Jesse, Sharpton, Waters, etc., are in it for the money and power, not for the interest of the people! I began to see how they play on white "guilt" and prejudice. I also began to see how they must keep perpetuating the victim and slavery mentality of "40 acres" to maintain power and influence.

*I laughed at the election of 2000. I had (regrettably) voted
for Gore, and thought, like everyone else, that there was some
type of cheating in the "Powers-That-Be" or the media was to
blame. I thought it was scandalous . . . until 9/11. Then I jumped
ship and realized that—like you say all the time—most black folks
are conservative and Bush was the right man for the right time. I
believe in empowering young people and teaching them resiliency.
I teach them not to blame the past of their circumstances
(poverty, molestation, abuse, gangs, learning disabilities, etc.)
but to use those experiences as fuel to the future.*

Joel W.

Talented, bright, charismatic Senator Barack Obama simultaneously delivers an uplifting message yet maintains his street
cred, "keepin' it real," by exaggerating the obstacle of racism.

On the one hand, when *60 Minutes*'s Steve Kroft asks whether
Obama expects his race to hurt his pursuit of the Democratic
nomination, or, if nominated, to get elected, Obama said, "I think
if I don't win this race, it will be because of other factors. It's
gonna be because I have not shown to the American people a vision for where the country needs to go that they can embrace."[13]

But Obama, on the other hand, delivered a speech at Virginia's
historically black Hampton University—Booker T. Washington's
alma mater—where he repeatedly referred to Los Angeles's 1992
Rodney King riots, which resulted in fifty-five deaths, over two
thousand injuries, and three thousand businesses looted or
burned. Obama declared that such violence erupted after a build-
up of "quiet riots" that could explode again. "[T]hose riots didn't
erupt overnight;" said Obama, "there had been a 'quiet riot' building up in Los Angeles and across this country for years."[14]

"Those quiet riots that take place every day," said Obama,
"are born from the same place as the fires and the destruction
and the police decked out in riot gear and the deaths. They happen when a sense of disconnect settles in and hope dissipates.
Despair takes hold, and young people all across this country

look at the way this world is and believe that things are never going to get any better. You tell yourself, my school will always be second-rate. You tell yourself, there will never be a good job waiting for me to excel at."[15]

"That despair quietly simmers," said Obama, "and makes it impossible to build strong communities and neighborhoods. And then one afternoon a jury says, 'not guilty.' Or a hurricane hits New Orleans. And that despair is revealed for the world to see."[16] Obama added, "This is not to excuse the violence of bashing in a man's head or destroying someone's store and their life's work. That kind of violence is inexcusable and self-defeating. It does, however, describe the reality of many communities around this country."[17] Liberal *New York Times* columnist Maureen Dowd, writing about Obama's speech, merely noted that he "talked with a preacher's passion,"[18] but never mentioned the absolutely asinine comparison of Katrina to the Rodney King riots—one wrought by weather, the other by the hand of man.

Obama's schizophrenia abounds. At CNN's "YouTube debate," Barack Obama dismissed a suggestion that he is not "authentically black enough" with a joke about catching a cab in Manhattan. He then stopped smiling and said, "Race permeates our society. It is still a critical problem."[19] So the American racist, Obama tells *60 Minutes*'s Steve Kroft, lacks the power to stop Obama from becoming president, but "race permeates our society."

Obama gave a speech at Brown Chapel, a black church in Selma, Alabama, on the forty-second anniversary of the Bloody Sunday Selma March across the Edmund Pettus Bridge that turned violent, shocked America, and helped to spark the passage of the Voting Rights Act of 1965 five months later. Obama rattled off the usual litany of social programs and government spending he claimed necessary to improve the plight of blacks.

"We've got forty-six million people uninsured in this country despite spending more money on health care than any nation on earth," said Obama. "Makes no sense. As a consequence we've got what's known as a health care disparity in this nation because many of the uninsured are African-American or

Latino. Life expectancy is lower, almost every disease is higher within minority communities—the health care gap. Blacks are less likely in their schools to have adequate funding. We have less qualified teachers in those schools. We have fewer textbooks in those schools. We have got in some schools rats outnumbering computers. That's called the achievement gap. You have got a health care gap. You have got an achievement gap. You have got Katrina still undone. Went down to New Orleans three weeks ago. Still looks bombed out. Still not rebuilt."[20]

But then, as Obama did in the 2004 Democratic convention, he said that "sometimes" blacks create problems by failing to exercise personal responsibility and accountability. "We have too many children in poverty in this country and everybody should be ashamed," said Obama, "but don't tell me it doesn't have a little to do with the fact that we got too many daddies not acting like daddies. Don't think that fatherhood ends at conception. I know something about that because my father wasn't around when I was young and I struggled. . . . Don't tell me that we can't do better by our children, that we can't take more responsibility for making sure we're instilling in them the values and the ideals that the [previous] generation taught us about sacrifice and dignity and honesty and hard work and discipline and self-sacrifice. . . .

"Sometimes it's easy to just point at somebody else and say it's their fault, but oppression has a way of creeping into it. Reverend, it has a way of stunting yourself. You start telling yourself, Bishop, I can't do something. I can't read. I can't go to college. I can't start a business. I can't run for Congress. I can't run for the presidency. People start telling you—you can't do something, after a while, you start believing it and part of what the civil rights movement was about was recognizing that we have to transform ourselves in order to transform the world. Mahatma Gandhi—great hero of Dr. King and the person who helped create the nonviolent movement around the world—he once said that you can't change the world if you haven't changed."[21]

So while Barack Obama votes liberal and supports government-to-the-rescue programs, he at times couples the message with that of personal responsibility. But in calling for more government and more programs, he fails to preach what he practices. What he practiced was hard work, getting a good, strong education, attending both Occidental and Columbia, becoming a "community organizer" for two years in Chicago (focusing on job-training and after-school programs), then going to Harvard Law School where he became the first black president of the *Harvard Law Review*. He then became a well-regarded professor of constitutional law at the University of Chicago Law School. Obama passed on opportunities to pursue tenure, but he decided to go into politics, where, again, he earned praise for his hard work.

So while Barack Obama votes liberal and supports government-to-the-rescue programs, he at times couples the message with that of personal responsibility. But in calling for more government and more programs, he fails to preach what he practices.

But like many liberals who engage in race-hustling, Obama couples his message of hope with a litany of the woes experienced by blacks as a result of government indifference or incompetence. In his speech at the Democratic convention, he said that government takes us only so far without hard work, personal responsibility, and appropriate moral behavior. He even castigated fathers who refuse to take responsibility. (Indeed, Obama's own father abandoned his family and returned to Africa when Obama was a young boy.)

I posed the following question to my listeners. On a scale from zero to one hundred, where does America rank as to black/white race relations? If 0 percent is slavery, and 100 percent is nirvana, paradise, the complete realization of Martin Luther King's dream of a color-blind America, where does America rank in 2007?

Some callers said 65 percent, others 75 percent, but most said either 90 percent or higher. Then I asked a two-part follow-up question. Take Jesse Jackson. As to this question, what does Jackson a) think, and b) truly believe?

Most listeners said that Jesse Jackson publicly asserts that America is at 10 percent and remains 90 percent racist. Remember, Jesse Jackson's sons own an Anheuser-Busch distributorship, another son serves in the United States House of Representatives, and, by 1988, when Jesse Jackson ran for president, disclosure forms showed a very comfortable net worth. Journalists reported Jackson earned a pretty substantial annual income from various sources. So when asked, "What does Jesse Jackson actually *think?*" virtually every listener said that, when the blinds close and the lights dim, Jesse Jackson actually believes that America is about 90 percent nonracist.

But what about Barack Obama? How do you suppose he feels about the same question? Here's what Obama said at his Selma speech: "There's still some battles that need to be fought, some rivers that need to be crossed. . . . [T]he previous generation—the Moses generation—pointed the way. They took us 90 percent of the way there, but we still got that 10 percent, in order to cross over to the other side."[22]

Ten percent?

Obama, flat-out said that America has evolved to the point where it is only "10 percent" racist. Given the number of "black leaders," guilt-ridden whites, and those who simply refuse to acknowledge change, 10 percent appears awfully small. Imagine Sharpton or Jackson suggesting that America was 90 percent of the way toward providing equal opportunity for others. Yet Obama, with an audience of several black clergy and "black leaders," painted an extremely optimistic view of America.

Newspapers across the country showed a panoramic photo of Barack Obama, Senator Hillary Clinton, and Bill Clinton reenacting the forty-two-year-old Selma March across the Edmund Pettus Bridge. But examine the photo closely. There is Obama—smiling. On the other side of the photo walked Bill and Hillary Clinton—again, smiling—arm-in-arm with others. If America is so bad, why are these people smiling? Sure, this is a photo op, but doesn't this also show that despite our often petty squabbles, Americans share more similarities than differences?

Obama recognizes that racists do not prevent kids from studying, racists do not demand that men father children outside of wedlock, that the complete and total eradication of racism cannot instill the necessary moral values that create healthy, prosperous communities.

Thus, Obama poses a contradiction, especially unsettling for the old guard. He proposes the same old liberal "solutions" as does every other liberal candidate—health care for all, affirmative action, programs to close the "wealth gap," and so on. But unlike Clinton, Democratic National Committee Chairman Howard Dean, and former presidential candidates Jesse Jackson and Al Sharpton, Obama recognizes that racists do not prevent kids from studying, racists do not demand that men father children outside of wedlock, that the complete and total eradication of racism cannot instill the necessary moral values that create healthy, prosperous communities. Small wonder that Sharpton recently said at a forum, "Just because you're our color doesn't make you our kind."[23]

But Obama, too, practices with one foot in and one foot out. Barack Obama attends Chicago's popular Trinity United Church of Christ. He described its minister, Reverend Jeremiah A. Wright Jr., as his "spiritual mentor."[24] On its Web site, Trinity United Church of Christ describes itself: "We are an African people, and remain 'true to our native land,' the mother continent, the cradle of civilization. . . . It is God who gives us the strength and courage to continuously address injustice as a people, and as a congregation. We constantly affirm our trust in God through cultural expression of a Black worship service and ministries which address the Black Community."[25]

Consider the grief President George W. Bush attracted when he gave a speech at Bob Jones University, an institution that formerly banned interracial dating. Imagine a Republican attending a church that professed "Caucasian-centric" Bible readings. According to an article in Rolling Stone, Reverend Wright said, "Racism is how this country was founded and this country is still run! . . . We are deeply involved in the importing of drugs, the exporting of guns and the training of professional KILLERS. . . . We believe in white supremacy and black inferiority and believe it more than we believe in God. . . . We conducted radiation experiments on our own people. . . . We care nothing about human life if the ends justify the means! And. And. And! GAWD! Has GOT! To be SICK! OF THIS SHIT!"[26]

Jeremiah Wright also helped to organize the Million Man March,[27] spearheaded by the anti-Semitic, homophobic, anti-Catholic Minister Louis Farrakhan. Wright also, accompanied by Farrakhan, visited Muammar el-Qaddafi of Libya.[28] In an interview about whether this kind of activity might hurt Obama's prospects, Wright said, "When his enemies find out that in 1984 I went to Tripoli [to visit Qaddafi] with Farrakhan, a lot of his Jewish support will dry up quicker than a snowball in hell."[29]

At the first Sunday service following the terrorist attacks of 9/11, Wright preached that the attacks were a consequence of violent U.S. policies. And four years later, Wright wrote that the 9/11 attacks were proof that "people of color had not gone away, faded into the woodwork or just 'disappeared' as the Great White West went on its merry way of ignoring Black concerns"[30]

Obama, showing his pragmatism again, disinvited Reverend Wright to the senator's announcement that he intended to run for president. According to Wright, on the eve of the announcement, "Fifteen minutes before Shabbos [or Shabbat, the Sabbath observed from sundown on Friday through nightfall on Saturday] I get a call from Barack. One of his members had talked him into uninviting me."[31]

So, the writer of *The Audacity of Hope* claims anyone can be what they want to be, but attends an Afrocentric church with a mission to fight racism while simultaneously urging blacks to embrace personal responsibility. But Obama's pastor then pals around with the anti-Semitic, white-man-blaming Minister Farrakhan and visits Muammar el-Qaddafi of Libya, a country then listed as an official state sponsor of terrorism. But then, when Senator Obama announces his presidential candidacy, he disinvites Reverend Wright, presumably because of Wright's off-putting, separatist baggage.

Confused?

Obama then puts back on the black-anger-serves-no-productive-purpose hat. In his first book, *Dreams From My Father*, written after he became the first black to head the *Harvard Law Review*, he criticized a black prep school friend for his phony rage against the white man:

> Our rage at the white world needed no object, he seemed to be telling me, no independent confirmation; it could be switched on and off at our pleasure. Sometimes . . . I would question his judgment, if not his sincerity. We weren't living in the Jim Crow South, I would remind him. We weren't consigned to some heatless housing project in Harlem or the Bronx. We were in goddamned Hawaii. We said what we pleased, ate where we pleased; we sat at the front of the proverbial bus. None of our white friends treated us any differently than they treated each other. They loved us, and

we loved them back. Shit, seemed like half of 'em wanted to be
black themselves—or at least Dr. J.

Well, that's true, Ray would admit.

Maybe we could afford to give the bad-assed nigger pose a
rest. Save it for when we really needed it.[32]

Obama wrote about a friend named Marcus, whom he met
while studying at Occidental College. He said that Marcus "took
to wearing African prints to class and started lobbying the administration for an all-black dormitory. Later, he grew uncom-
municative. He began to skip classes, hitting the reefer more
heavily. He let his beard grow out, let his hair work its way into
dreadlocks." After college, Obama saw Marcus playing bongos at
a street fair in Compton, a predominately minority suburb of
Los Angeles. "Through the haze of smoke that surrounded him,
his face was expressionless; his eyes were narrow, as if he were
trying to shut out the sun. For almost an hour I watched him
play without rhythm or nuance, just pounding the hell out of
those drums, beating back untold memories."[33]

A few weeks after Barack Obama announced his presidential
candidacy, when he gave his speech at the black church in
Selma, Alabama, he was introduced by Congressman Artur Davis
(D-AL). "All the times you've told your kids they could grow up
to be anything they wanted to be, you know you've been lying
to them," Davis said. "But I know a man who will make you into
a truth-teller when you tell your grandchildren that."[34]

Lying to them?

It is unfortunate that so many blacks need a black president
before they can *believe* they, too, could be president. When I was
seven years old, my own mother sat with me as I read a book on
presidents of the United States. Pointing to one page showing all
their portraits, she told me, "Larry, if you work hard enough,
some day *your* picture will be in this book." My mother believed
it. And I never doubted her. But that attitude threatens the very
viability of someone like Al Sharpton.

While Obama's liberalism and failure to understand the threat posed by Islamofascism undermine his candidacy, he does offer something worthwhile: he can inspire black victicrats who believe that barriers thwart their progress. I reject the necessity of the election of a black president to show blacks that, with application, their potential can be realized. But if the strong candidacy, if not the nomination and election, of Barack Obama shuts up or turns down the volume of those who say, "You can't make it in America if you're black," I'll take it.

Obama, after the collapse of the immigration reform bill in the Senate, accused Republicans of racism. Obama characterized those opposed to the immigration bill as "both ugly and racist in a way we haven't seen since the struggle for civil rights."[35] He refused to accept that many Republicans' opposition to the bill rested on skepticism about the government living up to its border enforcement promises, or because many aliens make demands that suggest a sense of entitlement. No, Obama equated opposition to the bill as opposition to Hispanics, whether legal or illegal.

Racial ambulance-chasers hurt the country. They divide us. They emphasize our differences rather than our similarities. A recent study led by researchers at Howard University found that black women who *think* that they are "everyday" victims of racial discrimination face a greater chance of developing breast cancer. The "everyday" instances of discrimination that these women claim to experience include getting poor service in stores, being around people they believe are "afraid" of them, being around people they believe act superior to them, and the like.[36] Doctors say that attitude affects health. People with optimistic outlooks on life engage in more healthful behavior, and negativity can actually have negative physiological effects. So believing that "The Man" seeks to get you can actually harm your health.

Who puts stuff like this in the minds of so many blacks? The Sharptons, Jacksons, Clintons, liberals who prattle about the "unfinished" business of racism in America, and other public figures, including some sports figures and entertainers—all claiming to "keep it real" by stirring the pot and keeping blacks angry, pessimistic, less productive, less proactive, and less willing to invest in themselves since they fail to see a hopeful future.

Who puts stuff like this in the minds of so many blacks? The Sharptons, Jacksons, Clintons, liberals who prattle about the "unfinished" business of racism in America, and other public figures, including some sports figures and entertainers—all claiming to "keep it real" by stirring the pot and keeping blacks angry, pessimistic, less productive, less proactive, and less willing to invest in themselves since they fail to see a hopeful future.

No one doubts the existence of racial discrimination. Utopia doesn't exist. But the persistent emphasis on the alleged "pervasive racism in America" turns minor incidents and inconveniences—that can be explained in a number of ways—into "acts of discrimination."

Whom does this help? It helps the Democratic Party to retain their monolithic black vote. It helps the race exploiters like Jesse Jackson and Al Sharpton to retain their power base. And it helps America's enemies, like al Qaeda and other Islamofascists, to exploit black anger for their own self-serving means.

It's time to stop the madness.

ENDNOTES

PREFACE

1. "Clinton Speech on Race Relations in San Diego," June 14, 1997, www.usembassy-israel.org.il/publish/civic/archive/107a.html.

2. Claiborne, William, "From Cheers to Tears: Verdict Splits America," *Washington Post*, October 4, 1995, 1.

3. Pew Research Center, "The 2004 Political Landscape, Part 4: Success, Poverty and Government Responsibility," November 5, 2003, www.people-press.org/reports/display.php3?PageID=753.

4. McGeveran, William A. Jr., ed., *The World Almanac 2007*, (New York: World Almanac Education Group, 2007), 65.

5. *Popular Quotations of John F. Kennedy* (Boston: John F. Kennedy Library and Museum, March 1, 2006), www.jfklibrary.org/jfkquote.htm.

1. IT'S THE MEDIA, STUPID

1. O'Sullivan, John, "A Yale Colloquy on Race," *Wall Street Journal*, April 17, 1997, 22.

2. Clemetson, Lynette, "Younger Blacks Tell Democrats to Take Notice," *New York Times*, August 8, 2003, 1.

3. Higgins, Sean, "Groups Push for Reparations to Right U.S.' Racial Wrongs," *Investor's Business Daily*, August 23, 2002, 16.

4. *The Steve Malzberg Show*, WABC Radio, August 18, 2002.

5. "Dr. Bill Cosby Speaks," www.eightcitiesmap.com/transcript_bc.htm.

6. Dyson, Michael Eric, interview by Al Roker, *Today*, NBC, May 3, 2005.

7. Ibid.

8. Ibid.

9. Ibid.

10. Ibid.

11. Ibid.

12. "Imus Called Women's Basketball Team 'Nappy-Headed Hos,'" *Media Matters*, April 4, 2007, www.mediamatters.org/items/200704040011.

13. Imus, Don, interview by Al Sharpton, *The Al Sharpton Show*, Syndication One, April 8, 2007.

14. Caruso, David B., "Sharpton Says He Wouldn't Object to an Imus Comeback," Associated Press, July 18, 2007.

15. Sharpton, Al, interview by David Gregory, *Today*, NBC, August 15, 2007.

16. "Imus and Andy," *Investor's Business Daily*, April 11, 2007, 12.

17. Bremner, Charles, "Trials Spotlight Blacks' Hatred of 'The White Judicial System,'" *London Times*, August 7, 1990.

18. "Brutality and Judgment," *Washington Post*, August 21, 1990, 22.

19. "Punish the Traitor," *Time*, April 16, 1984, www.time.com/time/magazine/article/0,9171,954236,00.html.

20. Thomas, Evan, "Pride and Prejudice," *Time*, May 7, 1984, www.time.com/time/magazine/article/0,9171,954291-5,00.html.

21. Willman, Chris, "A Look Inside Hollywood and the Movies," *Los Angeles Times*, December 27, 1992, 7.

22. Mercurio, John, "Lott Apologizes for Thurmond Comment," *CNN.com*, December 10, 2002, www.archives.cnn.com/2002/ALLPOLITICS/12/09/lott.comment/.

23. "ABC's Roberts Unfazed by Spike Lee Charge That Lott in Klan," *CyberAlert* 7, no. 199 (December 18, 2002), www.mediaresearch.org/cyberalerts/2002/cyb20021218.asp.

24. Tapper, Jack, "Obama: Fire Imus," *ABC News*, April 11, 2007, www.abcnews.go.com/politics/story?id=3031317&page=1.

25. Taranto, James, "Imus and Obama's Daughters," *Opinion Journal*, April 13, 2007, www.opinionjournal.com/best/?id=110009939.

26. Ibid.

27. "Clintons Go Bi . . . Coastal," *TMZ.com*, May 31, 2007.

28. "Hillary Responds—Or Does She?" *Washington Times*, May 11, 2007, 16.

29. "Michael Richards Hecklers Tell Their Story," *MSNBC.com*, November 22, 2006, www.msnbc.msn.com/id/15855423/.

30. "Kramer's Racist Tirade—Caught on Tape," *TMZ.com*, November 20, 2006, www.tmz.com/2006/11/20/kramers-racist-tirade-caught-on-tape/.

31. Ryan, Joal, "No *Seinfeld* for You?" *E! Online*, November 27, 2006, www.eonline.com/news/article/index.jsp?uuid=a0d80f54-2bde-4927-80a7-717b41f6d02f.

32. Masada, Jamie, interview by Larry Elder, *The Larry Elder Show*, ABC Radio Networks, November 28, 2006.

33. Canzano, John, "Miles' Bluster Dares Blazers to Make a Choice," *Oregonian*, January 28, 2005, D-1.

34. Quick, Jason, "Cheeks Is Ready to Forgive," *Oregonian*, January 29, 2005, E1.

35. *The World Almanac 2006*, ed. William A. McGeveran Jr. (New York: World Almanac Education Group, 2006), 181.

36. Stein, Charles, "For Black Men, Job Market Hurdles Grow Ever Larger," *Boston Globe*, July 31, 2005.

37. Pierce, Greg, "Inside Politics," *Washington Times*, February 16, 2006, 6.

38. NAACP, "Comedian's Comments Are Indicative of Deeper Racism in America," news release, November 22, 2006, www.naacp.org/news/press/2006-11-27-01/index.html.

39. O'Brien, Richard, and Hank Hersch, "Tiger: New Following, Old Stereotypes," *Sports Illustrated*, April 27, 1997.

40. Ibid.

41. "Tavis Smiley: Blacks Too 'Emotional' to Obey Rules," *World Net Daily*, June 29, 2007.

42. Magnuson, Ed, "Drama and Passion Galore," *Time*, July 30, 1984, www.time.com/time/magazine/printout/0,8816,926698,00.html.

43. Associated Press, "Andrew Young Resigns from Wal-Mart Group," *MSNBC.com*, August 18, 2006, www.msnbc.msn.com/id/14406528/.

44. Lambro, Donald, "GOP Leaders Condemn Gore Aide's Remarks," *Washington Times*, January 7, 2000, 4.

45. Williams, Walter, "Racial Censorship," *Jewish World Review*, October 15, 2003, www.jewishworldreview.com/cols/williams101503.asp.

46. Montgomery, Alicia, "Hillary Denies 'Jew Bastard' Slur," *Salon*, July 17, 2000, www.archive.salon.com/politics/feature/2000/07/17/trail_mix/print.html.

47. "More Than Sex: The Secrets of Bill and Hillary Clinton Revealed by Arkansas State Trooper," NewsMax.com, September 14, 1999, www.newsmax.com/articles/?a=1999/9/13/220611.

48. Homnick, Jay D., "Race to the Top," *American Spectator*, January 12, 2006, www.spectator.org/util/print.asp?art_id=9269.

49. Wallace, Amy, "Connerly, Sen. Watson Engage in Shouting Match Legislature," *Los Angeles Times*, February 21, 1996.

50. *Allred & Taylor*, KABC TalkRadio, January 3, 2001.

51. "Still Divided by Race," *Washington Post*, November 1, 1994.

52. Clyne, Meghan, "President Bush Is 'Our Bull Connor,' Harlem's

Rep. Charles Rangel Claims," *New York Sun*, September 23, 2005, www
.nysun.com/article/20495.

53. "Belafonte Won't Back Down from Powell Slave Reference,"
CNN.com, October 18, 2002, www.archives.cnn.com/2002/US/10/15/
belafonte.powell/.

54. Peyser, Andrea, "True or Not, Sickening Story Is All Too Easy to Believe," *New York Post*, July 18, 2000, 5.

55. Trotta, Liz. "Sharpton to Go to Jail, but He Won't Be Solitary;
Black Activist Basks in Media Spotlight," *Washington Times*, March 16,
2000, 1.

56. Dershowitz, Alan, "Has Carter Crossed the Line?" *Jerusalem Post*, December 21, 2006, www.jpost.com/servlet/Satellite?cid=1164881943132&
pagename=JPost%2FJPArticle%2FShowFull.

57. Kaplan, Karen, "People Who Feel Wronged Can Really Take It to
Heart," *Los Angeles Times*, May 15, 2007, 9.

58. Ibid.

59. Malveaux, Julianne, *The Larry Elder Show*, KABC, December 22, 1998.

60. "Julianne Malveaux: USA, Bush Are Terrorists," *NewsMax*, July 11,
2005, www.newsmax.com/archives/ic/2005/7/11/170630.shtml.

61. Ibid.

62. "Chris Matthews Blames Racist White Conservatives if Harold Ford
Loses," November 5, 2006, www.newsbusters.org/node/8847.

63. Dionne, E. J. Jr., "Republicans' Double Negatives," *Washington Post*,
October 31, 2006, 21.

64. "A Political Outrage," *New York Times*, October 28, 2006.

65. Ford, Harold, interview by Chris Wallace, *Fox News Sunday*, Fox
News, October 20, 2006, www.foxnews.com/story/0,2933,226104,00
.html.

66. Nordlinger, Jay, "Tiger Time," *National Review*, April 30, 2001, 41.

67. *The World Almanac 2007*, ed. William A. McGeveran Jr. (New York: World Almanac Education Group, 2007), 563.

68. Wallace, Amy, "Connerly, Sen. Watson Engage in Shouting Match Legislature," *Los Angeles Times*, February 21, 1996.

69. "Spike Hates Your Cracker Ass," *Esquire*, October, 1992, 138.

70. Wickham, DeWayne, "Civil Rights Outrage Should Begin at Home," *USA Today*, August 2, 2005, 11.

71. Carty, Sharon Silke, "Iacocca Does Ads to Aid Battle Against Diabetes," *USA Today*, August 4, 2005.

72. Rhoden, William C., "Toughened by Adversity, Robinson Sets the Tone," *New York Times*, August 22, 2005, 3.

73. Ibid.

2. DEMOCRATS, STUPID BLACKS, AND REPUBLICANS

1. " 'Live' with Shelby Steele," April 2006, www.taemag.com/issues/articleID.19044/article_detail.asp.

2. Virasami, Bryan, and Glenn Thrush, "Martin Luther King Day Holiday Controversy," *Newsday*, January 17, 2006, 5.

3. Tanner, Michael, "Disparate Impact: Social Security and African Americans," Cato Institute Briefing Papers no. 61, February 5, 2001.

4. Teela, James, B., "Bush, Unlike Democrats, Shares Values of Black Voters," *Detroit Free Press*, October 26, 2004.

5. "In Praise of the Other Milton Friedman," *Centre Daily Times*, November 22, 2006, 8.

6. Ibid.

7. Kirsanow, Peter, "Black Back to the Back of the Line," *National Review*, April 19, 2006.

8. Perez, Evan, and Corey Dade, "Reversal of Fortune: An Immigration

Raid Aids Blacks—For a Time—After Latinos Flee," *Wall Street Journal*, January 17, 2007, 1.

9. Hicks, Joe R., "Civil Rights? How About Lawlessness?" *Los Angeles Times*, April 1, 2006, B15.

10. Rubenstein, Ed, "The Real Reagan Record," *National Review*, August 31, 1992, 38.

11. Ibid, 42.

12. "Blacks Prospered Under Reagan," *NewsMax*, June 10, 2004, www .newsmax.com/archives/ic/2004/6/10/110117.shtml.

13. Rubenstein, Ed, "The Real Reagan Record," *National Review*, August 31, 1992, 42.

14. Ibid.

15. "Quotes: A Nation Reacts," *Fox News*, June 6, 2004, www.foxnews .com/story/0,2933,121884,00.html.

16. Fears, Darryl, "Coretta Scott King's Legacy Celebrated in Final Farewell," *Washington Post*, February 8, 2006, 1.

17. Fausset, Richard, and Peter Wallsten, "A Eulogy for King, a Scolding for Bush," *Los Angeles Times*, February 8, 2006, 1.

18. Kloer, Phil, and Rodney Ho, "Latest Updates from the Funeral," *Atlanta Journal Constitution*, February 7, 2006.

19. Fausset and Wallsten, "A Eulogy for King, a Scolding for Bush."

20. Lewis, Dwight, "Belafonte's Absence at King Funeral Is Noticeable," *Tennessean.com* February 16, 2006, www.tennessean.com/apps/ pbcs.dll/article?AID=/20060216/COLUMNIST0107/602160390/1101/ NEWS.

21. Ibid.

22. "Belafonte Calls Bush 'Greatest Terrorist,'" January 8, 2006, www .msnbc.msn.com/id/10767465/.

23. Ibid.

24. Montgomery, David, "Tally Mon Come, Name Belafonte; The Singer's Latest Hits Find an Enthusiastic Audience in Washington," *Washington Post*, April 2, 2006, D1.

25. Bositis, David, "Black Elected Officials 2001," Joint Center for Political and Economic Studies, www.jointcenter.org/publications1/publication-PDFs/BEO-pdfs/2001-BEO.pdf.

26. Gray, Kathleen, "GOP Trying to Win Over Blacks. Party Wants to Show Its Umbrella Is a Wide One," *Detroit Free Press*, February 17, 2003.

27. Sokolove, Michael, "Why Is Michael Steele a *Republican* Candidate?" *New York Times*, March 26, 2006, www.nytimes.com/2006/03/26/magazine/326steele.html?ex=1301029200&en=5f68414aa2308c51&ei=5090&partner=rssuserland&emc=rss.

28. Miller, S. A., " 'Party Trumps Race' For Steele Foes," *Washington Times*, November 2, 2005, www.washtimes.com/metro/20051101-104932-4054r.htm.

29. "Slurs Against Michael Steele," *Washington Times*, October 21, 2005, www.washtimes.com/op-ed/20051030-100352-4066r.htm.

30. Miller, " 'Party Trumps Race.' "

31. Miller, S. A., "Steele Decries Black Critics as Racists," *Washington Times*, November 7, 2005, www.washtimes.com/functions/print.php?StoryID=20051107-122435-8462r.

32. Wyatt, Kristen, "Obama Tells Md. Blacks Not to Support Steele Because of His Race," Associated Press, November 3, 2006.

33. Schelzig, Erik, "Sen. Obama Stumps for Ford in Tennessee," Associated Press, November 6, 2006, www.foxnews.com/wires/2006Nov06/0,4670,TennesseeSenate,00.html.

34. Ward, Jon, "Snub by Blacks in PG Sank Steele," *Washington Times*, November 9, 2006, www.washtimes.com/metro/20061109-122539-9504r.htm.

35. Ibid.

36. Maxwell, Bill, "Black Republicans Are Strange Indeed," *St. Petersburg Times*, December 8, 1999, 21.

37. Gillespie, Nick, "Ted Rall's Latest Outrage," *Reason*, July 24, 2004.

38. Urbina, Ina, and Robert Pear, "Arrest of Former Bush Aide Shocks Friends, President: Claude Allen Accused of Series of Store Thefts," *New York Times*, March 12, 2006.

39. Ibid.

40. Reichman, Deb, "Bush Shocked by Arrest of Former Adviser," Associated Press, March 11, 2006.

41. Kaplan, Erin Aubry, "Claude Allen's Life Sentence," *Los Angeles Times*, March 15, 2006.

42. Ibid.

43. Lengel, Allan, "FBI Says Jefferson Was Filmed Taking Cash," *Washington Post*, May 22, 2006, 1.

44. Lengel, Allan, and Charles Babington, "Congressman Tried to Hide Papers, Justice Dept. Says," *Washington Post*, May 31, 2006, 4.

45. Lengel, "FBI Says Jefferson Was Filmed Taking Cash."

46. Kaplan, Jonathan E., "Former Conyers Aides Press Ethics Complaints," *The Hill*, March 1, 2006, www.hillnews.com/thehill/export/TheHill/News/Frontpage/030106/news2.html.

47. Kaplan, Erin Aubry, "Rice and the New Black Paradigm," *L.A. Weekly*, January 27, 2005, www.laweekly.com/news/news/rice-and-the-new-black-paradigm/994/.

48. Ibid.

49. Ibid.

50. Flanders, Laura, "Beware the Bushwoman," *Nation*, March 22, 2005, www.thenation.com/doc/20040322/flanders.

51. "Powell Defends Affirmative Action," CBS News, January 20, 2003, www.cbsnews.com/stories/2003/01/21/politics/main537363.shtml.

52. Apple, R. W. Jr., "Powell On Target For The White House," *Sydney Morning Herald*, May 27, 1995, 21.

53. Rice, Condoleezza, interview by Wesley Pruden, *Washington Times*, March 12, 2005, www.washingtontimes.com/world/20050311-102521-9024r.htm.

54. "Investigation Cost Too Much, Did Little," *Reading Eagle, Pa.-Knight Ridder/Tribune Business News*, March 27, 2006.

55. Power, Samantha, "It's Not Enough to Call It Genocide," *Time*, October 04, 2004, www.time.com/time/magazine/article/0,9171,995282,00.html.

56. VandeHei, Jim, "In Break with U.N., Bush Calls Sudan Killings Genocide," *Washington Post*, June 2, 2005, 19.

57. Morano, Marc, "Jesse Jackson Says GOP Pushing 'Ideology of the Confederacy,'" *CNSNews*, June 30, 2004.

58. Navarette, Ruben Jr., "Offense Taken, But Not for Name Calling," *San Francisco Gate*, August 31, 2006, www.sfgate.com/cgi-bin/article.cgi?file=/chronicle/archive/2006/08/31/EDG0SJ7NHT1.DTL.

59. Shear, Michael D., and Tim Craig, "Allen Quip Provokes Outrage, Apology," *Washington Post*, August 15, 2006; 1, www.washingtonpost.com/wp-dyn/content/article/2006/08/14/AR2006081400589.html.

60. Shear, Michael D., and Tim Craig, "Allen Denies Using Epithet to Describe Blacks," *Washington Post*, September 26, 2006, B1.

61. Shear, Michael D., "Webb Denies Ever Using Word as Epithet," *Washington Post*, September 28, 2006, 1.

62. Stirewalt, Chris, "Byrd Has Changed Since Letter from Klan Days," *Charleston Daily Mail*, April 8, 1999, 1.

63. "Trooper: Clinton Called Black People He Didn't Like 'N——gers,'" *NewsMax.com*, September 20, 1999, www.newsmax.com/articles/?a=1999/9/20/50808.

64. Dunleavy, Steve, "We Don't Need a Lie Detector with the Clintons," *New York Post*, August 23, 2000, 6.

65. "Did Hillary Commit a Hate Crime?" *Human Events*, July 28, 2000, www.findarticles.com/p/articles/mi_qa3827/is_200007/ai_n8910772.

66. "Hillary Has History of Racial Gaffes," *NewsMax.com*, January 7, 2004, www.newsmax.com/archives/ic/2004/1/7/13308.shtml.

67. Kennedy, Helen, and Michael McAuliff, "I'll Fight Like Harriet Tubman, Hil Tells Her Young Backers," *New York Daily News*, April 24, 2007, 19.

68. "Africans in America: Harriet Tubman, Part 4," PBS, April 26, 2007, www.pbs.org/wgbh/aia/part4/4p1535.html.

69. Walden, Andrew, "Farrakhan's Candidate," *Frontpage Magazine*, September 19, 2006, www.frontpagemag.com/Articles/ReadArticle.asp?ID= 24482.

70. Sultoon, Sarah, "Farrakhan: Racist or Righteous," *CNN.com*, July 12, 2001, www.archives.cnn.com/2001/WORLD/europe/07/12/farrakhan .case/index.html.

71. Ibid.

72. Gerstein, Josh, "Historic Primary Takes Shape in Minnesota," *New York Sun*, September 5, 2006.

73. Dewan, Shaila, "Election Ad Aggravates a Racial Divide in Atlanta," *New York Times*, January 22, 2007, 12.

74. Ibid.

75. Ibid.

76. "The Dog Days of July: White House Bites Back at NAACP's Attack," *Washington Post*, July 10, 2001, 7.

77. Miller, John J., and Ramesh Ponnuru, "Back On Track," *National Review Online*, December 5, 2001, www.nationalreview.com/daily/ nrprint120501.html.

78. Bond, Julian, "Campaign For America's Future Take Back America Conference," June 2, 2004, 3:50–5:30 session, www.ourfuture.org/ document.cfm?documentID=1607.

79. Taranto, James, "Whitewashing a Black Leader—II," *Opinion Journal*, February 6, 2006, www.opinionjournal.com/best/?id=110007929.

80. Horowitz, Jason, "Biden Unbound: Lays Into Clinton, Obama, Edwards," *New York Observer*, February 5, 2007, 1, www.observer.com/20070205/20070205_Jason_Horowitz_pageone_newsstory1.html.

81. "Labor Force by City & Unincorporated Community Los Angeles County. Recent Preliminary Data," November 2004, www.laalmanac.com/employment/em03.htm.

82. Liebau, Carol Platt, "Leading a Parade Down the Road to Nowhere," CaliforniaRepublic.org, April 19, 2004, www.californiarepublic.org/archives/Columns/Liebau/20040419LiebauParade.html.

83. City data, Inglewood, California, January 8, 2007, www.city-data.com/city/Inglewood-California.html.

84. Galvin, Andrew, "Wal-Mart on Ballot in Inglewood," *Orange County Register*, April 6, 2004, 1

85. "Wal-Mart in the Crosshairs," *Orange County Register*, April 8, 2004.

86. Biddle, RiShawn, "Sam's Curse," *Reason*, March 18, 2004, www.reason.com/news/show/32724.html.

87. Liebau, Carol Platt, "Leading a Parade Down the Road to Nowhere."

88. "Wal-Mart in the Crosshairs Series: Seiler," *Orange County Register*, April 8, 2004.

89. Biddle, RiShawn, "Sam's Curse."

90. Liebau, Carol Platt, "Leading a Parade Down the Road to Nowhere."

91. "Major Ordinance Passed at City Council Meeting," *Inglewood Today Weekly*, July 20, 2006, www.laane.org/pressroom/stories/inglewood/060823inglewoodToday.html.

92. Ibid.

93. "The Wal-Mart Timeline," January 9, 2007, www.walmartfacts.com/content/default.aspx?id=3.

94. *Meet the Press*, NBC, January 14, 2007, www.msnbc.msn.com/id/16577874/.

95. Hook, Janet, "The *Times/Bloomberg* Poll; Voters Favor McCain over Clinton in '08," *Los Angeles Times*, December 14, 2006, 1.

96. Ibid.

97. Kennedy, Edward, interview by Tim Russert, *Meet the Press*, NBC, April 23, 2006, www.msnbc.msn.com/id/12407213/page/4/.

98. Bartlett, Bruce, "Media's Coverage of Scandal Exposes Bias," *Townhall*, January 24, 2006, www.townhall.com/columnists/column.aspx?UrlTitle=medias_coverage_of_scandal_exposes_bias&ns=Bruce-Bartlett&dt=01/24/2006&page=full&comments=true.

99. "The First Black Congressmen," *IPOAA*, www.ipoaa.com/1st_black_congressmen.htm.

100. "African-Americans in the Twentieth Century," www.liunet.edu/cwis/cwp/library/african/2000/1930.htm.

101. "African Americans in Congress," *Encarta*, www.encarta.msn.com/media_521506343/African_Americans_in_Congress.html.

102. "Appendix to the Congressional Globe," Library of Congress, 1854, www.memory.loc.gov/cgi-bin/ampage?collId=llcg&fileName=036/llcg036.db&recNum=762.

103. "African Americans in Texas Politics," www.texasgop.org/site/PageServer?pagename=library_aa.

104. "Free Negroes, 1619–1860," Answers.com, www.answers.com/topic/free-negroes-1619-1860.

105. Barton, David, "Black History Issue 2002," www.wallbuilders.com/resources/search/detail.php?ResourceID=63.

106. Ibid.

107. Ibid.

108. Barton, David, "Black History Issue 2003," www.wallbuilders.com/resources/search/detail.php?ResourceID=95#_ednref53.

109. "People & Events: Rise of the Ku Klux Klan," *American Experience*, PBS, www.pbs.org/wgbh/amex/grant/peopleevents/e_klan.html.

110. "The 1957 Civil Rights Act," www.historylearningsite.co.uk/1957_civil_rights_act.htm.

111. Barabak, Mark Z., "For Many Blacks, Election Isn't on Radar," *Los Angeles Times*, October 17, 2000, 1.

112. "Civil Rights Act of 1964," Wikipedia, www.en.wikipedia.org/wiki/Civil_Rights_Act_of_1964.

113. Ibid.

114. Kane, Tim, "Who Are the Recruits? The Demographic Characteristics of U.S. Military Enlistment, 2003–2005," October 26, 2006, www.heritage.org/Research/NationalSecurity/cda06-09.cfm.

115. Buchanan, Patrick J., "The Neocons and Nixon's Southern Strategy," The American Cause, December 30, 2002, www.theamericancause.org/pattheneoconsandnixons.htm.

116. Sanger, Margaret, "The Pivot of Civilization," World Wide School, January 27, 2007, www.worldwideschool.org/library/books/socl/social concerns/ThePivotofCivilization/legalese.html.

117. Innes, Roy, "Gun Control Sprouts from Racist Soil," *Wall Street Journal*, November 11, 1991, 14.

118. Ibid.

119. Lott, John R., Jr., "More Laws Won't Cure Gun Problems," *Los Angeles Times*, June 17, 1999, 9.

120. Byrne, Bridget, "GOP Guns for Spike," E! online, May 26, 1999, www.eonline.com/News/Items/0,1,4822,00.html.

121. Tempest, Rone, "A 'Community Tragedy' Deepens," *Los Angeles Times*, July 23, 2005, B3.

122. "Democrats Clash in Early Debate," *Inside Politics*, CNN.com, May 4, 2003, www.cnn.com/2003/ALLPOLITICS/05/04/dems.debate/index.html.

123. Hasson, Judi, "Mayor D.C. Crime Rate's Low," *USA Today*, March 24, 1989, 2.

124. Barabak, Mark Z., "For Many Blacks, Election Isn't on Radar."

125. Sowell, Thomas, "Trying to Attract the Wrong Blacks," *Baltimore Sun*, February 2, 2006, 13.

126. Stoddard, Ed, "Many Conservative Blacks Still Vote for Democrats," Reuters, November 1, 2006.

3. STUPID BLACK LEADERS

1. "Cosby Rips Blacks for Abuse, Poor Parenting," July 2, 2004, www .msnbc.msn.com/id/5345290/http://www.msnbc.msn.com/id/ 5345290/.

2. Bond, Julian, "Civil Rights, Now and Then," speech at Agnes Scott College Martin Luther King Jr. Convocation, January 27, 1999, www .agnesscott.edu/about/p_newsarticle.asp?id=44.

3. Hamburger, Tom, and Stuart Silverstein, "NAACP Chief Gordon Resigns, At Odds with Board," *Los Angeles Times*, March 5, 2007, 7.

4. DeBose, Brian, "NAACP to Target Private Business," *Washington Times*, July 12, 2005.

5. Ibid.

6. Magill, Ken, "From J. P. Morgan Chase, an Apology and $5 Million in Slavery Reparations," *New York Sun*, February 1, 2005.

7. Ibid.

8. Mooney, Kevin, "'Stealth Racism' Still Pervasive in America, Says NAACP," *CNSNews.com*, December 19, 2006, www.cnsnews.com/View Culture.asp?Page=/Culture/archive/200612/CUL20061219b.html.

9. Ibid.

10. "A Curriculum of Indoctrination," *Issues and Views*, Fall 1992.

11. Ibid.

12. Ibid.

13. Ibid.

14. Richardson, Lisa, "Funeral Service Celebrates Williams Conversion from Violence to Peace," *Los Angeles Times*, December 21, 2005.

15. Hall, Carla, "Mesereau's Fame Doesn't Alter Focus," *Los Angeles Times*, November 23, 2005.

16. "Transcript of Bush's Address to N.A.A.C.P." *New York Times*, July 20, 2006.

17. Riechmann, Deb, "Bush Acknowledges Racism Still Exists," Associated Press, July 20, 2006, www.breitbart.com/news/2006/07/20/D8IVQT000.html.

18. Sharpton, Al, interview by Bill O'Reilly, *The O'Reilly Factor*, Fox News, July 20, 2006.

19. Wallsten, Peter, "Bush Vows to Patch Up His Ties to the NAACP," *Los Angeles Times*, July 21, 2006, 17.

20. "The Dog Days of July: White House Bites Back at NAACP's Attack," *Washington Post*, July 10, 2001, 7.

21. Miller, John J., and Ramesh Ponnuru, "Back On Track," *National Review Online*, December 5, 2001, www.nationalreview.com/daily/nrprint120501.html.

22. Bond, Julian, "Campaign For America's Future Take Back America Conference," June 2, 2004, 3:50–5:30 session, www.ourfuture.org/document.cfm?documentID=1607.

23. "Finally, the NAACP," *Los Angeles Times*, July 21, 2006.

24. Stolberg, Sheryl Gay, "Bush in First Speech to N.A.A.C.P., Offers Message of Reconciliation," *New York Times*, July 21, 2006, 15.

25. "Jane Bolin, 98," *Los Angeles Times*, January 13, 2007, B12.

26. Rondy, John, "Milwaukee's Black Leaders Say the Enemy Is Within," Reuters, July 7, 2005.

27. Simmons, Ann M., "The Storm This Time: An Outburst of Crime," *Los Angeles Times*, June 23, 2006, 5.

28. Lopez, Steve, "A Glaring Omission from Legacy of the Riots—Apologies," *Los Angeles Times*, May 1, 2002, B1.

29. Gresko, Jessica, "Watts Riots Remembered," *Los Angeles Times*, August 6, 2005, B3.

30. Reitman, Valerie, and Landsberg, Mitchell, "Watts Riots, 40 Years Later," *Los Angeles Times*, August 11, 2005, 1.

31. Postrel, Virginia, "The Long-Term Consequences of the Race Riots in the Late 1960s Come into View," *New York Times*, December 30, 2004, 2.

32. Ibid.

33. *The Larry Elder Show*, ABC Radio Networks, August 16, 2005.

34. Brooks, Arthur C., "Religious Faith and Charitable Giving," *Policy Review Online*, November 10, 2005, www.policyreview.org/oct03/brooks .html.

35. Ibid.

36. "1997 Economic Census Minority- and Woman-Owned Businesses United States," U.S. Census Bureau, November 11, 2005, www.census .gov/epcd/mwb97/us/us.html/#PDF.

37. "2002 Survey of Business Owners Preliminary Estimates of Business Ownership by Gender, Hispanic or Latino Origin, and Race: 2002," U.S. Census Bureau, November 11, 2005, www.census.gov/csd/sbo/state/ st00.HTM.

38. "African-American Entrepreneurship Reaching Higher Heights," *Jet* 108: no. 10 (September 5, 2005):6.

39. "The Buying Power of Black America—2003," *Target Market News*, November 3, 2005, www.targetmarketnews.com/buyingpowerstats .htm.

40. *The World Almanac 2006*, ed. William A. McGeveran Jr. (New York: World Almanac Education Group, 2006), 854.

41. Leo, John, "Shocking, But Not True," *US News & World Report*, November 22, 1999, 18.

42. Ibid.

43. Young, Yolanda, "Tough Choices for Tough Times," *USA Today*, April 2, 2004, 9.

44. Leo, "Shocking, But Not True."

45. Peterson, Jonathan, "Racial Gap in Loans Is High in State," *Los Angeles Times*, September 29, 2005, C1.

46. Ibid.

47. Hudson, Mike, and E. Scott Reckard, "More Homeowners with Good Credit Getting Stuck with Higher-Rate Loans," *Los Angeles Times*, October 24, 2005, 1.

48. Thibault, David, "Payday Loans Blamed for Trapping Poor in 'Quicksand,'" *CNSNews.com*, December 1, 2006, www.cnsnews.com/Nation/Archive/200612/NAT20061201a.html.

49. Karger, Howard, "Cut to the Chase; Swimming with the Sharks: Compared to Your Average Predatory Lender, Tony Soprano Looks Like a Nice Guy," *Chicago Sun-Times*, January 15, 2006.

50. "The Bottom Line," *San Antonio Express-News*, December 5, 2005, B5.

51. "Report: Company Sharpton Hawks Is Banned in His Own State," Associated Press, December 2, 2005.

52. Karger, "Cut to the Chase."

53. "Al Sharpton's New Campaign," *New Republic Online*, December 22, 2005, www.tnr.com/doc.mhtml?i=20051219&s=notebook121905twp.

54. Ibid.

55. "Loan-Shark Sharpton," *New York Post*, December 3, 2005, 18.

56. Ibid.

57. Brown, Stone C, "Predatory Lending," *New Crisis* 108, no. 3 (May 1, 2001): 28.

58. Nordlinger, Jay, "Power Dem," *National Review*, March 20, 2000, 32–34, www.nationalreview.com/20Mar00/nordlinger032000.html.

59. Sherman, Scott, "He Has a Dream," *Nation*, April 16, 2001, 15.

60. Kurtz, Howard, "Sharpton Pleads Not Guilty to Tax-Evasion Charges in N.Y.," *Washington Post*, July 1, 1989, 6.

61. Sack, Kevin, "Guilty Plea by Sharpton in Tax Case," *New York Times*, January 6, 1993, 1.

62. Nordlinger, "Power Dem," 34.

63. Ibid.

64. Feder, Don, "Dems Court Homicidal Race-Hustler," *Jewish World Review*, February 22, 2000, www.jewishworldreview.com/cols/feder022200.asp.

65. Nordlinger, "Power Dem," 34.

66. Ibid, 34–35.

67. Boteach, Shmuley, "Sharpton's Missed Opportunity," *Jerusalem Post*, November 9, 2001, 8B.

68. Siegel, Fred, "New Sharpton? Only to Old Fools," *New York Observer*, March 13, 2000.

69. Nordlinger, "Power Dem," 35.

70. Sharpton, Al, *The Larry Elder Show*, ABC Radio Networks, December 20, 2001.

71. "Sharpton Sues HBO Over Cocaine Tape," *Fox News*, July 24, 2002, www.foxnews.com/story/0,2933,58638,00.html.

72. Ibid.

73. Ibid.

74. Ibid.

75. Drury, Bob, Robert E. Kessler, and Mike McAlary, "The Minister and the Feds," *Newsday*, January 20, 1988, 1.

76. Bishop, Ian, "Feds Probe Rev. Al," *New York Post*, April 12, 2005, 4.

77. Ibid.

78. Kessler, Ronald, "HUD Secretary Attacks Black Victimhood," *News-Max*, January 3, 2007, www.newsmax.com/archives/articles/2007/1/2/174405.shtml?s=lh.

79. Ibid.

80. "Bush Chooses Alphonso Jackson to Serve as HUD Secretary," U.S. Department of State, Bureau of International Information Programs, December 12, 2003, www.usinfo.state.gov/xarchives/display.html?p=washfile-english&y=2003&m=December&x=20031212160443ssoro.1845514.

81. Kessler, "HUD Secretary Attacks Black Victimhood."

82. Ibid.

83. Ibid.

84. *The World Factbook, 2005,* www.cia.gov/library/publications/the-world-factbook.

4. STUPID BLACK POLITICIANS

1. Benac, Nancy, "Dean Ready to Take Charge of Democrats," Associated Press, February 11, 2005.

2. "District Profile: North Carolina—12th District," *CNN.com*, September 1, 2005, www.cnn.com/ALLPOLITICS/1996/states/NC/NC12.shtml.

3. Watt, Melvin, interview by Brian Lamb, "Q&A," C-span, February 20, 2005, www.q-and-a.org/Transcript/?ProgramID=1011&QueryText=+Mel+Watt.

4. White, Jerry, "Michigan Judge Condemns 16-Year-Old to Life Sentence with No Parole," www.wsws.org/articles/1999/mar1999/high—m18.shtml.

5. "Census 2000 Supplementary Survey Profile, Population and Housing Profile: Congressional District 14, Michigan," www.census

.gov/acs/www/Products/Profiles/Single/2000/C2SS/Narrative/500/
NP50000US2614.htm.

6. "Census 2000 Supplementary Survey Profile, MI Congressional District 14, Table 2. Profile of Selected Social Characteristics," www.census.gov/acs/www/Products/Profiles/Single/2000/C2SS/Tabular/500/50000US26142.htm.

7. "Major Issues—Reparations," statements from briefing: The Impact of Slavery on African Americans Today, April 6, 2005, www.house.gov/conyers/news_reparations.htm.

8. Payne, Henry, "Eminem's Real Detroit," *National Review*, November 18, 2002, www.nationalreview.com/script/printpage.p?ref=/comment/comment-payne111802.asp.

9. Ibid.

10. Ibid.

11. Ibid.

12. Ibid.

13. Waters, Maxine, *The Larry Elder Show*, KABC TalkRadio, June 8, 2000.

14. Seper, Jerry, "Agents Cite 'Political Interference': DEA Ends Probe after Profiling Claim," *Washington Times*, December 7, 2000, 4.

15. "Cuba No Enemy to U.S. Fugitives," *Palm Beach Post*, February 7, 1999, 1E.

16. "New Jersey Top Cop Rips Lawmaker on Chesimard," *Star-Ledger*, January 14, 1999, 4.

17. Ford, Andrea, and Michael K. Frisby, "Maximum Effect," *Emerge*, April 1997, 46.

18. Newman, Maria, "The Angry Insider U.S. Rep. Maxine Waters Is a Combative but Effective Voice of the Disenfranchised," *Kansas City Star*, May 30, 1992.

19. Murphy, Dean E., "Waters: No Apologies for Her Calling the President a Racist," *Los Angeles Times*, August 9, 1992, 14.

20. Barone, Michael, *2006 Almanac of American Politics* (Washington, D.C.: National Journal, 2005), 462.

21. Laksin, Jacob, "A Profile in Corruption," *FrontPage Magazine* June 16, 2006, www.frontpagemag.com/Articles/ReadArticle.asp?ID=22965.

22. Barone, Michael, *2006 Almanac of American Politics.*

23. Ibid.

24. Ayres, B. Drummond Jr., "Black Congressman Fires Shot for Blacks," *New York Times*, April 6, 1998, 16.

25. d'Oliveira, Steve, "Putting His House in Order," *Sun Sentinel Ft. Lauderdale*, October 6, 1996, 8.

26. Laksin, Jacob, "A Profile in Corruption."

27. "Rep. Charles Rangel's Cuba Trip Subsidized by Castro," *NewsMax*, June 8, 2006, www.newsmax.com/archives/ic/2006/6/8/84327.shtml.

28. "Illinois Senate Candidate Barack Obama," transcript, *Washington Post*, July 27, 2004, www.washingtonpost.com/wp-dyn/articles/A19751-2004Jul27.html.

29. Allen-Mills, Tony, "Obama's Charm Lost on America's Black Activists," *Sunday Times*, January 14, 2006, www.timesonline.co.uk/article/0,,2089-2546081.html.

30. Ibid.

31. Kramer, Marcia, "Sharpton Rips Obama, Keeps Endorsement on Hold," WCBS, March 12, 2007, www.wcbstv.com/topstories/local_story_071165711.html.

32. "Sharpton's Barack Attack," *New York Observer*, March 19, 2007, 18.

33. Burchfiel, Nathan, "Black Liberals Hesitant to Endorse Obama for President," *CNSNews.com*, January 22, 2007, www.cnsnews.com/ViewPrint.asp?Page=/Politics/archive/200701/POL20070122a.html.

34. "2008 Presidential Candidates: Barack Obama on the Issues," www.ontheissues.org/Barack_Obama.htm.

35. Allen-Mills, "Obama's Charm Lost on America's Black Activists."

36. Ibid.

37. Curry, Tom, "Clinton Versus Obama: Is There Any Difference?" MSNBC.com, November 29, 2006, www.msnbc.msn.com/id/15920730/.

38. Mitchell, Mary, "Why Are Black Lawmakers Already Jumping on Clinton Bandwagon?" *Chicago Sun-Times*, February 15, 2007, 14.

39. Davenport, Jim, "Endorsement Raises Doubts About Obama," Associated Press, February 13, 2007.

40. Richards, Sarah, E., "Murphy Drops His Caucus Bid," *Chicago Tribune*, July 17, 2001.

41. Hearn, Josephine, "Black Caucus: Whites Not Allowed," January 22, 2007, www.politico.com/news/stories/0107/2389.html.

42. Ibid.

43. Ibid.

44. Scales, Ann, "Race, Politics and Perception," *Boston Globe*, April 12, 1996, 3.

45. Hicks, Jonathan P., "Winning Isn't Everything," *New York Times*, March 14, 1997, 1.

46. Colgan, Jim, "Home State Record: Al Sharpton," New Hampshire Public Radio, January 9, 2004, www.nhpr.org/node/5584.

47. Dionne, E. J. Jr., "Jackson Share of Votes by Whites Triples in '88," *New York Times*, June 13, 1988, B1.

48. Flannery, Mike, "Poll: Many Black Voters Don't Identify with Obama," CBS News, January 25, 2007, www.cbs2chicago.com/local/local_story_025191728.html.

49. "Hot Topic: Uncle Charlie Wants You!" *Wall Street Journal*, November 25, 2006, 8.

50. Scarborough, Rowan, "Middle Class Filling Up Military, Study Says," *Washington Times*, November 8, 2005, 6.

51. "Backdoor Bill on Draft," *Palm Beach Post*, November 26, 2006, E2.

52. "John Kerry Thinks," *Washington Times*, November 1, 2006, 16.

53. Ibid.

54. Miles, Donna, "Official Debunks Myths About Military Recruits," *American Forces Press Service*, December 5, 2005.

55. Soloman, John, "Kerry's '72 Army Comments Mirror Latest," Associated Press, November 2, 2006.

56. Miles, "Official Debunks Myths about Military Recruits."

57. Scarborough, Rowan, "Middle Class Filling Up Military, Study Says."

58. Horowitz, David, "Black America at War," *Front Page*, November 5, 2001.

59. Wallsten, Peter, "Kerry's Fighting Words Give Way to Apology," *Los Angeles Times*, November 2, 2006, 15.

5. STUPID BLACK ENTERTAINERS

1. "The 40 Most Obnoxious Quotes of 2006," *Right Wing News*, December 18, 2006, www.rightwingnews.com/archives/week_2006_12_17 .PHP#006999.

2. Parham, Marti, "Queen Latifah Still Reigns as Artist, Activist and Entrepreneur," *Jet*, July 23, 2007, 63.

3. Ibid.

4. Ibid.

5. "Diddy Declared Richest Person in Hip Hop," EURweb.com, August 9, 2006, www.eurweb.com/printable.cfm?id=27931.

6. Strong, Nolan, "Diddy Says Bush Has to Go, Q-Tip Educates Young Voters," February 20, 2004, www.allhiphop.com/Hiphopnews/?ID= 2881.

7. Combs, Sean "P Diddy," interview by Bill Hemmer, *American Morning*, CNN, November 2, 2004, www.transcripts.cnn.com/TRANSCRIPTS/ 0411/02/ltm.05.htm.

8. Ibid.

9. "Against the Odds," August 18,2005, www.judgemathis.net/againsttheodds.htm.

10. Morano, Marc, "Bush, GOP Labeled 'Thieves' Who 'Need to Be Locked Up,'" Crosswalk.com, August 8, 2005, www.crosswalk.com/news/1344556.html.

11. Ibid.

12. Cosby, Camille, "America Taught My Son's Killer to Hate Blacks," *USA Today*, July 8, 1998.

13. "Powell, Rice Accused of Toeing the Line," *Fox News*, October 22, 2002, www.foxnews.com/story/0,2933,66288,00.html.

14. Ingram, Dexter, "Belafonte Should Stick to Singing," Heritage Foundation, October 27, 2002, www.heritage.org/Press/Commentary/ED102702.cfm.

15. Ibid.

16. "Mistaken Identity," *Investor's Business Daily*, August 10, 2005, 12.

17. Farah, Joseph, "Belafonte, Glover Trash U.S. in Cuba," *World Net Daily*, December 16, 2002, www.worldnetdaily.com/news/article.asp?ARTICLE_ID=30011.

18. "People in the News," *News Tribune*, January 21, 2003, www.newstribune.com/stories/012103/ent_0121030037.asp.

19. "Belafonte Says U.S. Leaders 'Possessed of Evil,'" Reuters, March 4, 2003, www.abcnews.go.com/wire/Entertainment/reuters20030304_173.html.

20. Williams, Juan, interview by Sean Hannity, "Comic Artist Calls Condoleezza Rice a Murderer," *Hannity & Colmes*, Fox News, February 4, 2004.

21. McGruder, Aaron, speech at Emory University, September 10, 2002.

22. *CyberAlert* 6, no. 182 (November 19, 2001), Media Research Center, www.mediaresearch.org/cyberalerts/2001/cyb20011119.asp#5.

23. *CyberAlert* 8, no. 28 (February 12, 2003), Media Research Center, www.mediaresearch.org/cyberalerts/2003/cyb20030212.asp#4.

24. *CyberAlert* 7, no. 188 (November 25, 2002), Media Research Center, www.mediaresearch.org/cyberalerts/2002/cyb20021125.asp#4.

25. Orin, Deborah, "Dirty Trick: Lewd Whoopi Bashes Bush," *New York Post*, July 9, 2004, 1.

26. De Moraes, Lisa, "Kanye West's Torrent of Criticism Live on NBC," *Washington Post*, September 3, 2005, www.washingtonpost.com/wpdyn/content/article/2005/09/03/AR2005090300165.html.

27. Williams, Zoe, "Quite Contrary," *Guardian*, December 17, 2005, www.arts.guardian.co.uk/features/story/0,,1669258,00.html.

28. "Mary J. Blige," *Billboard*, January 3, 2007, www.billboard.com/bbcom/retrieve_chart_history.do?JSESSIONID=FcGWpW1LNXK-bGLH81jQBLxST3HRYwvBwkBW24Vh9rLnWKqSwC1Kf!-500187014&model.vnuArtistId=43746&model.vnuAlbumId=752044.

29. "Mary J. Blige's Achievements and Awards," January 3, 2007, www.en.wikipedia.org/wiki/Mary_J._Blige's_achievements_and_awards.

30. Ibid.

31. Ibid.

32. Ibid.

6. STUPID BLACKS AND KATRINA

1. Daunt, Tina, and Robin Abcarian, "Katrina's Aftermath; Survivors, Others Take Offense at Word 'Refugees'; Dictionary Definitions Aside, Many Consider the Term Inappropriate—Even Racist—When Applied to Hurricane Katrina Evacuees," *Los Angeles Times*, September 8, 2005, 12.

2. Ibid.

3. "Question of Race Hurricane and the Poor," *ABC News*, September 2, 2005.

4. Rush, George, and Joanna Molloy with Patrick Huguenin and Cristina Kinon, "Summers Recalls Sting-Ing Rebuke," *New York Daily News*, October 6, 2006.

5. Shafer, Jack, "The Rebellion of the Talking Heads," *Slate*, September 2, 2005, www.slate.com/id/2125581/.

6. Ibid.

7. Kalette, Denise, "Dean: Race Played a Role in Katrina Deaths," Associated Press, September 7, 2005, www.breitbart.com/news/2005/09/07/D8CFNMPG0.html.

8. Dvorak, Petula, "Hurricane Victims Demand More Help; Federal Government Not Doing Enough to Aid Rebuilding, Survivors Say," *Washington Post*, February 9, 2006, 12.

9. Moore, Art, "Barney Frank Accuses Bush of 'Ethnic Cleansing.' " *World Net Daily*, January 5, 2007, www.worldnetdaily.com/news/article.asp?ARTICLE_ID=53650.

10. Lucas, Fred, "Katrina 'Ethnic Cleansing' Remarks Causes Stir," Cybercast News Service, January 9, 2007, www.cnsnews.com/ViewCulture.asp?Page=/Culture/archive/200701/CUL20070109a.html.

11. Lee, Spike, interview by Bill Maher, *Real Time with Bill Maher*, HBO, August 25, 2006.

12. Ibid.

13. Ibid.

14. Farley, John, "Kids and Race," *Time* November 24, 1997.

15. Taranto, James, "Is Katrina Racist?" *Wall Street Journal*, September 2, 2005.

16. Leo, John, "Most Media Got Katrina Wrong," *Townhall*, January 9, 2006.

17. "Katrina Death Stats Contradict Racial Complaints," December 12, 2005, www.newsmax.com/scripts/printer_friendly.pl?page=http://www.newsmax.com/archives/ic/2005/12/12/103853.shtml.

18. Johnson, Allen, "Hurricane-Wracked New Orleans to Elect Mayor," May 20, 2006, news.yahoo.com/s/afp/20060520/wl_afp/usstormneworleanspolitics_060520114121.

19. Moore, "Barney Frank Accuses Bush of 'Ethnic Cleansing.'"

20. Ibid.

21. Douglas, William, "Blacks Gathered in D.C. Focus on Katrina," *Houston Chronicle*, October 16, 2005, 3.

22. "Video: Blanco Assured Washington Levees Not Breached," www.foxnews.com/story/0,2933,186688,00.html.

23. Ray Nagin, interview by Soledad O'Brien, *American Morning*, CNN, September 5, 2005, www.transcripts.cnn.com/TRANSCRIPTS/0509/05/ltm.01.html.

24. "History's Happenings for October 8," www.csamerican.com/Event.asp?page=10/8/2006.

25. "Mary, Mary, Quite (to the) Contrary," *Investor's Business Daily*, September 12, 2005, 18.

26. Silverstein, Ken, and Josh Meyer, "Louisiana Officials Indicted Before Katrina Hit," *Los Angeles Times*, September 17, 2005, 17.

27. "Media Learn an Amazing Fact: Reality," *Chicago Tribune*, February 12, 1992, 12.

28. Ibid.

29. Woodrow, Stephanie, "The 50 Richest Members of Congress; Lawmakers' Fortunes Continue to Increase," *Roll Call*, September 11, 2006.

30. Coile, Zachary, "Bay Lawmakers Among Wealthiest Feinstein and Pelosi Continue to Top the List of the Richest Members of Congress," *San Francisco Gate*, June 26, 2004, www.sfgate.com/cgi-bin/article.cgi?f=/c/a/2004/06/26/BAG7B7CDMQ1.DTL.

31. Leibovich, Mark, "Talk of Pelosi as Speaker Delights Both Parties," *New York Times*, May 30, 2006, 1.

32. "Hillary Clinton Praises Belafonte's Anti-US Rant," *NewsMax.com*,

September 24, 2005, www.newsmax.com/archives/ic/2005/9/24/102013.shtml.

33. "The 2004 Political Landscape," Pew Research Center, www.people-press.org/reports/display.php3?PageID=753.

34. "Eye-Opening Statistics from *Who Really Cares*," www.arthurbrooks.net/statistics.html.

35. Gelinas, Nicole, "Who's Killing New Orleans?" *City Journal*, Autumn 2005, www.city-journal.org/html/15_4_new_orleans.html.

36. "Louis Farrakhan: Levees Were 'Blown Up,' " *Newsmax.com*, September 14, 2005, www.newsmax.com/archives/ic/2005/9/14/201055.shtml.

37. "Wash Postie: 'Reasonable' Blacks Believe Levee Plot," *NewsMax.com*, September 18, 2005, www.newsmax.com/archives/ic/2005/9/18/124302.shtml.

38. Feder, Don, "The Worst Offenders of the Year Gone By," *Boston Herald*, January 2, 1992, 21.

39. *The Larry Elder Show*, ABC Radio Networks, December 7, 2005.

40. "New Orleans Evacuees and Activists Testify at Explosive House Hearing on the Role of Race and Class in Government's Response to Hurricane Katrina," *Democracy Now*, December 9, 2005, www.democracynow.org/article.pl?sid=05/12/09/1443240.

41. "ABC, CBS and NBC Jump to Push Racism Charges of Katrina Victims," Media Research Center, December 7, 2005, www.mediaresearch.org/cyberalerts/2005/cyb20051207.asp#1.

42. Rudd, Shayna Y., "After Unfair Media Coverage, Blacks Work to Restore Community," *New York Times*, October 18, 2006, www.nytimes-institute.com/23media.html.

43. "The Buying Power of Black America-2000," *Target Market News*, November 2001, www.targetmarketnews.com/numbers/index.htm.

44. *The World Almanac 2002*, ed. William A. McGeveran Jr.(New York: World Almanac Education Group 2002), 106.

45. McCaskill, Claire, interview by Tim Russert, *Meet the Press*, NBC, October 8, 2006.

46. *The Larry Elder Show*, ABC Radio Networks, September 14, 2005.

47. Feran, Tim, "55th Annual Primetime Emmy Awards," *Columbus Dispatch*, September 22, 2003, B8.

48. "Discovering Hidden Washington: Special Presentation—Nannie Helen Burroughs," *Library of Congress Live*, www.loc.gov/loc/kidslc/sp-burroughs.html.

49. Ibid.

50. Burroughs, Nannie Helen, *Twelve Things the Negro Must Do to Improve Himself*, November 29, 2006 www.blackmeninamerica.com/12.htm.

51. Stern, William J., "How Dagger John Saved New York's Irish," *Wall Street Journal*, March 17, 1997, 18.

52. Stern, William J., "How Dagger John Saved New York's Irish," *City Journal*, Spring 1997, www.city-journal.org/html/7_2_a2.html.

53. Ibid.

54. Ibid.

55. Stern, "How Dagger John Saved New York's Irish," *Wall Street Journal.*

7. THE CRIMINAL JUSTICE SYSTEM

1. Kennedy, Ted, "Opening Statement by Senator Edward M. Kennedy on Nomination of John Roberts to Chief Justice of the Supreme Court," Committee on the Judiciary, September 12, 2005.

2. "Opening Statement of Senator Kennedy (D- MA), Senate Judiciary Committee Member," Tuesday, September 10, 1991, morning session, www.people.virginia.edu/~ybf2u/Thomas-Hill/0910a03.html.

3. Kennedy, Edward M., "Why Roberts's Views Matter," *Washington Post*, August 19, 2005, 21.

4. "Memorable quotes for *Menace II Society* (1993)," May 17, 2007, www.imdb.com/title/tt0107554/quotes.

5. "Jackson Wins Case, Loses Battle for Public Opinion," *Yahoo!*

News, June 14, 2005, www.news.yahoo.com/s/afp/20050614/en_afp/afpentertainmentus_050614181052.

6. "Poll: Most Think Jackson, Bryant, Stewart Will Get Fair Trials," KABC and Associated Press, January 15, 2004, www.abclocal.go.com/kabc/ontv/print_011503_nw_poll_trials.html.

7. Schlesinger, Arthur Jr., "A New Era Begins—But History Remains," *Wall Street Journal*, December 11, 1991, 16.

8. "Jermaine Jackson: Brother's Arrest a 'Modern-Day Lynching,'" *CNN.com*, November 21, 2003, www.cnn.com/2003/LAW/11/20/cnna.jackson/.

9. "Jackson Jury Candidate: 'I'd Be Worried If I Were Him,'" World Entertainment News Network, February 25, 2005.

10. Ibid.

11. "Stanley Tookie Williams Executed at San Quentin," December 13, 2005, www.democracynow.org/article.pl?sid=05/12/13/1524254.

12. Sheppard, Harrison, "A Matter of Life and Death," *Daily News*, December 9, 2005, N1.

13. Phillips, Joseph C., "Tookie Goes Hollywood," December 5, 2005, www.josephcphillips.com/html/EssayShow.asp?Essay=210.

14. Richardson, Lisa, "Drive Starts to Spare Life of Gang Leader," *Los Angeles Times*, December 7, 2005.

15. "NAACP Chief Stumps for Williams," *Houston Chronicle*, December 7, 2005, 13.

16. "NAACP Wants Williams' Execution Stopped," UPI International, December 7, 2005.

17. "Atkins Death Sentence Would Violate Spirit and Intent of Supreme Court Decision," July 16, 2005, www.naacp.org/news/press/2005-07-26/index.html.

18. "Byrd Vote-T.V.," October 2000, www.gwu.edu/~action/ads2/adnaacp.html.

19. "Third Defendant Is Convicted in Dragging Death in Texas," *New York Times*, November 19, 1999.

20. "Request for Clemency by Stanley Williams," *Statement of Decision*, office of Governor Arnold Schwarzenegger, December 12, 2005, www .deadlinethemovie.com/Williams_Clemency_Decision.pdf.

21. Sack, Kevin, "Affirmative Action Alive and Well in Atlanta," *New York Times*, June 10, 1996.

22. "Cross Country," *U.S. News & World Report*, June 26, 2006.

23. Jeffrey, Scott, and Beth Warren, "Campbell Squeaked Past Corruption Charges, Juror's Say," *Atlanta Journal-Constitution*, March 12, 2006.

24. "Ex-Atlanta Mayor to Begin Prison Sentence," Associated Press, August 4, 2006, www.washingtonpost.com/wp-dyn/content/article/ 2006/08/03/AR2006080301630.html?referrer=email.

25. Tucker, Cynthia, "Poor Little Big Man's Pity Party. No Reason to Feel Sorry for Campbell," *Atlanta Journal-Constitution*, January 18, 2006, 15.

26. Coen, Jeff, "Judge Lays Down Own Law: No All-White Juries," *Chicago Tribune*, July 25, 2005.

27. Herrera, Kevin, "Out of Tragedy May Come Unity," *Los Angeles Wave*, July 21, 2005, 1.

28. "McKinney Punches Cop," WXIA, March 30, 2006, www.11alive .com/news/news_article.aspx?storyid=77991.

29. "McKinney's Office Responds," March 29, 2006, www.11alive.com/ news/news_article.aspx?storyid=77995.

30. Hearn, Josephine, and Jonathan E. Kaplan, "McKinney in Fracas with Officer," *The Hill*, March 30, 2006, www.thehill.com/thehill/ TheHill/News/Frontpage/033006/news3.html.

31. "McKinney Decries 'Inappropriate Touching' by Capitol Police," Fox News, April 1, 2006, www.foxnews.com/story/0,2933,189940,00.html.

32. Ibid.

33. Ibid.

34. Neuman, Johanna, and Nick Timiraos, "The Lawmakers vs. The Police Officer; Was It a Scuffle or a Misunderstanding? Regardless, It's Building to a Political Fray," *Los Angeles Times*, April 5, 2006, 4.

35. Hampson, Rick, "Anti-snitch Campaign Riles Police, Prosecutors," *USA Today*, March 28, 2006, 1.

36. Armour, Jody, "Black Tax—The Tithe That Binds," *Los Angeles Times*, November 20, 2005, M5.

37. O'Reilly, Bill, *The O'Reilly Factor*, Fox News, October 22, 2002.

38. "2005 Crime Comparison," January 22, 2007, www.areaconnect.com/crime/compare.htm.

39. Ibid.

40. City-Data.com, January 22, 2007, www.city-data.com/city/San-Jose-California.html.

41. Ibid.

42. "2005 Crime Comparison," January 22, 2007, www.areaconnect.com/crime/compare.htm.

43. City-Data.com, January 22, 2007, www.city-data.com/city/Newark-New-Jersey.html.

44. "2005 Crime Comparison."

45. City-Data.com, January 22, 2007, www.city-data.com/city/Cleveland-Ohio.html.

46. "2005 Crime Comparison."

47. City-Data.com, January 22, 2007, www.city-data.com/city/Compton-California.html.

48. "2005 Crime Comparison."

49. Eckholm, Erik, "Plight Deepens for Black Men, Study Warns," *New York Times*, March 20, 2006, 1.

50. Ibid.

51. Whitlock, Jason, "Mayhem Main Event at NBA All-Star Weekend,"

AOL Sports, February 21, 2007, www.sports.aol.com/whitlock/_a/
mayhem-main-event-at-nba-all-star/20070220103009990001.

52. Adande, J. A., "Jones Incident Lumped in with NBA," *Los Angeles Times*, March 5, 2007, D1.

53. Lichtblau, Eric, and Lait, Eric, "Blacks Back Local Police, L.A. Poll Says," *Los Angeles Times*, June 4, 1999, 1.

54. Ibid.

55. Lopez, Steve, "A Glaring Omission from Legacy of the Riots—Apologies," *Los Angeles Times*, May 1, 2002, B1.

56. "UpClose: Charles Moose," *Nightline*, ABC, November 19, 2002.

57. Kouri, Jim, "Duke Rape Prosecutor Shares Evidence with Black Panthers," *Common Voice*, May 2, 2006, www.commonvoice.com/article.asp?colid=4784.

58. Ibid.

59. Pollard-Terry, Gayle, "For African American Rape Victims, A Culture of Silence; But as the Phenomenon Is Finally Addressed, Women's Voices Emerge," *Los Angeles Times*, July 20, 2004, E1.

60. "Details of Controversial Photo Lineup Revealed," WRAL, April 21, 2006, www.wral.com/news/8893975/detail.html.

61. Miller, Stephen, "Duke Lacrosse: A Call to Action," *Duke Chronicle*, November 6, 2006.

62. Ibid.

63. "The Duke Case," *60 Minutes*, CBS News, January 14, 2007, www.cbsnews.com/stories/2007/01/11/60minutes/main2352512.shtml.

64. Miller, "Duke Lacrosse: A Call to Action."

65. Miller, Stephen, "Persecution," *Duke Chronicle*, August 28, 2006.

66. Wilson, Duff, and Jonathan D. Glater, "Files from Duke Rape Case Give Details but No Answers," *New York Times*, August 25, 2006, 1.

67. Miller, "Persecution."

68. Wilson and Glater, "Files from Duke Rape Case Give Details but No Answers."

69. Miller, "Persecution."

70. Eaglin, Adam, "Security Guard: Alleged Lax Victim Sought Money," *Duke Chronicle*, November 7, 2006.

71. Johnson, KC, "Nifong and the Black Vote," Durham-In-Wonderland, November 9, 2006, www.durhamwonderland.blogspot.com/2006/11/nifong-and-black-vote.html.

72. Beard, Aaron, "Duke Lacrosse Ethics Optional," Associated Press, December 28, 2006.

73. Ibid.

74. Ibid.

75. Ibid.

76. Ibid.

77. Ibid.

78. "The Duke Case."

79. Zucchino, David, "Duke Rape Case Prosecutor Quits," *Los Angeles Times*, January 13, 2007, 1.

80. "N.C. Bar Issues Order Disbarring Nifong," Associated Press, July 12, 2007, www.charlotte.com/nation/story/194447.html.

81. Holberg, Mark, "What Grabs Media's Eye in Rape Case?" *Richmond Times-Dispatch*, May 14, 2006, B1.

82. Campbell, Tom, "Rape Trial Ends with One Plea, Dismissal," *Richmond Times-Dispatch*, December 6, 2006.

83. Mansfield, Duncan, "Media Criticized over Tenn. Slayings," Associated Press, May 18, 2007.

84. Manzer, Tracy, "10 Youths Charged in Halloween Beating," *Long Beach Press Telegram*, November 6, 2006.

85. Ibid.

86. Becerra, Hector, and Rong-Gong Lin II, "8 Youths Are Charged with Hate Crime in Long Beach," *Los Angeles Times*, November 23, 2006, 1.

87. Coe, Kate, "Long Beach Hate Crime," *Los Angeles Weekly*, January 5–11, 2007, 23.

88. Ibid.

89. Herrera, Kevin, "Out of Tragedy May Come Unity," *Los Angeles Wave*, July 21, 2005, 1.

90. Barrett, Beth, Troy Anderson, and Sue Doyle, "LAPD Violence: Same Old Story? Cell-Phone Photo Shows Officers Beating Suspect Police Use Force on Suspect and Everyone Can Witness It," *Los Angeles Daily News*, November 10, 2006, N1.

91. "Turnpike Profiling Ruled Out," *The Record*, March 25, 2005, 4.

92. Westfeldt, Amy, "Researchers Debate Best Method to Detect Racial Profiling," *St. Louis Post-Dispatch*, April 7, 2002, 7.

93. "Turnpike Profiling Ruled Out."

94. Hepp, Rick, "Independent Report Finds No Profiling in Pike Trooper Stops," *Star-Ledger*, March 24, 2005, 24.

95. Ibid.

96. "Turnpike Profiling Ruled Out."

8. AFFIRMATIVE ACTION

1. Washington, Booker T., *Up From Slavery*, The Free Library, www.washington.thefreelibrary.com/Up-From-Slavery/2-1.

2. Greenhouse, Linda, "Context and the Court," *New York Times*, June 25, 2003.

3. "Bush Pursuing 'White Supremacist' Policies, Congresswoman Says," *Cybercast News Service*, June 24, 2003, www.townhall.com/news/politics/200306/POL20030624b.shtml.

4. Ibid.

5. Ibid.

6. Ibid.

7. Vandenabeele, Janet, and Jodi Upton, "Colleges' Retention of Blacks Dismal," *Detroit News*, July 15, 2001, www.detnews.com/2001/schools/0107/15/a01-247739.htm.

8. Keeton, Claire, "Race Quotas Cripple Hospitals," *South African Sunday Times*, June 3, 2007.

9. Irvine, Reed, and Joseph C. Goulden, "The 'Blame Whitey' Media," *USA Today Magazine*, January 1, 1994, 78.

10. Sack, Kevin "Affirmative Action Alive and Well in Atlanta," *New York Times*, June 10, 1996.

11. Ibid.

12. Modrowski, Roman, "Color Us Hypocrites," *Chicago Sun Times*, September 10, 2006, 78.

13. Xirin, Dave, "Racism and Coaching in the NFL," Alternet, January 6, 2006, www.alternet.org/story/30460/.

14. "GM: 'He Better Stay out of White Sox Business,'" ESPN, February 27, 2006, www.sports.espn.go.com/mlb/news/story?id=2345972.

15. Becker, Lee B., Tudor Vlad, Maria Tucker, and Renée Pelton, "2005 Enrollment Report: Enrollment Growth Continues, But at Reduced Rate," *Journalism and Mass Communication Educator* (Autumn 2006), 309, www.grady.uga.edu/ANNUALSURVEYS/Enrollment06/Enrollment_J&MCE_Report_2006_v1.pdf.

16. "ASNE Census Shows Newsroom Diversity Grows Slightly," American Society of Newspaper Editors, April 25, 2006, www.asne.org/index.cfm?id=6264.

17. "Year of Extremes," *Communicator*, July/August 2006, 27, www.rtnda.org/research/2006diversity.pdf.

18. Ibid.

19. Blanchette, Aimee, "The Disappearing Male Anchor," *Star Tribune*, September 19, 2006, 1D.

9. STUPID BLACK MEN AND SPORTS

1. Lincoln, Abraham, letter to William H. Herndon, July 10, 1848. *Collected Works of Abraham Lincoln*, vol. 1, (Piscataway: Rutgers University Press, 1953, 1990), 497.

2. Perazzo, John, "Finding Racism Everywhere," *FrontPage Magazine*, April 17, 2002, www.frontpagemag.com/Articles/ReadArticle.asp?ID= 1313.

3. *The Larry Elder Show*, ABC Radio Networks, March 6, 2002.

4. Ryan, John, "Make Up Your Mind Already," *San Jose Mercury News*, May 10, 2006, M1.

5. Palmquist, Matt, "Satanic Hacking," *San Francisco Weekly*, August 24, 2005, www.sfweekly.com/issues/2005-08-24/news/apologist.html.

6. Kroner, Steve, "KNBR Makes The Call: Krueger Is Fired. Program Director and Morning Show Producer Also Let Go," *San Francisco Gate*, August 10, 2005, www.sfgate.com/cgi-bin/article.cgi?file=/c/a/2005/08/ 10/KNBR.TMP.

7. Matthews, Wallace, "Better Watch What You Own Worst Enemy," *Newsday*, August 9, 2005, 62.

8. Gonzales, Mark, "Curses! Guillen-Ordonez Flap Erupts," *Chicago Tribune*, April 24, 2005.

9. Matthews, "Better Watch What You Own Worst Enemy."

10. "Guillen Fined, Ordered to Take Sensitivity Training For Slur," ESPN.com, June 22, 2006, www.sports.espn.go/espn/print?id=2496753 &type=story.

11. Welch, Matt, "Dusty Inroads: Baker's 'Heat' Statement, True or False, May Signal New Era," July 10, 2003, www.reason.com/news/show/33661 .html.

12. Morrissey, Rick, "Baker Raises Heat in Unusual Way," *Chicago Tribune*, July 6, 2003.

13. "KNBR Makes the Call: Krueger Is Fired," *San Francisco Chronicle*, August 10, 2005, www.sfgate.com/cgi-bin/article.cgi?f=/c/a/2005/08/10/SPG9OE5KV71.DTL&hw=KNBR+makes+the+call&sn=001&sc=1000.

14. "Statement by Tony Salvadore, Senior Vice President and General Manager, KNBR," Hispanic PR Wire, www.hispanicprwire.com/news.php?l=in&id=4604&cha=5.

15. Verducci, Tom, "A Slugger Arrives He's Always Had Power and Style, But When Sammy Sosa Found a Little Discipline, He Went on the Greatest Homer Tear Ever Seen," *Sports Illustrated*, October 7, 1998, 48.

16. Ibid.

17. Reaves, Joseph A., "Talk-Show Host Far Off Base with Rant about Giants," *Arizona Republic*, August 7, 2005, C10.

18. "Major League Baseball; Alou Regrets Firings, But Won't Back Down," *Duluth News-Tribune*, August 11, 2005.

19. Plaschke, Bill, "A Long Way from the Summer of '42," *Los Angeles Times*, April 15, 2007, D1.

20. "Lack of Black Players a 'Crisis,' Indians Ace Says," Associated Press, March 14, 2007.

21. Ibid.

22. Plaschke, Bill, "50 Years, Still Fears," *Los Angeles Times*, April 15, 1997, C1.

23. "Honoring A Pioneer," *Augusta Chronicle*, April 15, 2007, C7.

24. Brown Tim, "Truckload of Talent," *Los Angeles Times*, July 11, 2005, D1.

25. Ibid.

26. Ibid.

27. Plaschke, Bill, "Andrews Is in the Minority on College Baseball Fields," *Los Angeles Times*, May 22, 2005, D1.

28. Ibid.

29. Coyne, Tom, "Jackson Pushes for Black ND Coach," Associated Press, December 20, 2001.

30. "AD Cites Lack of On-Field Progress," ESPN, November 30, 2004, www.sports.espn.go.com/ncf/news/story?id=1935138.

31. "Williams Trio Busy Supplying Exactly What Tennis Needs," *Chicago Sun Times*, April 1, 2001, 120.

32. www.dbireport.com/

33. Johnson, Greg, "He Won't Be Sold Short," *Los Angeles Times*, January 30, 2007, D1.

10. EDUCATION

1. "Bill Cosby: Poor Blacks Can't Speak English," May 20, 2004, www.worldnetdaily.com/news/article.asp?ARTICLE_ID=38565.

2. Moore, Stephen, and Julian L. Simon, *It's Getting Better All The Time*, (Washington D.C.: Cato Institute, 2000), 74.

3. Springer, Steve, "From Champion to King," *Los Angeles Times*, June 29, 2006, D1.

4. Ibid.

5. Ibid.

6. Ibid.

7. Samuels, Allison, "Oprah Winfrey's Lavish South African School," *Newsweek*, January 8, 2007.

8. Simon, Stephanie, "High Cost for Low Grades," *Los Angeles Times*, May 18, 2001, 1.

9. Ibid.

10. Ibid.

11. Ibid.

12. Stossel, John, "Myth: Schools Don't Have Enough Money," *Townhall*,

January 18, 2006, www.townhall.com/columnists/column.aspx?UrlTitle =myth_schools_dont_have_enough_money&ns=JohnStossel&dt=01/18/ 2006&page=full&comments=true.

13. Simon, "High Cost for Low Grades."

14. Clowes, George A., "Study: KC Dollar Deluge Fails to Raise Test Scores," *The Heartland Institute: School Reform News*, October 1998, www .heartland.org/Article.cfm?artId=13160.

15. Teicher, Stacey A., "An African-Centered Success Story," June 8, 2006, www.csmonitor.com/2006/0608/p14s01-legn.html.

16. Ibid.

17. Aguilar, Marcos, interview by Maribel Santiago, *Teaching to Change LA* 4: no. 1–3, (2003–2004), www.tcla.gseis.ucla.edu/equalterms/dialogue/2/ aguilar.html.

18. McIntyre, Doug, interview by Bill O'Reilly, *The O'Reilly Factor*, Fox News, June 15, 2006.

19. Williamson, David, "Despite Common Beliefs, Study Shows Young Blacks Have Higher Self-Esteem," UNC News Services, www.unc.edu/ news/archives/jan00/graylit012400.htm.

20. Sharpton, Al, interview, *National Public Radio*, January 31, 2003.

21. Williams, Walter, "School Choice Will Create Schools," *Dallas Morning News*, October 16, 1993, 27.

22. Banks, Sandy, "The Times Poll: School Voucher Initiative Narrowly Trails, 45–39%," *Los Angeles Times*, September 16, 1993, 1.

23. Bulldog, "Blacks Support Vouchers in Capitol, *Los Angeles Times*, October 31, 1993, N10.

24. "Joint Center Poll Shows More Blacks Than Whites see Deterioration in Public Schools," National Center for Political and Economic Studies: Press Room, January 10, 2000, www.jointcenter.org/ pressroom1/PressReleasesDetail.php?recordID=64.

25. "In Praise of the Other Milton Friedman," *Centre Daily Times*, November 22, 2006, 8.

26. Farragher, Thomas, "Ebonics May Spur Fund Ban," *Houston Chronicle*, January 24, 1997.

27. Boghossian, Naush, "LAUSD's Graduation Rate: 44% District 6th Worst Among U.S. Cities, New Study Finds," *Los Angeles Daily News*, June 21, 2006, N1.

28. "Class Warfare," *Investor's Business Daily*, July 7, 2005, 16.

29. Owsiany, David, "Cleveland's School Voucher Program Worth Maintaining," January 28, 2002, www.buckeyeinstitute.org/article.php?id=351.

30. "Class Warfare."

31. Greene, Jay P., "Graduation Rates for Choice and Public School Students in Milwaukee," *School Choice Wisconsin*, September 28, 2004, 2.

32. "Class Warfare."

33. "The State of Our Nation's Youth 2005–2006," Horatio Alger Association, 2005, 2.

34. Ibid, 20.

35. Ibid, 52.

36. Ibid, 20.

37. Klein, Joe, "How the Teachers Killed a Dream," *Time*, November 3, 2003, www.time.com/time/magazine/article/0,9171,1006074,00.html.

38. Snell, Lisa, "Teacher Unions Crush Philanthropy and Volunteerism," *School Reform News*, December 1, 2003, www.reason.org/commentaries/snell_20031201a.shtml.

39. McHugh, Jack, "Detroit School Establishment Turns Away $200 Million Gift," *Michigan Education Report*, October 3, 2003, www.educationreport.org/article.aspx?ID=5811.

40. Snell, "Teacher Unions Crush Philanthropy and Volunteerism."

41. Klein, "How the Teachers Killed a Dream."

42. Payne, Henry, "An Offer They Could Refuse," *Weekly Standard* 11, no. 3 (October 3, 2005).

43. Sowell, Thomas, "The Education of Minority Children," www
.tsowell.com/speducat.html#N09.

44. "Marva Collins Preparatory School," January 9, 2007, www
.marvacollinspreparatory.com/.

45. "Marva Collins Preparatory School," January 9, 2007, www
.marvacollinspreparatory.com/faq.html#8.

46. "Brave New Schools: District to 'Affirm' Ebonics," July 18, 2005,
www.worldnetdaily.com/news/article.asp?ARTICLE_ID=45334.

47. Hayasaki, Erika, "Reading, 'Riting and Rap Teachers Are Using the
Song Lyrics to Make Literary Classics Relevant," *Los Angeles Times*, January 14, 2003, 1.

48. Ibid.

49. Williams, Walter, "Is the Language They're Using Really Black English?" *State Journal-Register*, December 26, 1996, 6.

50. Sowell, Thomas, "Bad Teachers and Learning Dip," *Dallas Morning News*, October 30, 1985, 18.

51. "A School Bus Driver Made Black High School Students. . . . ," Associated Press, December 19, 2006.

52. "Teacher on Leave After Distributing Letter," *Pasadena Star-News*, October 21, 2002.

53. Ibid.

54. Banks, Sandy, "Debate on Black Students Rages," *Los Angeles Times*,
December 1, 2002, B1.

55. Kaplowitz, Joshua, "How I Joined Teach for America—and Got Sued
for $20 Million," *City Journal* 13, no. 1 (Winter 2003), www.city-journal
.org/html/13_1_how_i_joined.html.

56. Ibid.

57. Ibid.

58. Ibid.

59. "Equity and Race Relations," May 23, 2006, www.seattleschools
.org/area/equityandrace/definitionofrace.xml.

60. *The Attitudes and Behavior of Young Black Americans: Research Summary,* (University of Chicago, February 2007), 18, www.blackyouthproject .uchicago.edu/writings/research_summary.pdf.

61. Ibid.

62. Ibid, 10.

63. Glazer, Nathan, "The Shape of the River: A Case for Racial Preferences." *The Public Interest,* April 1, 1999, 45–63.

64. *2006 College-Bound Seniors, Total Group Profile Report,* The College Board, www.collegeboard.com/prod_downloads/about/news_info/cbsenior/ yr2006/national-report.pdf.

65. Ibid.

66. "What Does a Social Disaster Sound Like?" *Chronicle,* April 6, 2006, www.google.com/search?hl=en&lr=&q=cache%3Ahttp%3A%2F%2Fwww .duke.edu%2Fweb%2Fafricanameric%2Flistening.pdf&btnG=Search.

67. Copeland, Rob, "The Ad in Question," *Chronicle Online,* November 7, 2006, media.www.dukechronicle.com/media/storage/paper884/news/ 2006/11/07/News/The-Ad.In.Question-2444770.shtml?sourcedomain= www.dukechronicle.com&MIIHost=media.collegepublisher.com.

68. "An Open Letter to the Duke Community," January 16, 2006, www .concerneddukefaculty.org/.

69. Van Voorhis, Scott, "Hungry for Attention; MIT Prof Mulls No-Food Strike as Tenure Protest," *Boston Herald,* December 22, 2006, 3.

70. Schweizer, Peter, *Do As I Say (Not As I Do): Profiles in Liberal Hypocrisy,* (New York: Doubleday, 1995), 208.

71. Ibid, 209.

72. "Belafonte Blasts Bush as 'Greatest Terrorist,'" *Newsday,* January 9, 2006, 2.

73. Schweizer, *Do As I Say,* 204.

74. Ibid., 205.

75. Ibid., 205.

76. Ibid., p. 207.

77. Ibid., p. 208.

11. BLACK MUSLIMS IN AMERICA

1. X, Malcolm, as told to Alex Haley, *The Autobiography of Malcolm X* (New York: Ballantine Books, 1992), 199.

2. "Muslim 'Reverts,'" *Investor's Business Daily*, March 8, 2007, 13.

3. "Obama Blows His OBL Moment," *Investor's Business Daily*, May 14, 2007, 19.

4. Silverberg, Mark, "Wahhabism in the American Prison System," May 6, 2006, www.jfednepa.org/mark%20silverberg/wahhabi_america.html.

5. Seper, Jerry, "Terrorists Recruited from U.S. Seen as a Rising Threat," *Washington Times*, June 18, 2002, 3.

6. Phares, Walid, "Terrorist Strategies against the West and Other Democracies," Accuracy In Media, January 15, 2007, www.aim.org/guest_column/5158_0_6_0_C/.

7. Klebnikov, Paul, "Who Is Osama Bin Laden?" *Forbes*, September 14, 2001, www.forbes.com/charitable/2001/09/14/0914whoisobl.html.

8. Silverberg, "Wahhabism in the American Prison System."

9. Gabriel, Brigette, *Because They Hate* (New York: St. Martin's Press, 2006), 142.

10. "The New Face of Terror?" *Investor's Business Daily*, June 28, 2006, www.investors.com/editorial/IBDArticles.asp?artsec=20&artnum=4&issue=20060.627&rss=1.

11. *The World Almanac 2007*, ed. William A. McGeveran, Jr. (New York: World Almanac Education Group, 2007), 712.

12. "The Muslim Program: What Muslims Want," Nation of Islam, www.noi.org/muslim_program.htm.

13. Ibid.

14. "Farrakhan in His Own Words: Introduction," January 16, 2007, www.adl.org/special_reports/farrakhan_own_words2/farrakhan_own _words.asp.

15. Ibid.

16. "Farrakhan in His Own Words: On Whites," January 16, 2007, www .adl.org/special_reports/farrakhan_own_words2/on_whites.asp.

17. "Farrakhan in His Own Words: On the US Government," January 16, 2007, www.adl.org/special_reports/farrakhan_own_words2/on_govt.asp.

18. "Farrakhan in His Own Words: On the Holocaust," January 16, 2007, www.adl.org/special_reports/farrakhan_own_words2/on_holocaust.asp.

19. "Farrakhan in His Own Words: On 'Jewish Conspiracies,'" January 16, 2007, www.adl.org/special_reports/farrakhan_own_words2/on _jewish_con.asp.

20. Salinas, David, "Farrakhan Stirs Division, Not Unity," *Daily Cougar*, February 3, 2005.

21. "Nation of Islam," December 29, 2006, www.pbs.org/wnet/ aaworld/reference/articles/nation_of_islam.html.

22. "Conversion of the Muslims," *Time*, March 14, 1977, www.time.com/ time/magazine/article/0,9171,947278,00.html.

23. Van Biema, David, "In the Name of the Father," *Time*, January 23, 1995.

24. "Farrakhan Admission on Malcolm X," *CBS News*, www.cbsnews .com/stories/2000/05/10/60minutes/main194051.shtml.

25. X, *The Autobiography of Malcolm X*, 199, 200.

26. Spencer, Robert, "The PC Jihad," *FrontPage*, February 10, 2003.

27. "The New Face of Terror?"

28. Elliott, Michael, "The Shoe Bomber's World," *Time*, February 16, 2002.

29. "The New Face of Terror?"

30. Ibid.

31. "Fresh Evidence Cited vs 'Lackawanna 6,' " CBS News, September 28, 2002, www.cbsnews.com/stories/2002/10/08/attack/printable524645 .shtml.

32. Gartenstein-Ross, Daveed, "Wahhabism in the Big House," *Weekly Standard* 11, no. 2 (September 26, 2005).

33. Kouri, Jim, "Four Terrorists Arrested in Terror Conspiracy," Opinionet.com, September 3, 2005, www.opinionet.com/article.php?id= 3232.

34. "The New Face of Terror?"

35. Robinson, Mike, "Man Charged in Shopping Mall Jihad Plot," Associated Press, December 8, 2006.

36. "Ace Terrorism Prosecutor Targets 'Wanna Be,' " CBS News, December 9, 2006, www.cbsnews.com/blogs/2006/12/09/primarysource/ entry2243829.shtml.

37. "The New Face of Terror?"

38. Garrett, Amanda, "Columbus Man Accused of Terror Ties," *Plain Dealer*, April 13, 2007, 1.

39. Oberman, Mira, "Accused Terrorist Faces Possible Life in Prison," *Vancouver Sun*, April 13, 2007, 10.

40. Ibid.

41. "The New Face of Terror?"

12. THREE THINGS THAT NEED TO BE SAID TO STUPID BLACK PEOPLE: "GROW UP, GROW UP, GROW UP"

1. "Today in History—Sept. 20," Associated Press, September 20, 2006.

2. Lynn, Michael, "Ethnic Differences in Tipping: A Matter of Familiarity with Tipping Norms," *Cornell HRA Quarterly* 45, no. 1 (February 2004).

3. Ibid., 13.

4. Ibid.

13. CHANGE IN THE AIR: THE MARCH OF PERSONAL RESPONSIBILITY

1. McLaughlin, Seth, "Wilder Praises Obama Strategy; Appeal Larger Than Blacks," *Washington Times*, February 23, 2007, 1.

2. Balmer, Crispian, "Berlusconi Denounced for West Superiority Claim," Reuters News, September 26, 2001.

3. Varadarajan, Tunku, "Overcooked," *Opinion Journal*, October 2, 2001, www.opinionjournal.com/columnists/tvaradarajan/?id=95001250.

4. Thomas, Pete, "Monroe Is No Longer Like a Fish out of Water," *Los Angeles Times*, May 30, 2006, D7.

5. Ibid.

6. Ibid.

7. Toner, Robin, "Democrats' Senate Hopes May Ride on Tennessee Race," *New York Times*, May 31, 2006.

8. Antlfinger, Carrie, "GOP, Democratic Parties at NAACP Summit," Associated Press, July 14, 2005, www.news.yahoo.com/news?tmpl=story&u=/ap/20050715/ap_on_re_us/naacp_convention_3.

9. *Inside Politics*, CNN, July 14, 2005.

10. Lambro, Donald, "GOP Leaders Condemn Gore Aide's Remarks," *Washington Times*, January 7, 2000, 4.

11. Ibid.

12. Bositis, David A., *2000 National Opinion Poll—Politics* (Washington, DC: Joint Center for Political and Economic Studies, 2000), 19, www.joint center.org/publications_recent_publications/national_opinion_polls/2000_national_opinion_poll_on_politics.

13. Obama, Barack, interview by Steve Kroft, *60 Minutes*, CBS, February 11, 2007.

14. "Obama Draws Attention to 'Quiet Riots'," *Fort Wayne Journal Gazette*, June 8, 2007, 8.

15. Ibid.

16. "Decoding Obama-ese," *Investor's Business Daily*, June 7, 2007.

17. "Obama Draws Attention to 'Quiet Riots.'"

18. Dowd, Maureen, "Can He Unleash the Force?" *New York Times*, June 6, 2007, 23.

19. Barabak, Mark Z. and Michael Finnegan, "YouTube Debate Brings Questioners into Picture," *Los Angeles Times*, July 24, 2007, 1.

20. Obama, Barack, "Obama, Clinton Speeches in Selma, Alabama," *Late Edition with Wolf Blitzer*, CNN, March 4, 2007.

21. Ibid.

22. Ibid.

23. Ibid.

24. "On The Vilsack Rebound," *Hotline*, March 6, 2007.

25. "About Us," Trinity United Church of Christ, www.tucc.org/about .htm.

26. Wallace-Wells, Ben, "Destiny's Child," *Rolling Stone*, February 7, 2007, www.rollingstone.com/politics/story/13390609/campaign_08_ the_radical_roots_of_barack_obama/.

27. Kantor, Jodi, "Disinvitation by Obama Is Criticized," *New York Times*, March 6, 2007, 17.

28. Ibid.

29. Ibid.

30. Kantor, Jodi, "A Candidate, His Minister and the Search for Faith" *New York Times*, April 30, 2007, 1.

31. Ibid.

32. Fergusan, Andrew, "The Literary Obama," *Weekly Standard*, February

12, 2007, 27, www.theweeklystandard.com/Content/Public/Articles/000/000/013/237rhfjc.asp?pg=2.

33. Ibid.

34. Henneberger, Melinda, "Selma Showdown: Obama, Clinton Converge on Activists," *Huffington Post*, March 4, 2007, www.huffingtonpost.com/melinda-henneberger/selma-showdown-obama-cl_b_42611.html.

35. Dinan, Stephan, "Obama Solicits La Raza Backing," *Washington Times*, July 23, 2007, 1.

36. "Bias May Hike Blacks' Breast Cancer Risk," Reuters, July 5, 2007.